Progress and Problems in Moral Education

'Do not give your children moral or religious instruction unless you are quite sure they will not take it too seriously.'

Bernard Shaw, *Man and Superman*. 'The Revolutionist's Handbook' on Education.

Progress and Problems
in Moral Education

edited by
Monica J. Taylor

NFER Publishing Company Ltd

Published by the NFER Publishing Company Ltd.,
Book Division, 2 Jennings Buildings, Thames Avenue,
Windsor, Berks., SL4 1QS
Registered Office: The Mere, Upton Park, Slough, Berks., SL1 2DQ
First Published 1975
© National Foundation for Educational Research in England and Wales
The copyright of the individual articles remains with their authors.

Typeset by Jubal Multiwrite Ltd.,
66 Loampit Vale, Lewisham SE13 7SN
Printed in Great Britain by
King, Thorne and Stace Ltd., School Road, Hove, Sussex BN3 5JE
Distributed in the USA by Humanities Press Inc.,
Hilary House—Fernhill House, Atlantic Highlands,
New Jersey 07716 USA.

Contents

PREFACE

All of these papers, excepting that by Mary Warnock, have been written specially for the volume. It represents the varied reflections and experiences of some who are most nearly concerned with moral education today. I am especially grateful to authors for their interest, flexibility and ready cooperation; the book testifies to their common concern to clarify some of the substantive moral issues in educating. Any shortcomings must, however, be attributed to the editor and to the limitations of communicating solely by written word in an area of such complexity.

M.J.T.

NOTES ON CONTRIBUTORS

H.J. Blackham taught for many years in secondary and adult education and is at present Chairman of the Social Morality Council which publishes reports, has initiated a moral education project and now has a Moral Education Centre at Goldsmiths' College, University of London (directed by Wendy Doeser). He is Chairman of the Editorial Board of the *Journal of Moral Education* and the author of several publications including *Six Existentialist Thinkers*, *The Human Tradition*, *Political Discipline in a Free Society*, *Religion in a Modern Society* and *Humanism*.

Celia Dusoir is a teacher at Barton Junior School, Oxford.

Cynthia Evans read theology at St. Hugh's, Oxford and is Head of the Religious Education Department, Hayes School, Bromley, Kent.

Brian Gates, at present Principal Lecturer in the Department of Religion, Goldsmiths' College, University of London, is shortly to become Head of the Department of Religious and Moral Studies, St. Martin's College, Lancaster. He is currently completing PhD work on the process of religious understanding in the life world of children and young people, and is the author of articles which have appeared in religious and educational journals.

John Hull taught in schools in this country and abroad and at Westhill College of Education before taking up his present post as Lecturer in Education (Theology), Birmingham University School of Education. He edits *Learning for Living* and has contributed to numerous educational and theological journals. He is the author of *Hellenistic Magic and the Synoptic Tradition* and *Sense and Nonsense about God*.

Judy Kyle taught for several years in elementary and secondary schools in Montreal before becoming Director of an independent junior school there. She is at present a graduate student at McGill University and a 'free-flow' part-time teacher.

Harold Loukes is Reader in Education, University of Oxford. His publications include *Friends and Their Children*, *Teenage Religion*, *New Ground in Christian Education*, and *Teenage Morality*.

Robert Lush is Chairman and Managing Director of the Richmond Design Group of Companies. His main connection with education is as Acting Chairman of the Warborough Trust which is continuing the work of the Farmington Trust in moral education.

Peter Newell was Deputy Editor of the *Times Educational Supplement* until 1971 and then Education Officer for the National Council for Civil Liberties until working at the White Lion Street Free School. He is editor of *A Last Resort? Corporal Punishment in Schools* and contributed (with Alison Truefitt) to *Education Without Schools*.

John Rose is Head of the Religious Education Department, Newton Abbot Grammar School.

Lawrence Stenhouse taught in Scottish schools and lectured in two Education Departments before taking up the post of Director of the Nuffield Foundation and Schools Council Humanities Curriculum Project (1967-1970). He is now Director of The Centre for Applied Research in Education, University of East Anglia and of an SSRC and Gulbenkian Foundation Project on the problems and effects of teaching about race relations. He is the author of *Culture and Education, An Introduction to the Study of Curriculum* and several articles, and edited *Discipline in Schools*.

Brenda Thompson is Headmistress of Northwold Infants' School in an educational priority area of East London. She is the author of *Learning to Read* and *Learning to Teach* and has also edited a series of children's books, *First Facts*.

Jasper Ungoed-Thomas who taught for several years in secondary modern and special schools, is Deputy Director, Schools Council Moral Education Project. He is the author of *Our School*, and (with Peter McPhail and Hilary Chapman) of *Moral Education in the Secondary School*, and of six booklets of classroom material from the Moral Education Project, as well as of several articles.

Mary Warnock, Research Fellow of Lady Margaret Hall, Oxford was for six years Headmistress of Oxford High School. Her publications include *Ethics since 1900, The Philosophy of J.-P. Sartre, Existentialism*, and *Existentialist Ethics* and numerous articles in philosophical journals.

J.P. White taught for several years in secondary schools and colleges of technology and is now Lecturer in Philosophy of Education at the University of London Institute of Education. He is the author of *Towards a Compulsory Curriculum* and (with Keith Thompson) *Curriculum Development: A Dialogue*, and several articles.

John Wilson is Lecturer and Tutor, Oxford University Department of Educational Studies and Director of the Warborough Trust Research

Unit. He was Housemaster and Second Master for several years at King's School, Canterbury, then held posts in religion and philosophy before directing the Farmington Trust Research Unit from 1965–1972. His numerous publications include *Introduction to Moral Education, Education in Religion and the Emotions, Practical Methods of Moral Education, Philosophy and Educational Research, The Assessment of Morality*, and many articles.

Derek Wright taught for many years in a secondary school and in schools for maladjusted children. He is now Reader in Psychology at the University of Leicester. He is currently engaged in research into the moral judgements of adolescents and is the author of many empirical, theoretical and 'popular' articles and (with others) of *Introducing Psychology: An Experimental Approach*, and *The Psychology of Moral Behaviour*. He also edits the *Journal of Moral Education*.

Michelle York has taught in both secondary and junior schools and is now at The Hermitage County Middle School, Woking.

Introduction

There is at present in the pluralistic society in which we live much general public interest in morality. Frequently this stems from concern with global social problems such as civil violence or pollution, or social phenomena like drug taking or delinquency. In recent years the accelerated breakdown of traditional authority structures[1], much documented by social scientists and efficiently relayed by the mass media, has, moreover, served to heighten an awareness of the tension and constantly shifting boundary between the private morality of the individual and the shared values of wider society. This is not, however, the place to enter into the confused arguments prevalent in much popular writing and discussion of these issues; neither is it necessary to stress the inevitability of our involvement in the moral life. Yet the need to make sense of conflicting and changing claims and demands and to get beyond social convention and self interest in unravelling society's moral problems remains urgent.

In some measure, however, one channel for the disinterested and rational inquiry prerequisite to sincere communication already exists. Significantly, it has been the school, that initial link between the morality of the home and the less certain, public morality of the world at large, which has historically played an important part educating the young in morality. Moral education in school is thus the meeting point for a study of these social problems. Yet, to date, it has lacked the coherence and structure of a subject in its own right, thereby often forfeiting a claim to merit serious attention as a part of the curriculum. In this connection the particular relevance of philosophical arguments on the nature of morality and the area which it covers, has been to a large extent overlooked.[2]

Notwithstanding some progress made in the last few years it would be wrong to underestimate the problems which arise in the school's on going work in moral education. The focus of interest in this collection is not therefore on specific aspects of moral education such as the assessment of morality or stages of moral development; the reader will find such (suitably scholarly and scientific) information elsewhere.[3] Instead our purpose here is to survey certain basic problems confronted in practice by those concerned with the moral function of education and to set up an interdisciplinary framework in which they may be discussed. In so doing, the aim has not been to supply definitive solutions but rather to present a conspectus on the kinds of questions which exercise teachers and to examine the extent and nature of their difficulties. Firstly, as a background to the problematic issues raised and debated by contributors in the body of the book, it seems appropriate to take a closer look at some perspectives on the school's role and review a few of the more influential developments in its concern with education in morality.

The school and moral education

Typically, the child's first encounter with morality is in the home. He gradually finds himself introduced to certain terms of approval and disapproval, with consequent praise and blame, so that his moral experience and thought is almost co-extensive with his linguistic experience. As he grows, the situations with which he is confronted become correspondingly less straightforward, so that by the time he reaches school he already has some idea of morality, and what it is to act morally, from his parents. It is at this point where the child has to learn to find his feet in the wider social community that the teacher is often seen as standing *in loco parentis*.

In practice, the school has always been concerned with something more than the imparting of factual knowledge or social skills. Often this additional dimension has been known as 'character training' or 'liberal education' or 'education of the whole man', and has been much influenced by the various views and entrenched interests of different 'authorities', primarily those connected with the Church, state, politics and specific social classes. Since the 1944 Education Act the school's task in educating in morality has, at least theoretically, taken place within a largely religious framework and in the Christian tradition, either directly as part of the curriculum in RI or RE lessons, or in school worship for which provision was expressly made (subject the conscience clauses and right of withdrawal). This has meant that for the most part instruction has been given in particular principles or codes, supported by the general ethos of the school (the 'hidden' curriculum) in the example set by teachers and their relationships with pupils, especially in 'pastoral care' sessions, and within the existing structure of rules and discipline. The pupil was thus supposedly provided with a strong and sound authoritarian basis for morality. But paralleling the deterioration in respect for and influence of these 'authorities' in recent years, and to substitute for them, the demand has since been made on those engaged in educating to promote in their pupils such things as 'a critical attitude', 'maturity', 'responsibility', and 'autonomy'.[4] This ill-defined, amorphous area is what we now know as moral education.

Moral philosophy

Moral education as a coherent subject however, is in its infancy and struggling to grow. From its inception it has been particularly associated with philosophy. But despite the firm foundations in moral philosophy on which to build, and notwithstanding the upsurge of interest in the last decade, the progress of solid constructive work in moral education has been slow. Although there is some evidence that the Pre-socratic philosophers made axiomatic ethical pronouncements, Plato, through his mouthpiece, Socrates, seems to have been the first in Western society to reason at length about the nature of morality and to ask whether virtue could be taught.[5] His successor, Aristotle, in his detailed treatise, *The Nicomachean Ethics*, regarded moral virtue as partly resulting from habit, but made the important distinction that to be so the virtuous man must not only do virtuous acts, but act as the virtuous man does, i.e. in the right frame of mind, with the right intentions and possessing and bringing to bear both theoretical and practical wisdom.[6] With the comparatively late introduction of Kant's categorical imperative of duty philisophical interest in ethics took a new turn.[7] In taking account of this influence when considering developments in this century, the theories of the Intuitionists and Emotivists in the earlier years may be dismissed; but mention should certainly be made of two controversial books by R.M. Hare: *Freedom and Reason* and *Language of Morals*.[8] Written in the Oxford linguistic tradition of philosophy, these works put forward an analysis of the respective places of reason and emotion in morality, pointing out the overriding, prescriptive and universal character of moral judgements. It is thus evident, from even the briefest survey, that throughout its close association with ethics, philosophy has concentrated on the emergence of a rational morality.

Education

By comparison, the study of education has until recently received relatively little analytic attention from philosophers; neither have there been many serious attempts to interrelate the different approaches of the educational disciplines.[9] Indeed, without belittling the sound work which goes on in many colleges of education, it seems for the most part true that energies in this field have long been expended empirically on the practical aspects of teaching and learning, even though there has been but partial understanding of how this takes place. For although many of the most renowned philosophers — Plato, Locke, Rousseau and others too — advanced considered reflections on education, it has been something of an innovation to submit the aims and objectives of education to prolonged theoretical examination and debate, and to subject the curriculum, teaching methods and school organization *inter alia* to the more rigorous scrutiny of scientific techniques and investigation.[10] Yet it is surprising that in a field where there is so much activity so little has been questioned or ascertained. But when we remember that the professional interest of philosophers such as Professors Hirst and Peters in contributing (along with psychologists, sociologists and historians) to the interdisciplinary study of education by clarifying educational concepts and analysing objectives, has only been operative for a decade or so, we may begin to see why this is the case.[11] If one takes the view, therefore, that it makes little sense to investigate areas such as classroom control before one has a clear idea of what is to count as control, what kind of teacher/pupil interactions are relevant — whether, for instance, it is only teacher-directed behaviour in which we are interested or also pupil-initiated change — then it is obvious that the groundwork has only just begun for a meaningful study of education.

Moral development and education

Just as education is only now beginning to undergo sustained and reasoned analytic inquiry, so in the last few years have there been signs of corresponding investigation in moral education. This seemingly new and sudden awareness of the importance of moral education amongst both teachers and parents may be traced, in part at least, to two major developments.

The first of these is in the background work in psychology and sociology which is of relevance to morality.[12] Since the initial reports of Hartshorne and May[13] on the nature of character, which elucidated certain moral traits, nearly fifty years ago, there have been a number of important psychological studies of the child's cognitive development. The exploratory work of Piaget, firstly on general conceptual development and later on moral judgement, is particularly significant.[14] As is now well-known, on the basis of careful and detailed analyses of data gathered from questioning a small number of children on their understanding of rules, he postulated three stages in their moral development. The child, he suggested, begins egocentrically, by seeing rules as examples rather than obligations; later, he accepts the rules transcendentally as emanating from adults, unalterable and backed by praise or blame; and, lastly, he passes from this heteronomous morality to a more autonomous position where rules are seen as changeable, depending on reciprocal respect for and cooperation with others.

Confirmation of this tentative analysis was later obtained by the wider cross-cultural investigations of Lawrence Kohlberg, who, in turn, refined the division of moral development into six stages.[15] He postulated that the child at 'Pre-moral' Level 1 sees rules as dependent on compulsion and requiring obedience, then as instrumental to gaining rewards. At Level 2, 'Morality of Conventional Role Conformity', they are ways of obtaining approval and avoiding censure and guilt in relation to others. The higher levels of the invariant hierarchical sequence may not be attained by all. Here, morality is firstly seen as a contract, and only finally as individual principles of conscience — especially that of justice — which are necessary in living together with others. Interestingly, Kohlberg has recently described parallel stages in the development of religious faith and proposed a Stage 7 'an ultimate stage of faith' towards which, he claims, the six stages of morality move and which 'integrates them with a perspective on life's meaning'.[16] From the evidence of these empirical studies by Piaget and Kohlberg it has widely accepted that, though the content of morality may vary, the form of the moral conscience follows an unchanging sequence in its development, and that this must be taken into account in any programme of moral education.

The second influential factor in the field of moral education was the emergence in this country in the late 1960s of two research projects. The first, set up in 1965, was the Farmington Trust Research Unit in Moral Education, under the direction of a philosopher, John Wilson. The Unit also employed a psychologist and sociologist, and their initial publication, *Introduction to Moral Education*,[17] was original in applying the findings of pure research in these disciplines to certain questions in the 'complex' and 'unclear' area of moral education. Though teachers and administrators were consulted during the Project, the position which evolved was largely theoretical and deductive. It was suggested, for instance, that the morally educated person was characterized by an ability to identify with others and take account of their feelings and interests; awareness of and insight into his own and other people's feelings, the possession of factual knowledge and social skills, and an ability to formulate rules and principles and to translate these into action.[18] This approach follows R.M. Hare in emphasizing the importance of understanding the rational form of morality. The Unit therefore advocated that pupils should be taught moral logic and methodology to enable them to grasp the part which right reasoning plays in the formation of correct moral judgements and in taking appropriate action. Practical methods for use in classroom teaching have been proposed,[19] and although no materials have been produced

to date, there are plans for the development of these in the research
now continuing in the name of the Warborough Trust at Oxford.

The second research project of note is the Schools' Council Moral
Education Project 13-18, directed by Peter McPhail. With the recent
work of the Farmington Trust in the background the aim of this Project
was somewhat different. Starting with action research in schools the
team collected statements from teachers on existing arrangements for
moral education and subsequently conducted interviews with 800
secondary school pupils in which they asked them to describe critical
incidents of 'good' and 'bad' treatment by adults. From these they
derived an inductive theory of morality which placed central emphasis
on the values of autonomy and consideration for others. They also
claimed from their inquiry to have identified the needs of adolescents,
and in relating their theory of morality to classroom practice they
subsequently developed stimulus materials and techniques covering the
kind of hypothetical situations which caused adolescents concern. The
Project's aim was therefore to help pupils in caring and choosing and to
live 'a considerate style of life', which, it was pointed out, was
self-rewarding. The materials thus stress treatment and behaviour
outcomes in attempting to facilitate pupils in moral decision taking and
to 'motivate boys and girls actually to treat people better'. With these
materials now in use in the secondary school, the Project is currently
being extended to develop materials appropriate to the 8 to 13 age
range.[20]

It will be apparent even from this brief synopsis that a number of
substantive differences in emphasis exists between these two projects;
for instance, whether morality can be 'caught' or 'taught'; or whether
the stress should be on understanding and reasoning leading to decision
making (Why should I do X?), or on feelings, actual decisions, and
behaviour. Yet with both these Projects a serious start has been made in
divesting the field of some of its muddled thinking and in giving moral
education a justification in its own right.

A new approach?

The interest in moral education has thus been reawakened, stimulated and even put on a surer footing. Yet in spite of its officialization
as a legitimate educational concern it finds itself in an anomalous
position. As a perennial feature of the school's affairs it has rarely been
reflected in the curriculum in any systematic or structured way. Having
a peculiarly integral relationship with education, this is no doubt in part
due to the image of considerable complexity and lack of clarity which
it purveys. Linked to this incoherence is the fact that it both cuts across
many different disciplines and has a strong practical element interacting
with the theory. In addition, it has often been seen as causing particular

personal difficulties for those teachers directly involved. To a large extent moral education has lacked a province and therefore provision. But the school's proper business is with *educating* its charges. If we accept that this implies the promotion and development of understanding and the ability to think and reason, as well as the acquisition of knowledge and social skills, it follows that, if the school is to continue to take an active interest in laying the foundations of morality (and it is difficult to see how it cannot), then the aims of education as a whole must be applied to moral education itself.

Logically, this means a thorough reappraisal of the school's role as a moral educator. There are signs, too, that moral education now sits uneasily as an official aspect of RE[21] and that it should be questioned whether the customary approach meets present requirements. Moreover, the claim of morality to be a distinctive form of thought[22] and intrinsically worthy of study gains support in practice from the arguments from social pluralism that one continually advanced. Considerable changes both in society and in educational thinking imply not only that educational administrators and practitioners should re-examine whether the provision that does exist is adequate — more specifically, whether direct teaching in morality should be more or less exclusively in the context of education in religion — but also whether the school should inculcate particular moral principles or codes (or should this be the province of parents in conjunction with religious teaching?); or whether it should perhaps indicate a more critical questioning and reflective approach to gaining possession of appropriate criteria to judge *between* various moral authorities. This is not to deny that some schools have already instituted a more genuinely educative approach towards the study of morality nor that there may be other alternatives. But much more hard and prolonged consideration of how the school can best help pupils learn in morality for themselves is urgently required. As a step in the direction of seeing how the teacher might take on this task it is necessary to start by clarifying the nature of moral education and its subject matter.

What is moral education?

It is crucial to begin by distinguishing different types of questions with which moral education is concerned. These questions in turn relate to different problems in which educators are involved and hence sometimes to the setting up of research to investigate particular areas of difficulty. For out of the confusion and complexity of morality it is at least clear that moral education is not just *one* field of inquiry. On the contrary, it involves both (1) many different disciplines and (2) many practical questions. Under (1) the further distinction has to be made between disciplines which attempt to answer conceptual questions and those disciplines concerned mainly with empirical questions. It is one of the functions of philosophy to analyse and clarify concepts integral to moral questions and, as has been noted in relation to education as a whole, it is essential that such questions as 'What is to count as "morally educated"?', or 'What is meant by "concern for others" or "sensitivity"?', should logically be the starting point for an investigation of these areas. The techniques of philosophy are thus used to explore and delimit the premises and underlying assumptions implicit in an inquiry, and, in so doing, to open up areas upon which empirical disciplines can be brought to bear. These empirical disciplines, dealing with factual questions, have their methodologies grounded in the natural sciences. Seeking primarily to describe experience, they proceed by observation and experiment to the construction of theory. Some person-oriented empirical disciplines — psychology, sociology and anthropology (so far under-applied) — are obviously of great relevance to considerations in moral education; others such as history, geography, literature and biology are of lesser significance. Within these disciplines are further subdivisions which specialize in certain kinds of questions. Thus in psychology, for instance, the work on personality factors in both developmental and experimental psychology is pertinent. Such questions as 'At what age does a child have the concept of stealing?' (i.e. does he understand why it is wrong to take money from his mother's purse without her permission or is he held back by the expectation or threat of punishment if he does), would fall into the province of developmental psychology. In experimental psychology, however, if the investigator's concern was with conscience it would be reasonable to test how long a small child left in a room with a forbidden packet of sweets on the table would resist the temptation to help himself, and what his reactions would be (e.g. guilt or shame) on the subsequent return of his parent. Similarly, there are specialisms in the discipline of sociology which take account of the social context in which people act. Sociology supplies evidence on such questions as how the home background and rearing of the child affects his capacity for education in school; or how the organization of the school influences pupils' moral learning: whether, for example, the prefect system helps older pupils assume responsibility, or whether democratic councils are more efficacious in promoting an understanding of rules.

The disciplines, as we see from these examples, are tools useful for doing different jobs in moral education. They are valuable more for their illumination or re-focusing of our ways of thinking about problems than for any scientifically 'proven' results or findings. When applied critically and appropriately they can be brought to bear with force and point on problems in moral education and can provide sound guidelines for researchers and practitioners alike. Yet although their evidence is complementary, there exists wide gulfs between one discipline and another — divergencies both in methodology and jargon. Much prolonged thinking and flexibility (as we shall witness later) amongst theorists familiar with these disciplines is therefore required to make sense of and integrate the relevant approaches. For just as we need to be clear about concepts involved in the making of moral judgements (philosophy) so we also need to know what personal characteristics influence people to act or to fail to act on their judgements (psychology) and what circumstances affect their actions (sociology).

Likewise, there are distinct gaps between theory and practice. Not only is it useful in moral education to make valid connections between the disciplines but it is also necessary to relate this evidence to classroom practice. Moreover, coordination is a two-way process: theory and practice, practice and theory modifying each other. Some of the concerns of the moral educator will, of course, be solely practical. Questions like 'Is moral education to be timetabled between 9.15 and 10.00 a.m. or 11.30 and 12 noon?', 'Shall we teach in discussion groups with pupils seated informally?', 'Shall we provide coffee?', or 'Shall we arrange for pupils to do community service as part of the moral education programme?' can all be decided quite straightforwardly either by an individual teacher or in conjunction with the Head or other members of staff or the team. Other questions may not be answered so simply. Often those which look *prima facie* direct questions of classroom tactics or organization are shown upon closer inspection to require some additional knowledge or appreciation of relevant theory. Imagine, for instance, that a class of 7-year-olds are turning out their lockers on Friday afternoon and the teacher notices that Jim has in his a number of letters which should have been posted to his grandfather. She asks him in the midst of the classroom activities why he failed to post the letters. If, on the other hand, she knows that two months ago his mother had another baby she may well choose to handle the situation differently. This again points out why teachers, having endured a certain professional training, may sometimes be better equipped to deal with these cases than parents, and how closely moral education is interwoven with both home and school.

Where the teacher needs guidance in the actual practical approach to direct teaching in moral education theoretical considerations are again to the fore. In thinking how to conduct moral education most efficiently and effectively the teacher will naturally bear in mind the age and abilities of the pupils, their interest and background and the relation of other subjects in the curriculum. Once he has decided whether he intends to teach ethics, the history of moral thought, moral methodology or actual moral principles his approach should reflect his

aims. Let us suppose the teacher is concerned to give his pupils
instruction in moral methodology. This will need to range from the
concrete to the more abstract and it will be important to get the right
mixture between abstract reasoning and real-life situations. The
methods for doing this may include written materials, drama sessions[23]
with role-play and simulated situations, or looking at films, and taking
part in debate or question and answer sessions or discussions. The
different techniques involved in these methods must be chosen for their
appropriateness in getting a particular point across and graded in
difficulty. A certain amount of verbalization — and this is what may
cause some difficulty either for those who are less articulate or who
lack confidence — is inevitable. Thus it may be possible to get the
pupils to see for themselves what kind of principles are continually
associated in inter-personal action. But they also need guidance to come
to realize how some principles are relevant to some situations but not
others, and how to weigh up aspects of situations and choose between
principles so that the overriding principle governing action in a
particular case emerges from a process of logical reasoning which they
have undergone on their own account. At certain points it may also be
helpful to introduce or return to some of the stimulus material, such as
that produced by the Schools Council Moral Education Project, in
order to give the pupils experience of practical reasoning and examining
certain features central to moral decision making, such as considering
the feelings of others or the consequences of actions. These particular
materials, as is well known, are illustrative situational examples using
hypothetical questions; but the teacher may, with caution, also start
from actual situations in which the pupil has found himself or in which
he is currently concerned and with regard to which he needs to make a
decision or commitment. In general, however, the distinctions marked
by 'methods', 'materials' 'techniques' and 'approaches' are somewhat
hazy, and only roughly related to the form or content of moral education lessons. There are conceptual problems here which require to be
tackled. More empirical clarification, too, is needed of the application
of the particular method or material more suited to the learning or
reinforcing of one concept rather than another.

Moral education, then, is a field of inquiry and discovery and for the
pupil a time of self-discovery. For pupils are, of course, already actively
engaged in morality but they need to be helped to understand and
behave morally in a more thoughtful, conscientious and serious way.
For this reason, the teacher's function will be to encourage the pupils
to monitor their own performances by a critical analysis of the
processes by which they arrive at their own judgements.[24]

Plan of the present volume

That moral education covers a wide and difficult area there can be no doubt. As has been shown, its complexity is compounded by its interdisciplinary nature and the number of complications inherent in attempting to relate theory to practical problems. This volume therefore sets out to consider four related areas in moral education which are beset by this dual difficulty. The problems discussed are both controversial and currently of pressing concern. The first section, on moral education and its place in the curriculum, debates whether moral education should be a timetabled subject, how it relates to other areas of the curriculum and how more meaningful communication can be promoted between all interested parties. Following this, we inquire into the teacher's attitude as to whether he could and should be neutral, either as to the content or the methods of his teaching. Thirdly, we probe the question of discipline which on any view must be a prerequisite of any serious moral education. Within this we examine the development of self-discipline in the individual, discipline as part of the school's organizational system and as it relates to society at large. The final section, prompted by the emergence of the multi-ethnic community,[25] considers the relation of RE to moral education and the nature of RE (as opposed to RI) in the multi-faith Britain of today. Each section has thus been planned as discrete although the reader will discern some overlap in issues.

The aim throughout has been to develop a dialogue demonstrating the value of interdisciplinary inquiry and to link theoretical suggestions to practice. To this end, and so that papers should in some way relate one to another within each section, the debate was originally structured as follows: The first contributor, generally a philosopher, was asked to clarify the concepts involved in the question. The next contributor added observation and argument, often in the form of evidence from an empirical discipline, psychology or sociology, but sometimes further elucidation from the philisophical standpoint. With the third paper it was often possible to introduce a practical slant by relating the work of a research project; and to further combine theory with practice a teacher was finally invited to comment on whether the theoretical proposals or accounts would be pragmatic. As a result, just as there is a variety in styles of contribution — analytic, descriptive, research-oriented etc. so the substance of the various arguments ranges in application through infant, junior and secondary schooling.[27]

As it happened, the section on Religious Education conformed most nearly with the envisaged framework, and within this there is a large measure of agreement about the role of RE in the school curriculum. Addressing themselves to the question of how existing provision can accommodate the new diversity in religious commitment, the contributors focus on three aspects singled out by the 1944 Education Act: lessons for religious instruction, denominational schools and school worship. John Hull advocates that the main function of Religious Education — hitherto a cluster of subjects — should be not just the biblical teaching or thematic approach of the past, but the descriptive teaching of living religions and secular philosophies. In this connection, Brian Gates makes the telling point that it is the politics of the various bodies with interests in RE that will shape the kind of religious understanding the child is likely to gain in school, whether this is secular or confessional as in the wider community. Evidence from his research on children's religious development highlights a major problem for pluralism: theological diversity. This is also stressed by Harold Loukes when he welcomes the discomforting need in a multi-faith society to question, examine and discover for the first time so that teaching and learning in religion (paralled by teaching in morality) can proceed by openness and sensitivity through experience to understanding and commitment. If priority were to be given to this approach it is evident, as John Hull points out, that the setting up of additional denominational schools, though possible in principle, would, in the long-term, only hinder integration. Instead, he recommends assemblies for sharing and exploring a variety of religious attitudes and beliefs. But Cynthia Evans argues that in practice these may only make the differences more obvious. Agreeing with Harold Loukes that the teacher's aim in RE should be to encourage pupils to search for meaning themselves (but differing with Brian Gates on their potential for knowledge and understanding of religion), she emphasizes that RE, unsupported by law, must be ordered by the same criteria as any other subject. For, she claims, whilst it cannot be entirely divorced from moral education the onus must be on the teacher to point out the particular religious viewpoint from which he visualizes the effect of religion on morality.

Variations in procedure

During the course of compiling the book, it became apparent, however, that in order to deal in any adequate way with certain issues raised by contributors, it was necessary to depart from the perhaps over-clinical schema which had been envisaged for each section. The subjects of discipline and moral education in the curriculum are cases in point. It is hoped that the extension of dialogue as necessary here has permitted the fullest treatment possible within the limitations (both of finance and length) of a book of this kind, balancing both the demands of conciseness on the writer in expressing his views and the reader's satisfaction in coordinating and evaluating the varying arguments.

In the section on discipline the discussion embraces a broader social perspective, for discipline, a persistently problematic and polemical area for the school,[28] has a particular bearing on both personal and social morality. Opening the discussion, Derek Wright stipulates a definition of discipline as effectively postponing immediate behaviour for some higher order value such as making a productive contribution to society, becoming a certain sort of person, or fitting in with other people personally and through institutional roles. Two main strands of psychological research — social learning and cognitive development theories — are shown to impinge on discipline, echoing to some extent the arguments of the traditionalists and progressivists in education, which are, in turn, reflected in modified forms in the remaining papers. Judy Kyle, for instance, demonstrates how discipline in the institutional context of the school can not only facilitate the ordering of the school's organization, but also foster the growth of self-discipline, whilst itself being educative. This is outlined in an hypothetical example, but based on her own experience, of democratic pupil participation in rule and decision making where the characteristics of discipline — order and restriction — are positive elements of the procedure itself.[29] Peter Newell, too, is concerned to promote the individual's 'capacity for real choice and control within his life', but in questioning the assumptions of schooling he examines to what extent discipline problems are 'real life' rather than institutional. Possibilities are noted for the social reform of education, working within the existing law and utilizing the full resources of the community: the free school is one example. Pursuing the social implications, Robert Lush points to the role of the school as a party in the 'contract to be educated' as an example of the importance of contract in interpersonal relations. It is unlikely that anyone will overlook the present significance of this discussion of contract, Kohlberg's fifth stage of morality, 'where the people accept both discipline and authority in the common cause'. Finally, Brenda Thompson eschews, contrary to Peter Newell, a community approach, asserting that the teacher, through his professionalism, should promote 'different and wider values than those of the immediate locality', thus helping to balance for the pupil the tension in loyalties between home, school and society — a common meeting ground on which all contributors converge.

Difficulties in communication

Given the rationale of the book, and bearing in mind the differing conceptual apparatus, logical structure, manner of expression and principles of application of the different disciplines involved in moral education, not to mention the variety in background and experiences of the contributors, it was perhaps to be expected that certain sections would lack even a common starting point for discussion. Whereas some authors share an appreciation of problems and sometimes even point towards solutions along similar lines, others start from fundamentally different conceptions of how the question at issue should be approached. This basic difficulty in communication appears to be highlighted where there are well known research projects, mediating between the disciplinary 'experts' and practising teachers at work in the area under discussion.

The section which aimed at a broad general discussion of the teacher and neutrality exemplifies this point. Both Mary Warnock and John Wilson are concerned at the outset to clarify the concepts of 'neutrality' and 'indoctrination' and to distinguish particular cases of these. Mary Warnock believes the teacher should take care to present the evidence fairly on both factual and value questions but that he should be 'a leader in argument', prepared to state his own view if necessary when showing how a judgement is made from the evidence, because of the nature of value judgements — that one wants others to believe the same. John Wilson, largely in agreement, distinguishes aims in educating given by the subject's methodology and contexts and methods of teaching determined by empirical evidence. Neutrality, he believes, may encourage pupils' self-confidence but is no substitute for a serious approach in disputed areas. Since, however, neither of these papers make reference here to empirical research on neutrality, they cannot be taken to imply direct criticism of the major empirical work of the Humanities Curriculum Project, which, under the direction of Lawrence Stenhouse, was set up in 1967 with the aim of producing materials to aid teachers in the handling of controversial 'human issues of universal concern' in the lower ability range of the secondary school.[30] For many teachers the Project is associated with the concept of the neutral chairman which it coined, and accordingly Lawrence Stenhouse was invited to explain the background to and function of the premise of procedural neutrality in the Project's work. He describes and evaluates some reactions to the teacher's role in the HCP which was defined empirically after a two-year experiment in schools, and it is indeed central to his position that any debate on neutrality in *teaching* should have 'an empirical referent in teacher behaviour and classroom events'. A true appreciation must be founded on a comparison of rigorously controlled observations of such events, not anecdotal illustrations of limited instances.[31] Lawrence Stenhouse wished, therefore, to commence the debate from the basis of the research findings, which was quite contrary to the position taken up initially. Yet in summing up, Celia Dusoir criticizes a 'monopolistic' empirical approach to neutrality on HCP's terms because of its application being limited to secondary pupils, and cites examples of the teacher as impartial chairman and arbitrator of daily events in the junior school. She calls, moreover, for clarification of the foundation of the Project's premises (especially 2 and 4, p. 125) as she contends the teacher has a duty to expose views which are mistaken or illogical. Thus the kind of impasse evidence by this section does throw into relief the difficulties and limitations of pursuing such a discourse solely by means of the written word.

Another disjunction in communication, but for different reasons, arose in the central question tackled by the book, on moral education and the curriculum. In the initial paper, John Wilson comes out in favour of timetabling moral education as a subject in the form of regular periods of instruction in moral methodology, a procedure to help pupils work out the right answers to moral questions, showing how these depend on good reasons which in turn relate to a welfare principle — 'human needs and interests'. To this H.J. Blackham adds the guided diversity of a humanized curriculum, linked to the localized and more concrete social context of the pupil's life, to enable him to understand more comprehensively how such principles are possible. This should, moreover, be contained within an overall direction in which he can see his own alternatives, take responsibility for action and share involvement, both in the school and the wider world. J.P. White questions whether Mr. Blackham intends diverse curriculum objectives or diverse routes to the same objectives, for the latter, he contends, are a necessary condition of *any* sort of education. Arguing that common terminal standards of achievement are a prerequisite of the morally educated person, he advocates a new 'architectonic of the curriculum' with the present individualistic aims of the subject-based curriculum subordinated to moral objectives. The content of a separate moral education programme, defined as 'the understanding of ethics' can only be discussed in the context of the moral foundations of the whole curriculum.

Up to this point, contributors thus adhered to the predefined limits of the discussion. Jasper Ungoed-Thomas, however, casting himself in the role of the teacher, chose with only oblique reference to moral education to analyse fundamental problems of communication, methodology and public relations in the curricular arena. Concentrating on a critical assessment of the philosopher's intervention, he maintains that this should be conditional upon his manifesting operational realism, professional insight into the teaching situation and an understanding of the logic of scientific research, since effective curricular methods should be derived inductively from the teacher's needs rather than deductively from independent theory. The paper's import is therefore provocative and essential: it disarmingly and originally brings to light some of the prejudices and interests of those educational philosophers, researchers and teachers engaged in curriculum development; it also strikes at the presuppositions underlying this collection. To have conformed to the sectional structure as planned would therefore have been both narrowing and inconclusive. And in the face of such an incisive challenge the charge could rightly have been levelled that the main concern was, by remaining bound to the initial framework and glossing over the divisions, to foster a seemingly harmonious picture rather than to establish a dialectic of communication. As a continuation of the analysis therefore John Wilson, as an interested (and named) educational philosopher, was accorded right of reply. He, too, is anxious to dispel the images of certain 'camps' selling various 'lines', but argues that the philosopher can claim to have the tools which equip him to clarify the curricular task and that this in itself is a large part of research. In conclusion two teachers — John Rose and Michelle York — in conversation comment on the materials presently available to a teacher of moral education, the support which is still required, and the ways in which teachers can take part in curriculum development.

To make progress

It would be wrong to claim that a collection of this nature had made more than a start in exploring any of these issues so crucial to moral education in schools today. From the difficulties in communication thus brought to the surface interdisciplinary approaches when linked with practical applications are seen to require sustained and painstaking interrelation not possible from the mere conjunction of discrete, albeit connected, papers. Indeed where contributors become wedded to different concerns they sometimes fail even within the same section to address themselves to the same kind of questions. Yet it is unlikely that any further dialogue would prosper without allowing participants the opportunity of meeting with the aim of getting somewhat clearer about the presuppositions, nature and range of their mutual undertaking. Even after conferences have been attended, however, other interdisciplinary inquiries in this field have revealed similar disjunction and often there is little or no attempt at interweaving the subsequent collation.[32] Not only is it apparent that there is a great diversity of opinion as to how common problems in moral education should be gauged, but the area is also underwritten by tradition, fears, prejudices and fantasies. Thus, though the bearing of interdisciplinary theory is complex, its application in practice is more so.

How then are we to make any useful progress? Firstly, it is at least plain that considerably more 'talk' and interaction involving *all* concerned parties is vital as a prelude to action. Just as the philosopher should be prepared to make clear his terms of reference and take pains to make himself understood, so the empirically oriented researcher must submit his proposed and ongoing task, whether it be large-scale action research or smaller in-depth 'illuminative' studies, both to the dissection of philosophic scrutiny and the modification entailed by teacher feedback. In turn, the onus is also on the teacher to make known the moral problems grounded in the daily confrontation of classroom experience, so that they are made available for diagnosis and exploration. Undoubtedly, teachers have an informed contribution to make, but are too often prevented by the constant pressures of teaching, and consequent lack of time and opportunity, from exploiting all the available channels for expressing their views or bringing their doubts and fears into the open. But it is most unlikely that any organized and coordinated approach to moral education can be soundly implemented without the full involvement, awareness and cooperation of teachers. The administrator too is implicated. He needs vigilance and alertness in reviewing policy decisions especially with regard to the present situation in moral education and Religious Education. Moreover, parents, whose major and proper influence in the education of the children in morality goes undisputed, often have strong feelings about the school's involvement. Both more active consultation and more positive participation by them in the school's work would strengthen its position as one link between the home and society at large. Lastly, attention must be paid to the voice of the pupil, whatever his age. Only by educing an accurate description of his needs and concerns can more effective guidance and support be supplied, both in direct teaching and the integrated and pervasive climate of the school. The challenge is to combine the multi-faceted interests of all these parties in establishing a context for deliberate and zealous communication with the object of devising an effective moral education programme to the benefit of both individuals and society.

To recognize a common involvement is, however, only a first step. Many of the problems in moral education remain largely uncircumscribed. More communication, consultation and participation undoubtedly constitute the necessary preliminaries to an increased synthesis of knowledge in this area. But, if this is not to degenerate in practice into confusion dictated by prejudice or the fashion of the times, the dialogue will require the ordering of a *structure*. Such a structure has yet to be forged. Any problem in moral education, as has already been outlined, contains a number of integral questions — philosophical questions, various genres of empirical questions and questions which only the experience of the teacher can answer. At present there is both a lack of appreciation of how the different disciplinary approaches cohere and a lack of scholarship with regard to educational problems. Thus there are many cases where, for example, a psychologist trespasses in the field of philosophy, failing either to give any indication that he is doing so, or to show awareness that some account should be taken of what may, for the particular aspect under consideration, be a more relevant expertise; equally, philosophers sometimes commit themselves to unsubstantiated empirical generalizations. Only the combined attention and enthusiasm of teachers and 'experts' in these disciplines will suffice firstly for disentangling and distinguishing these myriad questions, and subsequently demonstrating how the relevant evidence fits together in a certain order, and entails, in its turn, a particular conclusion and policy indication. In many respects, the required procedure would resemble the coordination of various specialists in building bridges or performing medical operations. The composition of such teams or working parties should, it seems evident, comprise members possessing knowledge appropriate to the problem in hand, led by an informed, sympathetic but firm chairman or director and with much more time and independence than is customary. Like the whole methodology of research and development in this area, the constitution of such teams and their working arrangements would be a matter for considerable and serious thought. No amount of working parties will, however, make the necessary headway without devising an effective structure by means of which an analysis and resolution of problems can be attempted. It is, nevertheless, imperative to embark on this undertaking if the future commitment of the school to educating children for the moral life is to be either sensible or coherent.

The intention of this collection has merely been to show what some of the immediate practical problems are. In so doing, it is to be hoped that our interdisciplinary debate is at least a pointer in the direction of much-needed serious communication. In that way only does certain progress in moral education lie.

M.J.T.
April, 1975

Notes

1 But a fascinating social-psychological investigation has recently shown how hierarchical authority structures can still induce unthinking conformity and obedience. See MILGRAM, S. (1974) *Obedience to Authority*, London: Tavistock Publications.

2 Some current positions can be seen from such works as FOOT, P. (ed) (1967). *Theories of Ethics*, London: Oxford University Press; WARNOCK, G. (1971) *The Object of Morality*, London: Methuen; WINCH, P. (1972) *Ethics and Action,* London: Routledge and Kegan Paul, and HARE, R.. See note 8 below.

3 See pp.14—16, for a brief account of present research and

development and Notes 15 and 18.

4 On the changing school role in moral education see P.H. HIRST (1974) *Moral Education in a Secular Society*, University of London Press.

5 PLATO, *Meno* translated by R.S. Bluck (1961) Cambridge University Press and *Republic*, translated by A.D. Lindsay (1935 edn) Dent, *passim*.

6 ARISTOTLE, *Nicomachean Ethics*, translated by Sir D. Ross (1925 edn), Oxford University Press, Book 2(1) and (4), but also *passim*.

7 Of course, many others — Plotinus, Aquinas, the Rationalists and Empiricists — were also concerned, like the Greek philosophers, with ethics as a part of their metaphysic but it was Kant whose stress on 'duty' in *The Groundwork of the Metaphysics of Morals*, (translated by H.J. Paton, Harper & Row) had such an influence on subsequent Western ethical thought.

8 HARE, R.M. (1963) *Freedom and Reason* and (1964) *Language of Morals*, both Oxford University Press.

9 One of the first such books was TIBBLE, J.W. (ed) (1966) *The Study of Education*. London: Routledge & Kegan Paul.

10 Educational research can of course now boast a vast array of inquiry methods ranging from participant research to longitudinal surveys with appropriate statistical techniques and evaluation methods.

11 See, for example, PETERS, R.S. (1966) *Ethics and Education*, Allen & Unwin and HIRST, P.H. and PETERS, R.S. (1970) *The Logic of Education*, London: Routledge & Kegan Paul. Even fewer philosophers have been prepared to apply philosophical techniques to educational research, but see WILSON, J. (1972) *Philosophy and Educational Research*, Slough: NFER.

12 Some more influential *sociological* works bearing on morality are: YOUNG, M. and WILLMOTT, P. (1963) *Family and Kinship in East London*; RIESMAN, D. *et al.* (1953) *The Lonely Crowd*, New York: Doubleday; and DOUGLAS, J.W.B. (1964) *The Home and the School*, MacGibbon & Kee, and more recently, SUGARMAN, B. (1973) *The School and Moral Development*, London: Croom Helm.

13 HARTSHORNE, H. and MAY, M.A. (1929) *Studies in the Nature of Character*, New York: Macmillan.

14 PIAGET, J. (1932) *The Moral Judgement of the Child*, London: Routledge & Kegan Paul.

15 KOHLBERG, L. (1963) *The Development of Children's Orientations Towards a Moral Order*, I Sequence in the Development of Moral Thought, Vita Humana, 6. II Social Experience, Social Conduct and the Development of Moral Thought, Vita Humana, 9.

16 KOHLBERG, L. (1974) 'Education, moral development and

faith', *Journal of Moral Education*, 4, 1, 5–16. Compare PETERS, R.S. (1973) 'The religious dimension of a rational morality', Lecture Four in *Reason and Compassion*, London: Routledge & Kegan Paul.

17 As a supplement to the inadequate summary here see: WILSON, J., WILLIAMS, N., and SUGARMAN, B. (1967) *Introduction to Moral Education*, Harmondsworth: Penguin.

18 See WILSON, J. (1973) *The Assessment of Morality*, Slough: NFER

19 See WILSON, J. (1972) *Practical Methods of Moral Education*, London: Heineman and (1973) *A Teacher's Guide to Moral Education*, Chapman.

20 MCPHAIL, P., UNGÓED-THOMAS, J.R. and CHAPMAN, H. (1972) *Moral Education in the Secondary School*, Longman. See also the critical review of this and the Project's materials *Lifeline* by R.S. PETERS in *Journal of Moral Education*, 3, 1, 413-5 and the reply by PETER MCPHAIL and J.R. UNGOED-THOMAS in *Journal of Moral Education*, 3, 2, 181-4. The Project does not, however, advocate the teaching of moral education as a subject:

'It makes little sense to conceive of moral education as a separate subject; we are concerned with all relations in the school, because behaviour is contagious'.

P. McPHAIL in *Set 74*, No. 2, NZCER.

21 Two recent papers have discussed the justification for RE and ME to be considered as either complementary or separate subject areas in the curriculum. See STRAUGHAN, R. (1974) 'Religion, morality and the curriculum', *London Educational Review*, 3, 3, 73–9. and PALMER, G. (1974). 'Religious education in the primary school', *Cambridge Journal of Education*, 4, 3, 123–33.

22 See P.H. HIRST (1965) 'Liberal education and the nature of knowledge' in ARCHAMBAULT, R.D., *Philosophical Anaylisis and Education*, London: Routledge & Kegan Paul, pp 113–38.

23 Some examples of moral education through drama are discussed in STEPHENSON, N. and VINCENT, D. (Eds) (1975) *Teaching and Understanding Drama*, Slough: NFER and also in TAYLOR, M. (Ed) (1974) *Team Teaching Experiments*, pp. 39–43. Indeed it would seem that a teaching team drawn from different disciplinary backgrounds could be a particularly effective approach in moral education. On the teaching of moral methodology see also CRITTENDEN, B. (1972) *Form and Content in Moral Education*, Monograph Series No. 12, OISE, Toronto: Canada.

24 This second-order monitoring function as a feature of human behaviour is discussed in HARRÉ, R. and SECORD P. (1973) *The*

Explanation of Social Behaviour, Oxford: Blackwell.

25 See TOWNSEND, H.E.R. and BRITTAN, E. (1973) *Multiracial Education: Need and Innovation,* Evans/Methuen.

26 It is an oft-voiced complaint today from all sections of education that much educational theory fails to relate to practice. It is hoped to have avoided incurring this charge both by starting from common school problems and by giving the last word to teachers.

27 To date there is little available on moral education in tertiary education except for a recent book COLLIER, G., WILSON, J. and TOMLINSON, P. (Eds) (1974) *Values and Moral Development in Higher Education,* London: Croom Helm.

28 As evidenced by the recent NAS Conference devoted to it and at which a discussion paper on discipline was presented. See 'Discipline in schools', *New Schoolmaster,* November, 1974.

29 Others too, including Kohlberg (See *Journal of Moral Education,* 4, 1, 77—8) have proposed a 'participatory program' in school management.

30 *The Humanities Project: an Introduction,* (1970) Heinemann Educational. See also other references in Lawrence Stenhouse's paper, pp. 123—133.

31 But see ELLIOT, J. (1974) 'Sex role constraints on freedom of discussion: a neglected reality of the classroom; in *New Era,* 55, 6, 145—55.

32 For example, the first interdisciplinary approach to moral education, NIBLETT, W.R. (1963). *Moral Education in a Changing Society.* See also MISCHEL, T. (ed.) (1974). *Understanding Other Persons,* Oxford: Blackwell; BECK, C.M., CRITTENDEN, B. and SULLIVAN, M. (1972) *Moral Education: Inter-disciplinary Approaches,* University of Toronto Press; WILSON, J. *et al.* (1967) *op cit.* even after two years' collaborative work hardly gives an adequate amount of the interrelation of the disciplines.

Section One

A. Moral Education and its Place in the Curriculum

'The young person should be taught
to reason morally, he cannot be brain-
washed into a state of true morality.'

*Religious Information and
Moral Development*, Report of
Committee on Religious Educa-
tion in the Public Schools
of Ontario by J. Keiller MacKay.
Toronto: Ontario Department of
Education. 1969. p. 50.

Moral Education and the Curriculum

John Wilson

Morality as a form of thought

Of the various fantasies sparked off by the words 'moral' and 'morality', perhaps both the commonest and the most obstructive is the idea that these words stand for some *one quality* (rather like being red-blooded), a quality which may in some mysterious way be 'transmitted' or 'infused' or 'caught' or 'inculcated': the agents for this process being 'society', 'the concerned teacher', 'the good example of parents', or whatever. 'Goodness', or 'virtue', or 'morality' somehow spreads by infection or transfusion (like a blood transfusion). It is this fantasy, I think, in one form or another, which causes hostility or indifference to the demonstrably correct idea of putting some aspects of moral education into the curriculum. To 'put morality into the curriculum' sounds a bit like putting God into the curriculum (or Virtue, or The Good, or Love, or something of that kind).

One aspect of this fantasy is the 'But-X-comes-into-everything' idea; it is noteworthy that we do not want to run this idea as an argument against putting X into the curriculum in the cases of (say) science, or mathematics, or English, but feel tempted to run it in other cases ('morality', 'personal relationships', etc.). Of course some people just react against any kind of specialized study at all: I actually heard one teacher say 'What! Learn mathematics as a separate subject! Ridiculous! Mathematics is all around you', he added, gesturing vaguely. If one is obsessed by the need to 'break down subject barriers' to the point of no return, there is not much that argument can do. But in general people, or educated people, do recognize that there just are different kinds of questions, issues, problems, 'forms of thought', or whatever, even though connections may be made between them. The argument that morality 'comes into everything' won't do, partly because it just isn't true (plenty of situations don't involve moral choices); and partly because, even if it were, that would not be a reason against giving special curricular consideration to (if one wants to insist on such a description) the 'moral aspect' of 'everything'.

Another aspect is the notion that morality has little to do with *thinking* or *learning* at all: that it is wholly concerned with 'feeling' or overt 'behaviour', and therefore in a strict sense unteachable: that hence all we can do (or need to do) is just to 'motivate' people in various ways (example, or inspiration, or cold baths and rugger, or tea and sympathy, or whatever). This could only be maintained by somebody who believed that educators were only interested in overt, photographable, 'brute' behaviour, for which the kind of reasons or motives or intentions did not matter. What such a person would want would be not morally educated pupils, but trouble-free ones: we leave him in the hands of Skinner and other operant conditioners, but do not pay him as a teacher or educator. As soon as reasons, purposes, motives and so on are allowed to walk onstage, we at once have to consider what *sorts* of reasons we are going to encourage pupils to use; and morality now can be clearly seen as partly, at least, a matter of thinking, learning, grasping concepts, noting what is relevant and irrelevant, and using what Aristotle called the right 'practical syllogisms': not, certainly, a matter just of a blood transfusion, nor even of some process of 'development' or 'maturation'.

This goes against quite a lot of grain, for reasons I am not clear about. A modified version of the idea above is that 'We all *know* well enough what's right, the problem is to *do* it': this does not totally abolish the notion of reasoning, but relegates it to a minor role. The idea is that we all know that (say) we ought to act out of love for our neighbour, so that there's no point teaching this to children: we should get on with the 'motivation', or inspiration, or whatever. One difficulty with this idea is that different people or societies that claim to 'know' make this claim on very different grounds, which not infrequently produce very different types of behaviour: consider the 'knowledge', or the sort of certainty, claimed by Christians, Nazis, Communists, members of the IRA and so on. There is indeed such a thing as moral knowledge; but most of us, most of the time, either do not possess it or do not use it as a basis for action. We have a strong resistance to the programme of (i) working out the answers for ourselves in the light of reason, and (ii) prescribing these answers for ourselves to act upon. We find this threatening, and too much like hard work. It is easier to act out our fantasies.

Leaving the amateur psychology aside, one would run the following straightforward argument: either

(1) we have some idea of how to get right answers to moral

questions — some notion of what counts as a good reason and what doesn't, perhaps something approaching a methodology, or
(2) we don't (maybe we think 'it's all relative', or maybe we are just muddled about what good reasons are in morality).

If (2), we have no right to be in the moral education business at all; thus if a pupil says 'I'm going to beat her up because it's Tuesday/ because I hate her/because she's black', or whatever reason you like, all we can say is 'Ah, well, that's a point of view'. Certainly *discussion* would be useless; for serious discussion presupposes the possibility of progress via relevant reasoning, of getting nearer to right answers or truth — otherwise we are just swapping feelings. Nor would we feel we had the right to know what *sort* of examples to set, inspiration to give, etc., since (on this view) we have no clue as to what can fairly count as a *good* example.

I don't think anyone seriously believes (2) (not even sociologists, if properly pressed). We have *some* idea how to do the subject, *some* grasp of what can fairly or intelligibly count as a reason, and of what we are committed to by the use of words like 'ought', 'right', etc. I think, of course, that we have a pretty good idea; that, at least on reflection, most sane people would accept that reasons — to count as good reasons — would have to be shown to relate to human needs and interests (rather than what some 'authority' says, or what one's inner feelings suggest to one, or what one selfishly wants, or what day of the week it is). If so, quite a lot follows: we need whatever skills, knowledge, abilities, aptitudes, etc. will best enable us to work out these reasons properly and act on them. I have spelled all this out often enough elsewhere[1]; here my point is simply that if we don't have any rational agreement on moral methodology and reasoning, we're not in business at all: but insofar as we do, we ought to teach it to pupils.

One might add to this basic point in three ways, defending the placing of 'moral thinking' (or whatever we want to call it) in the curriculum:

(a) First, it is *honest*. If we suppose that we are in a position to educate pupils morally at all, then we thereby claim to have some idea about the aims of moral education, about the qualities required by people for settling moral problems reasonably and acting on their decisions. That is, we claim some knowledge of morality as a subject. If so, how can we *not* put this before our pupils in some form without dishonesty? Why conceal this from them?

(b) Secondly, it is *professional*. By this I mean that we ought to, and now can, get well beyond the stage of merely 'discussing moral problems', 'arousing concern', 'stimulating interest', 'being open-ended', and so on. A lot of (no doubt useful) work has been done along these lines; but we must give our pupils a clear idea that there are *right and wrong answers* to moral questions, that there is a coherent *methodology* for settling them. We cannot encourage the feeling expressed in such words as 'It's all relative really, isn't it?', 'It's just a matter of how you feel', 'It's a matter of taste', etc. Just as, in science or other subjects, it is one thing to encourage and help pupils to find out the answers and the reasons behind them, but quite another to imply that there are no answers; so in morality, although we do not impose our individual views as right, we must not imply that one view is as good as another.

(c) Thirdly, it *gives the pupils something to hang on to*. I avoid here words like 'ideal', 'creed', 'faith', etc., because we are not out to give them any specific or partisan set of moral or metaphysical beliefs. What we are trying to give them is something far more important, for which 'methodology' is as good a word as I can think of. We are giving them the tools to do the job for themselves (which is the only way you can do morality anyway). Without these tools, there is bound to be the 'moral vacuum' ('alienation', anxiety, sense of being lost, 'drifting', or whatever we care to call it) that many people have talked about. The tools are not intellectually very complex: the concepts and reasoning required are well within the cognitive grasp of quite young children.[2]

All this is perhaps just a long-winded way of repeating what other philosophers have meant by saying that morality is a 'form of thought' in its own right,[3] and must be taught as such. There are, of course, some disagreements amongst moral philosophers about its logical basis; but not, in my judgement, enough to preclude our getting on with the job. Much graver is the divergence between those who want to get on with the job and those who, for whatever reasons, somehow react against the whole idea of putting it on the curricular map as a serious subject of study. I have been trying to argue that to be serious about moral education means, in part, to welcome this idea.

The use of materials

It seems clear, then, that — whatever else is needed for moral education — the teacher needs to have some coherent material on 'moral methodology' (to give it a grand name), that is, those concepts, procedures, types of reasons, abilities and so on which are basic to the subject. I should expect these to look not much unlike the list of 'moral components' published elsewhere[4] — that is, they would include the various concepts and principles involved in concern for people (PHIL), awareness of emotions (EMP), factual knowledge and 'know-how' (GIG), and alertness and determination (KRAT). I do not here want to argue for these in detail, but I shall assume that the material in question attempts the task of explaining what is required for moral thought and action, in a quite straightforward and workmanlike manner, and that the teacher using it at least thinks that this is a possible and important thing to do.

As a matter of fact I am not aware that any satisfactory material of *this* kind has been produced. A vast quantity has been produced, both in the U.K. and (even more) on the other side of the Atlantic, with apparently different aims: to stimulate thought about social or personal problems, discuss controversial issues, arouse general interest in 'values', and so on. These appear often under vague or trendy headings, like 'value clarification', 'personal development', 'learning to live', 'society today', etc. Much of this may, for various purposes, be extremely useful. But it seems to me fairly clear that it fights shy of the whole notion of a rational methodology, and (to say the least) does not stress the point that there are right and wrong, rational and irrational, serious and non-serious ways of making up one's mind about moral issues. The popularity of controversial issues, and of the large-scale 'social' issues (pollution, war, etc.), suggests this strongly. Issues of this kind of course exist, and are important: but they are clearly not easy to settle. To *begin* with issues of this kind seems an absurd policy for anyone who is really trying to initiate pupils into a particular methodology or form of thought. Much more naturally, as in other subjects, we should begin with clear cases of a non-controversial kind, where we have something like certain knowledge; also, with cases which are simple and nearest to the pupils' own experience — the behaviour of one pupil or family-member to another, for instance, rather than the wider problems of politics and society. Moral education, like charity, begins at home; and a good deal of contemporary material seems to me evasive in more than one way.

Let us assume, then, that we have some material or booklet of the required kind — a sort of 'First Steps in Morality'[5] — without arguing too much about its exact form (in fact, somewhat different forms will be suitable for different types of pupils). A number of important questions arise about how teachers should use such material, what methods of teaching may be appropriate for it, what specific difficulties might be encountered, and so on. I shall try and sketch out some answers to these questions which I think would apply to *any* satisfactory material of this kind. A lot, of course, would rightly be left to the individual teacher, but, assuming that the teacher has some such material actually in his hands, I should want to advise him roughly as follows.

I General

Whatever other methods of moral education the teacher may use, it is essential that the material be worked through in an ordered and serious way. First try to ensure, by reading and discussion, that the pupils grasp the points; then perhaps amplify and illustrate by whatever supporting methods seem valuable; and then return to the text to reinforce the understanding. There can be no harm, and much good, in testing pupils in some way, to see how far they have grasped the points. Naturally this needs a good deal of experiment, and it might for many reasons be unwise to institutionalize something called 'An Examination in Morality' in schools, before we have taken sufficient thought about its content, its form, and its title. But the teacher should not be deterred from making his own assessment of his pupils' progress.

Other school subjects — perhaps most obviously RE, English and history, but not they alone — are of course relevant to the area covered by this sort of material and much is to be gained in deploying these subjects in the interests of moral education. However, it would be fatal to regard this as a substitute for direct teaching. Morality has its own principles and methodology, and they are not the same as those of history, literary criticism, science or any other subject. They must be taught in their own right, however much advantage may be derived from what the pupil learns elsewhere. Granted that moral questions may arise in the course of a history or English lesson, granted also that some of the skills and abilities useful for morality are also fostered by other subjects, nevertheless, to treat morality as a kind of addendum or 'fringe' topic is to court disaster.

Head teachers and other teachers will make up their own minds about the title and arrangements under which such material should be taught. I would suggest 'Moral Thinking' as a possible title for the periods used, but it makes little difference whether it comes under RE, or English, or 'citizenship', or 'general periods', or any other title. What matters is that a definite number of periods — at least one or two a week — should be set aside, under the control of one teacher, for this purpose.

If any question arises of which teachers should use this material, I would remind the reader that personal commitment (whether to Christianity or to any other set of beliefs) is not a relevant criterion. All that matters is that the teacher should believe the material to be useful, and that he should be — above all — *clear-headed* about it. Deep personal concern for children, and other psychological characteristics, are of course important; but they are, in this context, less important than the desire to do a good, workmanlike job of educating pupils in the vital area, and the ability to understand and teach these principles without muddle, vagueness, irrelevance or dishonesty. Partly for this reason, I think it may be helpful to make some use of the 'moral components' described elsewhere.[6] They have the merit of avoiding vague terms like 'sensitivity', 'awareness', etc., and of forcing us to make quite sure that we understand what they mean.

II Teaching methods

The teacher will remember that he must go through the material step by step, making sure that the points in it are grasped by his pupils. But he will also need additional or supporting methods of teaching, to make these points 'real' to the pupils: to make them stick in their imagination and memory. To what extent, and in what ways, the teacher decides to introduce these supporting methods is up to him. All I can do here is to say something about the general principles which should underlie these methods.

(1) *Use of methods*

Most teachers will be very well aware of the difficulty their pupils experience in absorbing written material, or engaging in more 'abstract' thinking. They will naturally, and rightly, think of using more concrete or less 'verbal' methods: drama, film, role-playing, and so on. What we want to stress here is that these more concrete methods must be used *in a supporting or reinforcing role, and not in their own right*. The question to be asked about them is, not 'Do the pupils enjoy them?', 'Are they fun?', or 'Do they do the pupils some kind of good?', but 'Do they help the pupils to see the point?'.

For we are here trying to teach the pupils certain points and principles. When we give them the benefit of visual aids, 'real-life' experiences, and so on, what we should be doing is to give them extended *examples* of these principles, examples which we hope will be more 'real' to them and stick in their minds. But they will only *be* examples if we use them *as* examples. We have to correlate them with the principles: to move back and forth, from the principle to the examples and methods, back to the principle again, and so on — just as in any form of teaching. We must resist the temptation to feel, or vaguely hope, that a certain method will somehow just *rub off on* the pupils. They need to be *taught*.

This is not to say that the teacher should spend more time on direct verbal instruction about the principles, and less time on the supporting methods. Naturally this will depend on the pupils. Some may need a great many examples, a great deal of time spent on more concrete methods, before thy get the point at all. But every pupil — even those whom we sometimes write off as 'non-verbal', 'too unintelligent', 'incapable of abstract reasoning', etc. — must be made to see the point sooner or later: otherwise nothing has been achieved.

There is in fact no doubt that even quite young children are capable of grasping these points and principles; for instance, they do in fact often think and act in an 'other-considering' way — that is, they have some understanding of the equality of individuals and use it as a reason for action. The difficulty lies in the difference between a weak and a firm grasp of them, and this is something which afflicts adults as well as children. Intellectually, the points are simple enough. What happens is that we do not grasp them firmly or fully, because we are tempted to think in quite different ways. The obstacles are not 'intellectual' but 'psychological'; and a firm intellectual grasp, which a good teacher can provide, is of the utmost importance for practical action.

(2) *Types and range of methods*

Here, for the sake of illustration, are a number of general methods which will occur to the teacher:

(1) Going through the material point by point, giving examples in class and asking the children questions about it.

(2) Encouraging the children to use sources which illustrate the material, and to bring their own examples and material (newspaper cuttings, cartoons, etc.) to the classroom.

(3) Oral discussion on moral questions to which the material is relevant.

(4) Oral discussions with the teacher about their emotions and personal relationships.

(5) The use of films and other visual media.

(6) Acting, drama and role-playing.

(7) Making a tape or videotape recording of the children's discussions, or their actual behaviour, and playing it back to them afterwards for further consideration.

(8) Putting them in 'simulation situations' where they have to solve personal and moral problems.

(9) Giving them experience of people unlike themselves (coloured people, old people, etc.) to enlarge their understanding.

(10) Getting them to make up their own rules, or organize something inside or outside the school on their own responsibility.

The reader will notice that these methods are arranged in a particular order, along a scale which might be (rather inadequately) labelled 'abstract' at one end, and something like 'concrete' or 'real-life' at the other. Method (1), the direct explanation of the material, may be 'abstract' and 'unreal' for some pupils; in method (10), on the other hand, the pupils are more or less forced to think and act for themselves. Films and other visual aids (5) produce more personal involvement, for some pupils, than most types of discussion (3) and (4), but not so much as role-playing (6).

Rather than just picking one or two methods to support the material, the teacher should ideally try to get a proper 'mix' of methods, and make sure that he is not spending too much time at one end of the scale or the other — that he is not being too 'abstract' or too 'concrete'. It will be best if he tries to use a number of methods which cover the whole scale. For instance, if he is dealing with concern for others (PHIL), he might start by going through the material (1), get the pupils to do some role-playing which illustrates PHIL (6), refer back to the material (1), tape-record their behaviour and their talk in some PHIL-type situation, such as when a stranger or a new pupil appears, and get them to discuss the recording (7), back to the material again (1), and then get them to engage in a 'real-life' experience (making up their own rules about strangers or new pupils, or getting them to help old people in the area, or whatever) (10), and finally back to the material (1). By such a judicious mixture of 'abstract' and 'concrete' methods, the principle of PHIL may be firmly grasped. Naturally the proper 'mix' depends on the type of pupils, but almost all pupils will need supporting methods which run throughout the scale. Both 'abstract' methods and 'experience' are impotent by themselves. They have to be correlated.

This vast range of methods may seem somewhat alarming. Naturally, teachers are handicapped, not only by the kind of pupils they teach, but by the time and resources available. Thus the use of videotape may be financially out of the question; and the more 'real-life' methods of giving the children responsibility for practical tasks, and experience of out-of-school situations, may be difficult for severely practical reasons. Some teachers may also feel unfamiliar and uncertain about such methods as 'simulation-situations', and perhaps even the use of drama and role-play. However, of these ten general methods or techniques it seems clear that all teachers should be able to use at least (1), (2), (3) and (4). That is, all teachers can go through the material point by point, encourage the children to bring their own examples and material to class, discuss this material, and discuss how they and the pupils feel about it and about each other. Here the importance of (2) should be stressed, that is, of using the pupil's own material and examples. This material — cuttings or cartoons from a newspaper which the pupils see, for instance — may not be particularly high-minded or 'respectable'; but it is *theirs*, and real to *them* — in a way, the more 'down to earth' it is the better.

Most teachers, I hope, could go further. Certainly the use of drama and role-play, which is now common and well-documented, requires no particular expense or complicated arrangements (6); tape-recorders are not hard to come by (7); references to films and popular TV programmes cost nothing, even if the films themselves do (5); and the situations described in (8), (9) and (10) require imagination rather than anything else.

Of one thing, however, I am reasonably sure. This is a subject which requires intellectual *coherence* even more than it requires to be made 'real' to the pupils. There will, therefore, be many occasions on which the teacher needs to be in full control of the class as a whole. For this purpose, 'discipline' — perhaps in a rather old-fashioned sense — is essential. The teacher may wish to split the class into groups for some purposes, or to allow individual pupils to pursue various lines on their own: and here he may encourage 'activity methods' to advantage. But the nature of the subject logically requires that there are times when the whole class needs to be firmly controlled, *instructed*, attentive, and so on in a quite straightforward sense. The right mixture of 'instruction' and 'activity' will vary from one class to another but it must *be* a mixture: no *one* disciplinary or social setting can do the whole job. Here I am really making the same point that I have made earlier about the *content* of the subject, but it applies also to the *context* of teaching.

(3) *Language*

In thinking about the use of language in regard to these methods, it is very important to draw a distinction between two things. First, on these occasions when we are concerned to give the pupils a firm and clear grasp of the principles in a straightforward way, we need to use pedestrian and simple language. Second, when we are trying to illustrate the principles imaginatively, to give pupils the 'inner feel' of them or to involve their emotions, we need so far as possible to use language which is aesthetically effective. Both these aspects are important, but they must not be confused.

With regard to the first, we have to remember that the points to be made (in this material) are themselves very pedestrian and simple. They stand on their own feet. We must resist the temptation to dress them up in borrowed clothes, and talk of 'an intuition of human value', 'the dignity of human beings', 'the brotherhood of mankind', as well as specifically religious or partisan phrases such as 'sons of God', 'fellow-members of the working-class', etc., which are to be avoided. And if we go further, and try to justify morality in some external way, as resting on some particular metaphysic, then we do positive harm: for now we have hired morality out to some other master. Whatever our personal beliefs, we must teach the principles as a matter of logic and common sense, and in the clear, simple language appropriate to such teaching.

With regard to the second, here again vague phrases and high-sounding terms are useless. It is no good talking of 'concern', 'caring', etc. if these words are not made real. For this task of imaginative illustration, we do better to make use of available literature which does the job better than we can hope to do it. Thus one does not have to be a committed Christian to realize that the parable of the Good Samaritan is an excellent illustration of PHIL, of the concept of a person and of the relevant type of action. Good fictitional illustrations, or any language which *particularizes* the principles in an imaginative way, are much better than general talk of 'concern for others', or vaguely topical considerations of war, pollution, poverty, and so forth.

III Some predictable difficulties

Finally, the teacher needs to be forewarned against certain difficulties which will inevitably crop up. I am not thinking here of obvious difficulties like lack of intelligence or understanding, or the problems of getting the points across by the methods we have been considering. The real difficulties are of a different kind, and better called *resistances* or prejudices. Unlike some other subjects, morality is something in which pupils are already engaged before they have any instruction at all: they already have built-in ways of thinking about what to do, derived from their parents, or their friends, or their own inner desires and compulsions. Consequently they will resist the kind of methodology, the way of 'doing morals', that we are trying to teach. The resistance may take various forms: hostility, anxiety, determined boredom, desire to please the teacher by 'going through the motions' of what they are taught without really believing it, and so on.

It is important that the teacher should be quite clear about these 'wrong ways' of thinking about morality — not least because adults, as well as pupils, are liable to think thus; we all have prejudices and psychological compulsions which prevent us from being reasonable in our morality. I have tried to criticize some of them at length elsewhere[7]; here we may put them under two general headings:

(a) 'Absolute' or 'arbitrary'

Many young people (and not a few adults) feel, *either* that there must be some complete and absolute set of 'right answers' in morality, some set of unbreakable rules which they can learn like the Ten Commandments *or* that morality is 'a matter of taste', 'purely relative', etc. Both these are attempts to evade any serious moral *thinking*: the former gives you all the answers ready-made, and the latter says there are no answers at all. In recent years the tendency has perhaps been for the latter mistake to gain ground, but the teacher must be prepared to meet both. Neither, in fact, will stand up to consideration; and it is doubtful whether many people really believe in these views as serious theories about morality — rather, they act as if they believed them because the effort of serious thinking is too great or too threatening. Few seriously believe that the whole of morality can be reduced to a simple, 'absolute' code that needs no further thought, and few seriously believe that important moral issues and actions, such as Hitler's killing of millions of people, are 'arbitrary', 'just a matter of taste', or entirely beyond the scope of rational criticism. The teacher may wish, of course, to take up this matter at a more advanced philosophical level with those (probably few) pupils who have serious and rational doubts about it; but he may well be inclined to regard some protests on the part of pupils in this area as essentially psychological resistance rather than intellectual difficulty — in which case he may be well advised to put the protests gently but firmly aside, and wait until the material has been thoroughly absorbed.

(b) Other modes of thought
The moral thinking of many pupils (and adults) is not done in terms of other people's interests at all, but in some other mode. Which mode affects particular pupils will depend on the stage of their development, and many other factors. It may be:

(i) the '*other-obeying*' mode, in which some external person, group of people, or code is taken as the ultimate authority on what to do. The 'other' may be the pupil's parents, or his friends, or 'what fashion says', or the Bible, or almost anything.
(ii) the '*self-obeying*' mode, in which some internal feeling on the part of the pupil determines what he thinks he ought to do. This may be guilt, or shame ('conscience') or perhaps some ideal of himself that he is wedded to (e.g. he sees himself as 'tough guy', 'modern', etc.).
(iii) the '*self-considering*' mode, in which some straightforward or selfish advantage dictates his thinking (he will get a reward, be detected and punished, be praised, make more money, etc.).

There is of course much more to be said about the kinds of mistakes mentioned above, and in particular about the kinds of emotions that engender them. Certainly the more the teacher is concerned with getting the pupils not just to understand the right way to 'do morality' — though this would be no mean achievement — but to be serious about applying it to their own case, the more he will find himself forced to enter the area of the education of the emotions. For it is other emotional pulls, pulls which have little to do with the attitude of concern (PHIL) which should operate in us, that distract us all from correct moral behaviour — and sometimes go so far as to distract us from correct moral thinking.

In this essay I hope (1) to have advanced *one* effective line of argument for some 'direct' teaching of moral methodology in the curriculum, or at least (2) to have defused some of the worries or fantasies that commonly stand in the way of doing so, and (3) to have given a very rough idea of the sort of way in which material for this can be used in practical teaching. This leaves many questions untouched, perhaps in particular (a) the contribution made by other curricular subjects; (b) the kind of difficulties that may arise (especially with pupils who reject, or seem to reject, a rational methodology); and (c) a host of practical questions about the precise form of any such material, the methods appropriate for pupils of particular ages, levels of intelligence, social background, and so forth. But I hope that succeeding contributors to this section of the book may have something useful to say about all or some of these.

Notes

1 Most fully in *Education in Religion and the Emotions*, (1971) London: Heinemann.

2 See Norman and Sheila WILLIAMS *(1970) The Moral Development of Children*, London: Macmillan.

3 See Paul HIRST'S (1974) *Moral Education in a Secular Society*. London: University of London Press with reference to his earlier work on 'forms of knowledge'.

4 The clearest lists will be found in my *The Assessment of Morality*, (1973), Slough: NFER; and *A Teacher's Guide to Moral Education*, (1973). London: G. Chapman.

5 I should add that I and some of my colleagues are engaged in preparing material which we hope to publish under this title shortly.

6 See *A Teacher's Guide to Moral Education*, (1973). London: G. Chapman.

7 *ibid.*

The Curriculum in Moral Education

H.J. Blackham

Direct teaching

I am in sympathy with John Wilson's plea for 'putting morality into the curriculum' in regular periods of direct teaching, but not altogether with what I think he means. To teach moral logic in a straightforward way as a self-contained method of getting right answers to moral questions is not enough even for its limited purpose, instruction in moral reasoning. It is not enough not merely because of the 'predictable difficulties' he speaks of as 'resistances', but mainly because it leaves out the conditions which justify the moral logic.

The making of choices is fast becoming a fundamental feature of our education from primary schools on; and 'guidance' is being built into the curriculum to help children to make the right educational decisions, that is, the most advantageous for their own development. (An NFER survey of methods of guidance in secondary schools in curricular choices is now in progress.*) The way in which informed decisions are made, therefore, is going to be taught more or less direct from early years. Moral decisions are specifically different in that the interests and feelings of others are likely to be affected, and the probable effect on them of alternative courses of conduct has to be considered impartially with the effects desired in my own interest. This equal consideration which marks and makes a moral decision, is rational only if there is a moral order presupposed based on mutual trust (as Hobbes insisted long ago). There is no point in my keeping my place in a queue which most others have quit, so that there is no longer a queue

---

* *Survey of Guidance Systems — Curricular Guidance Evaluation Phase 1,* supervised by Margaret I. Reid, is investigating methods guiding pupils in their subject choices in the third year of secondary schooling (Ed.).

situation. The point is that morality inescapably involves a share in the responsibility of maintaining, or bringing about, the conditions on which it is reasonable to make agreements and keep the rules in good faith.

This comes out clearly in the history of ethics and is clearer to more people in current attempts to run an incomes policy. If you are going to teach morality in the form of moral logic, how to get the right answers, you have to have the right answers also for the sharp boy with the questions of Thrasymachus, and even for the articulate rebel. It is not reasonable to pass by the fundamental questions underlying morality by starting from premises which rest on undisclosed assumptions. In other words, if we are going to teach morality credibly as a method of reasoning, it must be in the context of an understanding of the conditions on which agreements and mutual trust and equal consideration for the interests of others are feasible. These are not merely to be presupposed with society itself, for they are under constant threat and are all the time being eroded or undermined. This permanent truth about morality that used to be an obscure footnote is now in the headlines of our daily newspapers. Social morality is locked in a dilemma unless there is, and is felt to be, a genuine movement towards social justice. Teaching moral logic is not rational if it does not include the rationale of social morality.

There is a distinction between this sphere of social obligation and the other moral hemisphere, personal choice of ideals, values, virtues, which does not involve others in the same way. The two are usually confused, and although they are interrelated, not to make the distinction is liable to stultify thought and discussion about morality. The hemisphere of personal choice is the ground on which RE stands in its more open and inclusive new development, and RE teachers are becoming prepared and equipped to move in this direction.

A second weakness in the direct teaching of moral logic is more subtle, and more difficult to correct. Although exercises in working out the right answers to hypothetical situations are necessary, and teaching the material in this way for this purpose is educationally entirely justifiable, the teaching leaves out, again, the moral reality. Right answers are not right because they have been worked out correctly, as conclusions in a logical argument. They are the answers which on reflection I am prepared to take responsibility for. But this can never be the case in class. True, the argument is about applying principles which do justify me on reflection in taking responsibility for a certain course, but the principles are not instructions which faithfully followed bring about a predictable result; they cannot justify their application. So that there is risk of falsifying the very nature of the 'right' answer. Another aspect of this risk is the danger of encouraging the pupils to make moral judgements. Not only a particular judgement has to be justified; one's title to make a judgement is always in question. On whose behalf does one speak, and with what authority?

The danger of false abstraction, moral unreality, is far less if the teaching goes on in the context of a school which is striving, and is known and felt to be striving, to make itself a just society. Indeed, the teaching is not justifiable in any other context.

Direct teaching, then, is desirable, but there is a long way to go before it is feasible in a desirable form and teachers are equipped to cope with it. The kind of understanding which can and should be the object of such teaching would make the intellectual core of moral education which John Wilson wants. Devising a syllabus for discussion might make a useful start.

Having made this comment on direct teaching in a regular period, I want to go on to say something about the contribution of the curriculum indirectly by providing diversity, and then to say something about 'guidance' and 'orientation'.

Diversity

The main influence in moral education is the school community itself, or so it is often said: the human relations within it, the way it is organized and run, the ideals it stands for and inculcates. The moral education provided in this way by, say, Winchester College and Neill's Summerhill has been rather different, as the discipline of square-bashing and spit-and-polish produces a different morale from that produced by the training of a commando or a guerilla fighter. At least it seems reasonable to assume this in general, although I know of no empirical study which shows what it means in particular. However, even if the school community is the main influence, that influence is not independent of the curriculum. On the contrary, a school community is defined by its educational task, and that at once points to the curriculum.

A vocational or a trade school selects and brings together those who want or are presumed to want to train for the same future, who have similar intentions and hopes and a fairly equal chance. A grammar school brings (or brought) together for the study of more or less the same subjects boys or girls selected by tests of their performance in these subjects. Those who fail to qualify go (or went) to another kind of school, where they may or may not study the same subjects, aiming at a lower level of attainment. For those who scrape into the grammar school or are in the lower streams, there is some failure, under-achievement; they are not thriving members of the educational community. For those who fail to get in, who are segregated in a school which is not merely different but markedly inferior, doing the same work at a lower level, there is likely to be a shared and total feeling of inferiority or social rejection, and insofar as the work is the same, it is by definition what they are not good at, do not enjoy, by which they are chronically defeated.

This is not here put forward as an argument for comprehensive secondary education, but as an argument for diversity in the curriculum, because this is a necessary condition of there being an educational community to which all who are compelled to go along have a chance of feeling that they belong. I have seen boys in the C and D streams of a grammar school (which was interested only in scholarships and cricket) either coerced or ignored, educated for hooliganism, subversion, or mental sickness. I have seen a secondary modern school (whose head and staff were ready to profit by their freedom from university requirements) with sixteen activities to choose from, with a plot of land and beasts, a school that hummed with thriving activities that evoked a spontaneous public spirit and mutual discipline. This school might well have enjoyed 'parity of esteem' with a grammar school, and have offered a far better education to any discerning parent of a child who just succeeded at eleven in qualifying for a grammar school. These are merely personal impressions. There have been some empirical studies.[1]

The point I am making is that the curriculum, in what it offers or fails to offer, makes all the difference to the possibilities of moral education. In two ways. A child who is offered only what he is invincibly not good at can hardly feel respected or valued, and therefore can hardly respect or value himself. Moreover, the pattern of failure is liable to become chronic and crippling, reinforced by all he does. The school community cannot be a means of moral education for those who are alienated by it. Remedial reading may be the best form of moral education in a given case.

The other way in which moral education suffers if the curriculum does not offer a child enough that he can take to and be comparatively good at is that he is not stimulated and developed, does not find an independent footing with interests of his own; he has no stake in the community, is not engaged, has no reason for co-operation, no interests to protect and further in terms of the tasks of the school. The school community is a hostile or unfriendly environment from which to escape, not a theatre of enjoyed activities in which to thrive. For such reasons, the school with a narrowly traditional curriculum cannot be a community which trains pupils of diverse abilities and aptitudes for responsible roles.

There cannot be diversity in the curriculum unless and until there is staff which can offer the options. This is the time, with the reorganization of college curricula and the shaping of new courses for professional qualifications, to create these opportunities. If students can choose from courses which make a term's intensive work credited as modules or units towards their qualification, many teachers will come into secondary schools with more to offer than the traditional disciplines in which the graduate teacher specialized. These new options, if they are interesting and sensible and are taken up by some of the brighter pupils as well as being within the reach of the less able, will earn their status alongside the classical subjects in the time-table.

The school 'contract'

Apart from the intrinsic interest of particular subjects, their appeal to individuals, there is the way in which pupils take the curriculum for their own purposes. The traditional subjects of an academic curriculum which those in the upper streams of a grammar school can cope with and do reasonably well at, even if they were mumbo-jumbo, put in their hands the passport to where they want to go. In a poor developing country secondary education means a white-collar job, preferably in a government office, escape from slaving if not starving on the land. When Patrick van Rensburg in Botswana tried to gear secondary education to economic development by self-help, through 'brigades' in which pupils were organized for self-employment in production, related to their studies (farming, building, textiles, mechanical and electrical engineering, tanning), he encountered stubborn disaffection: this was not what they were in secondary schools for; this was not what happened to pupils in government secondary schools. There had to be a compromise between the secondary course which prepared the eligible for clerical employment and professional careers, and productive engagement and training in small-scale labour intensive industries which would provide employment and advance the economy.[2]

The comprehensive school here is also a compromise of this kind in a similar situation, in that there is an attempt to meet (and partly transform) the life expectations and possibilities of dissimilar groups within one educational community, to relate their education realistically to their future in a way they understand and accept. Unless this can be done, responsibility is not likely to be learned at school nor practised later on. How can it be done through the curriculum? Pioneer work in primary schools and in colleges of further education has shown the way.

The right start is made if school is related from the first to the on-going life of the child, and is not a set of imposed tasks to which the child makes whatever adjustment he can. If the primary teacher discerns and values what the child has to offer, as a preliminary to transforming it, instead of merely standing for what the school requires, the school is an expansion of the child's life, not a division within it. Then talking, reading, writing are regulative disciplines which promote sharing, thinking, planning and control, reflection; they are activities which serve the developing life of the child, not formal exercises for the acquisition of useful arts. This decisive difference in the teacher's mediation of the primary curriculum is already a teaching-guidance function rooted in a relationship. Whether or not it alters the timetable, it does affect training. Of course it has been abundantly exemplified.[3]

Teachers of general studies in colleges of further education in the early days when relevant material was scarce and they were faced with youngsters who had had too much of school, found their clue also in accepting and valuing the experience and thinking and feeling of their students, thus putting new heart into them. By this approach was developed new material concerned with the anxieties and problems of adolescents, about themselves and about the world, dealt with in a way that respected their opinions. This provided a model for much curricular material helpful to the early school leaver.[4] Part of the same theme, although not directly useful in the same way, is the incorporation (not uncritically, but not unsympathetically) of elements of the contemporary youth culture into the curriculum, or into the life of the school.

The curriculum if it is to relate to the lives of the pupils should have some local reference. If there are West Indian children and there is a bland unthinking assumption that the school is an English school for English children, with no recognition of their feelings or their needs or their difference, nothing in the curriculum for them, they are alienated, and their homes with them. Similarly, if there is a marked difference of social class between staff and neighbourhood, care has to be taken not to discredit the local culture. There are sturdy examples of those who loved the close and smelly neighbourhood around them and equally the larger world on to which the school opened its windows.[5] The realities of the two may well be ingredients in the same dish.

One or two more adventurous projects, outside the school curriculum but in a learning context, have been started for early leavers without jobs, including some chronic truants, in connection with a self-financing production or service project, say, building or maintenance work. Schools in some areas or with special difficulties might well encourage and co-operate with such projects if they cannot sponsor them.

This rough sketch of the contents of the curriculum relevant to moral education must mention the special topics that are usually dealt with at some point, like sex education or the use and abuse of drugs. The sensible view is that topics of this kind should be brought into a more general programme, not singled out for special attention. They are topics that parents are liable to be anxiously interested in, which therefore occasion a talking-point that can be used to bring school and home into closer touch.[6]

In multiplying options in the secondary school, which is necessary and is on the way, there is danger of dilution, dissipation, enfeeblement of the vertebrae of secondary education. This threat to the standards of academic excellence as well as to the status of traditional subjects and specialist teachers is equally a threat to moral education, if the social distance and impartiality of the teacher, representing the ruthless requirements of the intellectual discipline, is one of the four corners of moral education, as Barry Sugarman has argued.[7] This 'old-fashioned' corner is not to be displaced by the wide teacher-pupil relationship and the open learning situation, for it is the necessary complement.

The 'subject' must have its rights and its representative as well as the child. The successful teacher succeeds in communicating his own enthusiasm for his subject, perhaps for more than his subject ('gladly wolde he lerne, and gladly teche'), but mainly his passionate partiality for a particular subject; rather, for what he finds in it for himself. This room for personal preferences among subjects and within them, so that they relate to personal lives and singularities and attract a feeling response is as important as the impersonal standards of scholarship and research. Enthusiasm for the subject which allows and encourages attachments of pupils to the subject which are equivalent but different, making their own response to what they find for themselves, is the surest protection of standards — and of the place and status of the subject in the timetable. The production of good examinees is quite a different craft.

Guidance

The development of 'guidance' programmes or courses is a new ingredient answering to the options which the curriculum now offers. School counselling, following the much earlier development in the USA, is generally thought of as having three interrelated functions: personal counselling, educational guidance, and vocational guidance. Educational guidance is the core activity of the school counsellor, for the child is not likely to know nor to make the best use of the educational resources available to him. This guidance is of course an inescapable part of the teacher-pupil relationship; if it is now becoming also (not instead) an integral part of the curriculum, that is to go beyond child-centred teaching and attempt to involve the pupil in using the curriculum to plan his own future and to develop his self-awareness. Later this becomes vocational guidance. But throughout it relates what the school offers to the child's personal life and to the future for himself which he learns to see. As in all transactions, there is a 'contract', implied or expressed. The child is sent to school in the first instance, and is required by law to attend regularly till he reaches a certain age. He may not consent, and although he cannot contract out he may remain disaffected, an unwilling party. Educational counselling seeks the reality and the mutuality of a good contract. What does the pupil want, hope, expect to get from his time at school? What does his school actually offer? Patrick van Rensburg's pupils (or many of them) expected what he did not offer and was not minded to provide. The 'contract' was misunderstood, and had to be revised. Educational guidance does not necessarily prevent a pupil's rejection of what he is offered, but does make sure that he knows what he is doing and knows what his alternatives are. He has been taken into the partnership from very early on.

A guidance programme to help the child through his transition from primary to secondary school is as important as the vocational guidance that sees him into the world of his choice (more or less) beyond school. Such a programme begins before entry, takes care of actual entry, and is brought to an end in the post-entry phase. Indeed, regular timetabled periods for 'guidance' discussion may begin with and continue throughout the secondary career. Syllabuses have been published.[8] James Hemming has suggested relating the whole curriculum in a 'guidance' way to what concerns young people about growing up and about the world in which they are growing up. Otherwise, guidance as it is developing means special programmes and specially trained teachers.

Guidance is meant to try to carry forward in appropriate ways what was begun in the good primary school, where the child is not met with imposed tasks but helped with his faltering developing abilities, so that· he grows into the means by which he is enabled to become a capable self-moving adult, and to learn what he wants to do and how to do it. In general, he learns *that*, he learns about himself and about the world in which he performs: he is given and he gets information. He learns *how*, in making choices, in managing himself and his affairs: he gains a basic skill for the conduct of his life. He learns *to*, for he learns to accept and to reject, actively and reasonably. In sum, he becomes educable and takes in hand his own education. Unless this happens, school does more harm than good: 'de-schooling' is on. Guidance is a more systematic attempt than has ever been mounted to make sure that this does happen more usually than it used to happen.

Orientation

Guidance may mean orientation, and such courses are sometimes called 'orientation' courses, but I am here using the word to indicate something distinct from learning to find one's way about the educational scene or the employment scene, and learning to find and follow one's own line. In addition to my place in these local scenes there is man's place in the total scene. This sounds vague or visionary, likely to invite rhetoric or speculation or indoctrination, alien to any sound curriculum; but unless the young person learns to see and to feel his place and part in this perspective, the curriculum fails in education. How, then, can the curriculum provide orientation in this sense in a way which is educational?

The primary school curriculum might be mapped roughly in five main subject areas: the language arts, the expressive arts, mathematics and science, social studies, health education. Each of these groups has a distinctive contribution to moral education. The science area and social studies in particular lay the foundations of 'orientation' in the present sense. The roots of ecology and ethology are in early observation of plant life and animal behaviour: the cycle and balance of nature in the relations of organism and environment; the behaviour of animals, related to habitat, for survival as a species. Scientific achievement is seen in getting to the moon, but comes home in reducing the death rate and multiplying food production, with the train of troublesome side effects and other consequences. So there is an introduction to the global tasks and problems which have brought mankind together for the first time in history with recognized shared responsibility for the conditions of life for generations of children unborn. The variety of species of plants and animals has a minor parallel in the variety of human cultures, each with its particular economic basis. Home economics can study the model of any economy in immediate terms, the key to an understanding of what is happening on the world scale to irreplaceable resources. The upshot of these remarks is that there is in the primary curriculum material for an outline understanding of human development and human responsibility in present terms.[9]

In the upper forms of the secondary school, theme and team teaching is one obvious way of contributing to this orientation role of the curriculum. In the school in Botswana mentioned earlier Patrick van Rensburg and Robert Oakeshott worked out a syllabus for a course in Development Studies which was designed to show the students where they stood in the modern world and how it had come about. The idea was to make intelligible and acceptable the policy of the school in preparing them for an active, responsible, creative role in their own society. School assembly, virtually an untilled field, is also an occasion for bringing into the focus of attention in a memorable way topics which identify the tasks and problems of mankind at this turning point in history.

Orientation is the outline which gives the curriculum unity and perspective, sketched in the primary school, and gradually filled in with further information and deepening understanding. The time-scale is all-important, beginning with the biological evolution of species and continuing with the historical development of human cultures, with the dramatic change of tempo in the past half-century that has changed almost everything. This introduction to the world in which their lives are cast is due to young people, not merely piecemeal in the several subjects which figure in the timetable, but mainly articulated in an intelligible survey that is not tendentious.

How can any such view escape contention, however, since it involves an interpretation of human existence and destiny? The clauses on religion in the 1944 Education Act enjoin on the county schools what is in effect a Christian interpretation of human life, with due provision of course for dissenters. But the attempt to teach the Christian interpretation of life with the implied authority of the school and the nation has been virtually abandoned, as founded on an untenable assumption and as educationally unjustifiable. Instead, there is educational agreement on the study of religions, not least Christianity, and of non-religious convictions, in a spirit of inquiry with a view to accurate information and sensitive understanding. This study of the main religious and cultural traditions contributes to orientation both as an historical study and as an understanding of the present situation, although of course it explicitly denies the early possibility of a universal view of human nature and destiny.

There is an interim line of agreement which is being forced upon us by events. This education for uncertainty at which we have arrived coincides with the arrival of these global tasks and problems which are all too certain, and are universal: need for a world order that does not rely on a precarious balance of terror; population control; deterioration of the environment by pollution; destruction of irreplaceable resources; race conflict; urban squalour; the vast needs of developing peoples and the vast waste of the affluent. These items on the human agenda have priority for business over ultimate questions, although of course ultimate differences of view will sometimes affect agreement on practical decisions. The shared responsibility of mankind for the immediate human future in practical terms is the scenario for all our lives which should inform the thinking and shape the expectations of young people about the world in which they are growing up.

The argument

Before summing up this argument on the curriculum in moral education, I want just to mention one other resource, which is rather a method than a subject, namely, the use of small groups. This may be simply a discussion group small enough to be effective for full participation and for training in moral reasoning and decision making. Mixed groups may also be used for increasing social experience. Less tried in the school context is the quasi-therapeutic use of unstructured groups which bring together pupils or staff and pupils (perhaps also parents) in a meeting which allows plain speaking and free expression of feelings without subsequent answerability, licensed by the convention. At any rate, the small group situation has great possibilities for moral education, curricular and extracurricular, and its uses have to be explored and evaluated.

I have argued in this paper that the curriculum has four functions related to moral education, apart from the special contribution of each subject: direct teaching, provision of sufficient diversity, guidance, orientation. The direct teaching may be a course at the upper end of the secondary school which all will take and which should include not only practice in moral reasoning but also an understanding of the conditions and rationale of social morality and of the range of choice in the management of personal life. Diversity does not mean necessarily nor only options in the timetable, but may be provided by what is included under various subject heads, especially the admissibility of what is personal or close at hand. A fair representation of the natural abundance of the real world is essential to moral education, to avoid the worst discouragement of selection and elitism and to provide a soil in which all abilities and interests may root and thrive, the necessary condition on which mutual discipline and mutual help can be learned and practised. Guidance is the attempt to make the school 'contract' genuinely contractual, in which there is room for some negotiation, so that what is offered is felt to be relevant to the real interests of the beneficiary, and a genuine partnership is developed. Orientation, presents in the content of the curriculum, the pupil's own future in the context of the future of his society and of mankind, with a time span that stretches into the immemorial past, and a tempo of change that has abruptly accelerated. Guidance and orientation contribute to education in self-knowledge and self-management and in responsibility.

Moral education is not the whole of education, obviously. It is possible to take almost any subject area or discipline, and by a broad and liberal treatment make it the vehicle of a total education — as Herbert Read did with 'education through art'. This should not be an aspiration of moral educators. But they do have a stake in every subject and in all that goes on in school. Education which aims at the full development of human beings satisfies the criteria of moral education. The functions of the curriculum which I have stressed from the point of view of moral education are already found as current trends in education, answering to what has been discovered in the actual work with children in school.

This leads to the last point, that moral education is based on and follows study of the child's moral development. Research and experiment are preliminaries to well-founded policies and practices in the development of moral education. It is not too much to say that new knowledge about the child's moral development has been the main reason for the systematic attention now being given to moral education. The Schools Council's materials specifically designed for moral education are the results of operational research, and are out for further evaluation in use in different social contexts. Curricular material for this purpose is no longer merely what turns up in the market. At the same time, however proved and available specific material may be, it can never take care of the whole job even within the curriculum. This has been a main point of my argument.

Notes

1 HARGREAVES, D.H. (1967) *Social Relations in a Secondary School*. London: Routledge & Kegan Paul.

KING. R. (1969) *Values and Involvement in a Grammar School*. London: Routledge & Kegan Paul.

2 RENSBURG. P. van (1974) *Report from Swaneng Hill*. Education and Employment in an African Country. Stockholm: The Dag Hammarskjold Foundation. London: Wildwood House.

3 For example: ROSEN, C. and H. (1973). *The Language of Primary School Children*. Harmondsworth: Penguin Education for the Schools Council.

4 See Section V (a) of *Moral Education: An Annotated List*, (1971) London: National Book League. The list was intended as a topography of the area.

5 HOGGART, R. (1957).*The Uses of Literacy*. London: Chatto & Windus: Harmondsworth: Penguin.

WEST, P. (1963). I, Said the Sparrow. London: Hutchinson.

6 *Education and Drug Dependence* (1975). A Report to the Social Morality Council. London: Methuen Educational.

7 SUGARMAN, B. (1973). *The School and Moral Development*. London: Croom Helm.

8 HOWDEN, R. and DOWSEN, H. (1973). *Practical Guidance in Schools*. Educational and vocational guidance as an integral part of the school curriculum. London: Careers Consultants.

HEMMING, J. (1965). *Pupil Guidance in Secondary Schools*. Berkshire County Council.

MILNER, P. (1974). *Counselling in Education*. London: Dent.

9 *Moral and Religious Education in County Primary Schools*, (1975). A Report to the Social Morality Council.

The Moral Objectives of a Uniform Curriculum

J.P. White

Since what I want to stress in my contribution is the moral aim behind a general, non-specialized education, it would be useful to focus first on Mr Blackham's apparently very different emphasis on the moral value of guided diversity in the curriculum. I say 'apparently' very different emphasis because it is not *absolutely* clear what kind of diversity and guidance he has in mind. He could be meaning either (1) diverse curriculum objectives or (2) diverse routes to attain the same objectives. Of these, only (1) is incompatible with the notion of a general education for all, where pupils leave school with the same sorts of achievements. I am almost persuaded that Mr Blackham has (1) in mind where he talks about the school's role in 'training pupils of diverse abilities and aptitudes for responsible roles' (p. 51); of 'relating their education realistically to their future' (p. 52); of introducing into the curriculum non-traditional subjects within the reach of the less able and taken as options by *some* of the brighter pupils (p. 52); and of 'room for personal preferences among subjects and within them' (p. 54). It looks from comments like these as if Mr Blackham is advocating the 'cafeteria', counsellor-guided, curriculum found in the USA and increasingly in our own secondary schools. On the other hand, his notion of 'orientation' implies a *common* achievement. The problem is: how *extensive* is this area of common achievement? 'Orientation', he tells us, 'begins with the biological evolution of species and continues with the historical evolution of human cultures, with the dramatic change of tempo in the past half-century' (p. 56). Is this intended as a description of a complete liberal education, as it quite easily could be? Are all pupils to leave school with some understanding of biology, world history, the history of the arts and sciences, recent social and political history and perhaps economics, sociology and political thought? If so, is the point about diversity only about different routes to essentially the same goals, with the content more concrete and experience-related for slower learners? Or are we to lay most weight on a cafeteria-curriculum, with such common core as there is restricted to a small fraction of timetable time?

This uncertainty about what 'diversity' means obviously needs to be resolved before we can assess the claim that diversity can contribute to moral education. Ignoring the ambiguity for a moment, let us remind ourselves just what the claim is. Diversity in the curriculum 'is a necessary condition of there being an educational community to which all who are compelled to go along have a chance of feeling that they belong' (p. 51); Without diversity, children will often have to study what they are not good at: this will lead to a decline in their self-respect and mean that they have no stake in the community, no reason for cooperation (p. 51).

If we interpret 'diversity' in the weaker sense (2), part of the claim seems to be that unless steps are taken to marry curriculum content on to the varying conceptual equipment and interests of pupils, they will find learning difficult and hence become alienated from the school community. This seems reasonable enough. The difficulty, though, is in seeing much of a connection with specifically *moral* development. Suppose the curriculum is successfully diversified in this sense, so that all children make progress in what they learn and enjoy being at school; there is no guarantee, so far, that they will make any *moral* headway, since they could all in principle have started out as egoists or even psychopaths and in studying things they enjoyed have simply become more entrenched in their egoism or their psychopathy. True, it is only claimed that this sort of diversity is a *necessary* condition of moral education. But so are all sorts of other things — like having a brain or understanding language, for instance — which it would be not very illuminating to mention. Like these other things, diversity in this sense is a necessary condition of moral education only because it is a necessary condition of *any* sort of education, or, indeed, of any sort of successful teaching. We are a long way, as yet, from seeing what kind of distinctive contribution this type of curriculum organization can make to moral education.

Two further considerations may bring the two topics a little closer. The first is that absorption in a task is closer in one way to altruism than to egoism. Both of the former possess a characteristic which might be called 'objectification': the individual in each case is directing his attention not to his own interests but to an object independent of these — the novel he is reading, for instance, on the one hand, or the needs of the person to whom he is giving a helping hand. It is reasonable to suppose, therefore, that one way of helping to wean a child from a chronic egoism would be to get him so absorbed in an activity that he learned to forget about himself, if only for a while. Clearly, too, one would have a good reason for trying to interest him in activities where absorption was likely to be demanding in attention or in time, or both; for in the one case he would be psychologically very distant from self-concern and in the other he would have less time for it. This consideration might incline one more towards aesthetic and intellectual activities than to, say, reading thrillers or making furniture. Without pursuing in more detail what may here prove to be a rather fruitful line of thought about the moral relevance of curriculum activities, we can see, I think, that the moral case for curriculum diversity in the weak sense may be stronger than it first appeared. Even so, two qualifications must be made. First, there must be some further restriction on the *content* of curriculum activities if 'objectification' is to occur: apart from the point just made above about demandingness, activities might clearly be counter-productive which bolstered up rather than reduced a pupil's egoism. Secondly, the moral benefit is negative, rather than positive: a self-centred child might be turned into, say, a science-centred child, but still without much interest in or concern for other people.

The second way in which diversity (sense 2) might seem to have a moral pay-off is this. Mr Blackham claimed that it would lead to a closer involvement in the school community, to more co-operativeness. Now I see no reason, especially in the light of what I said at the end of the last paragraph, why diversity would in itself be likely to make pupils *more concerned for* other people in the school community: the more easily they learned, the more absorbed they might become in what they were studying and the less time they might have for others. It is true that they would (necessarily) be more co-operative and more involved in the school community in the very different sense that their behaviour would be in line with the wishes of their teachers. At its lowest, this is simply to say that they would allow the work of the school to run smoothly, not be troublemakers. But inmates of a prison could be co-operative with the prison authorities without being anything but several hundred individualistic atoms who don't care a fig for each other. 'Being co-operative' can mean very different things. Now I doubt very much whether Mr Blackham was arguing that there is any moral value in sheer obedience to authority; but the point is worth making because some people *would* erect obedience into a moral virtue and favour Blackham's ideal of a community of contented learners precisely because it was more likely than any other system to turn otherwise alienated pupils into models of obedience: moral education has traditionally been seen as consisting of obedience-training, but the traditional methods of conducting it, through punishments and threats of punishment, have long since been seen to be less effective than more 'progressive' methods.

I shall come back to this traditional conception of moral education in a moment. Meanwhile I want to turn from the weaker sense of Blackham's claim about diversity, with which I have so far been concerned, to its stronger sense, i.e. to the claim that there is moral value in making curriculum *objectives* diverse, rather than simply the means to these objectives. How could this new claim be defended? Blackham's argument that diversity is a prerequisite of an educational community is less effective here. Neither the point about the anti-egoistic value of absorption in activities nor the point about enhanced co-operativeness (compliance) is relevant, for each of these concerned the benefits of ensuring that curriculum content be married on to the varying conceptual equipment and interests of individual pupils: a system of curriculum organization in which common achievements were expected of all pupils at the end of the course would be less than rational if it did not individualize the routes through to these achievements in this way. Are there any other arguments which could be used to support the new claim? A familiar one would be that if one fixes common expected standards of achievement, the chances are that not all pupils will be able to meet these standards and those that do not will still be alienated, self-deprecating or unco-operative. But there is no reason why, if standards are to be fixed, they must be fixed so that only a fraction of children can attain them. We shouldn't be dominated in our thinking by the traditional grammar school tradition, about which Mr Blackham is quite rightly critical. Common standards do not necessarily mean an 'O' level pass in five subjects: in fixing them, we could, if we really wanted this, determine them in the light of what the average child might be expected to achieve, allowing some latitude in the satisfaction of these standards to accommodate the weaker pupil. This is not to be taken as implying that we should set our sights deliberately low. If the average child's eleven years of compulsory schooling were more rationally organized than they are in our own haphazard system, who knows what heights he might reach? I know of no evidence to suggest that he couldn't get further than the pitifully low expectations in Newsom, say, or in some of the Schools Council's ROSLA projects. There is as yet no reason, therefore, why imposing common terminal standards is likely in itself to promote the negative attitudes of alienation, etc. about which Mr Blackham is concerned. It is hard to see, more generally, why moral education should suffer if such standards were imposed. In subsequent sections I shall argue, indeed, that common standards are a *prerequisite of*, not a hindrance to, the formation of morally educated men and women.

II

I must confess to some surprise at first reading Mr Blackham's plea for the moral value of curriculum diversity and educational guidance, since, taken (perhaps wrongly) in the strong sense, an emphasis on guided diversity belongs to a tradition of educational thought in which moral education has been consistently played down. We may call this the 'conservative' tradition, not least because it has shaped the educational policies followed during British Conservative administrations throughout this century. The tradition originally stressed diversity between *schools*, between elementary and secondary schools until the Hadow reforms, and between different types of secondary school since that time. Whereas many of those backing the Labour Party's call for 'secondary education for all' in the 1920s had in mind a general education and one not specialized according to industrial requirements, the latter were dominant and grew increasingly so in Conservative thinking. Very crudely secondary (later grammar) schools were for the black-coated jobs, elementary for the blue-coated: not everyone could be given an academic education, for then the pressure for non-manual jobs would grow and industry would suffer.

A new stage began in the 1960s, with the challenge of the comprehensive school to the older dualist order. To meet this challenge, curriculum diversity began to be stressed not *between* different types of school, as previously, but *within* the same school. One finds this first adumbrated in the 1963 Newsom Report and later, more explicitly, in the early Young School Leaver projects of the Schools Council, set up in the last days of the 1959—64 Conservative government. Special kinds of course were recommended for the 'less able' pupil in comprehensive schools, the harsher outlines of dualism now being blurred by a new doctrine of pupil choice of curriculum options, to be guided by school counsellors. The new liberalism has not been at all at odds with the old industry-oriented policy. Letting older pupils choose their own curricula has, in fact, reinforced it, since vocational interests are likely to steer their choices and most children can be relied on to opt for intellectually more accessible occupations than the scarcer, more recondite jobs. The institution of counselling is also more than consistent with industrial aims: as Blackham points out (p. 54), educational guidance in curriculum options lower down the secondary school is intended to lead towards vocational guidance in the upper forms.

How has moral education fitted into this pattern of curriculum organization? Certainly the universal encouragement of a *reflective* morality, i.e. one which questions and does not blindly accept the mores and socioeconomic arrangements of a society, would be hard to square with it, because the traditional policy has taken existing socio-economic arrangements for granted in trying to fit pupils into existing slots in the industrial structure. The only compatible morality, at least for the great mass of pupils, would be a morality of obedience, of unquestioning acceptance of the existing social order. This is indeed what has been emphasized. Neither in the state-controlled elementary curriculum before 1926 nor in the informally controlled one (with the same content) after that date, was there any place for the political, sociological and economic reflection necessary to a reflective social morality. Conservative statesmen, like the President of the Board of Education responsible for the shift of policy in 1926, Lord Eustace Percy, explicitly inveighed against courses in citizenship or economics. On the latter, for instance, he epitomized the conservative tradition in stating:

> 'Do we wish to teach the child, even if we could, to reason theoretically about the production of goods and the performance of services by other people, or do we not rather wish to teach him first, in practice and in the concrete, to produce goods and perform services himself?'[1]

Instead of citizenship, the conservative tradition, Percy included, for long favoured religion as the basis of moral education: understandably so, since a religiously based morality would be both a morality of obedience and one which would stress the insignificance of existing social inequalities *sub specie aeternitatis*. RE was made compulsory in Butler's 1944 Act which continued the tradition. The problem which inheritors of that tradition face today is: how best to promote a morality of obedience now that it is clear that the religious means of doing this is no longer a starter? Hence a large part of the interest in cafeteria, guided curricula, as I hinted in Section I: if pupils can be induced to choose their own pattern of education, one which leads on to a certain type of vocation, then they cannot rationally kick against the system if they later find themselves in a dead-end job, for it is they, after all, who have decided what they want to become. Hence, too, perhaps — I advance this extremely tentatively in present company — one reason for the contemporary willingness to fund curriculum development in non-politically oriented forms of moral education. (Whether the results are always what are expected is quite another issue.)

III

Some of the points made in the last paragraph may be seen as unduly cynical. What one can safely say, at least, about the conservative tradition is that, in wanting to make the educational system mirror the division of labour, it has had to stress the individual differences between people, the things, in other words, which divide man from man, rather than the things which, in any other but an economic sense, bind them together. It has constantly had to face the problem, therefore, of incorporating into the curriculum something which will act as a social element and mitigate the socially destructive atomism to which it naturally tends, *without*, however, leading pupils to wish to make radical changes to the socioeconomic order.

It would be quite at odds with this tradition to see moral development as one of the *prime* objectives of a school curriculum, for this would be to put morality too close to the heart of education and the contradiction between moral demands and the demands of industry would be too glaring. Any moral education in the conservative tradition which rises above a crude morality of obedience cannot be more than a small part of, a mere addendum to, the main work of the school. It is quite in line with this tradition to support ME as a separate curriculum element: that way, some social cohesion is built into the curriculum, but, at the same time, its pretensions are kept within well-circumscribed bounds.

I wish now to contrast this conservative tradition with a quite different tradition of educational thought, one which, far from wishing to contain morality within an insignificant corner of the curriculum, makes it a central objective of education as a whole. It is hard to find a suitable name for this tradition. It could almost be called the 'socialist' tradition, owing to its prominence in such socialist educational systems as those of Sweden and the various Communist states (where it often appears in a perverted form), and, indeed, in British socialist thought before and after the First World War. But in the contemporary British context it would be more confusing than illuminating to attach this label to it. The British Labour Party has long since disclaimed any interest in the objectives and content of the curriculum (as is shown, for instance, in its apparent lack of anxiety about the way in which the comprehensive ideal is being undermined by the latest strategies in the conservative tradition). I propose, therefore, to label it the 'Herbartian' tradition, in honour of the educational thinker most closely associated in modern times, at least, with the centrality of moral aims in education, J.F. Herbart (1776–1841).

It is symptomatic of the strength of individualist ideas in educational circles today that Herbart's ideas are now virtually unknown. Seventy years ago, teacher training institutions were permeated by Herbartianism. The first director of what was to become The London Institute of Education, John Adams, was the leading Herbartian in the country; today not one of Herbart's works is in the Institute's main library — they are all in the archives.[2] Herbart's educational theory, as propounded in his *Science of Education*, is no doubt deficient in many respects, but many of its leading ideas still seem to me very sound and worthy of a wider audience.[3] In the absence of any comprehensive educational theory produced since 1806 which follows the Herbartian tradition but avoids Herbart's inadequacies, it will be best to go back to what he wrote in that year.

Morality is for Herbart the *highest* aim of education. It has another aim, preparing pupils to choose their personal life-aims, under the aegis of their own self-perfection; but the moral aim is overriding. This is *not* to say that when teachers aim at moral development they must constantly be relating the subjects they are teaching to moral considerations. On the contrary, Herbart holds that morality is best fostered through the growth of a 'many-sided interest' in different fields of human endeavour. We need not follow him in his intuitionist account of morality, and there are also difficulties, requiring a deeper analysis than we can give them here, in his central psychological assumption that the development of the will reduces to the inculcation of 'ideas'; but there is much of relevance in his allocation of types of interest to knowledge and sympathy, his stress on 'instruction', and his views on individuality. About each of these topics I must now say something in more detail.

The creation of a many-sided interest subserves both the personal and the moral aim. Interest has different objects. Herbart divides them into six main categories, three of which are forms of 'knowledge' and three of 'sympathy'. Knowledge is of (1) the 'manifold' of observable physical phenomena and human behaviour (2) the laws underlying these (3) aesthetic relationships. Leaving aside the difficulty of squeezing aesthetic development under the rubric of 'knowledge', Herbart's division between observational knowledge and knowledge of non-observable laws is acceptable, if unoriginal. What *is* distinctive of his theory, setting it apart from other theories which base a general education on forms of knowledge alone, is the equal weight it gives to 'sympathy' (owing to the centrality of the moral aim). The three divisions of sympathy are (1) sympathy with humanity (2) sympathy with society and (3) the relation of both humanity and society to the Highest Being. I shall say more about this trichotomy in a moment.

For Herbart education consists to a large degree in 'instruction'. The term has changed its sense in educational writings in the past three-quarter-century. We now reserve it largely for the mere imparting of information.[4] In Herbart it is essentially connected with his concept of 'many-sided interest'. To a limited extent the latter can grow out of one's everyday experience and, in the case of sympathy, one's everyday social intercourse. But experience and intercourse can only lay the foundation. Beyond a certain point instruction is necessary – the deliberate building up of carefully sequenced ideas within the pupil's mind in the different categories of interest. The stress on instruction rather than social intercourse in the development of sympathy makes Herbartian moral education very different from contemporary attempts to tie ME closely to the pupil's everyday moral experience. As that socialist manqué Rhodes Boyson recently stated (with perhaps the Schools Council ME Project in mind), there is no point in trying to teach most secondary children to be 'compassionate', since they have learnt this already from family and other non-school influences. There are three main areas where one needs to go beyond everyday life. Herbart is right, it seems to me, in his identification of these, though in elaborating their content in what now follows I shall not always stick very firmly to Herbart's own prescriptions but add some independent argument.

(1) *Sympathy with humanity*. This is concerned with moral attitudes to individuals rather than with wider social and political issues. The role of 'instruction' here is to extend and deepen sympathetic feelings (given that the pupil already possesses these in some measure). The pupil's sympathy will naturally at first only be extended towards those individuals with whom he is acquainted. But it is morally important to develop an imaginative understanding of people's points of view in different circumstances from his own. The value of human geography, history and above all, literature, in promoting this end has long since been recognized (e.g. by Herbart himself). A point which has not been much remarked on, however, is the moral advantage, if one may put it that way, that the broadly educated person has over the sparsely-educated. The former is often able to enter into the thoughts, feelings, interests and ambitions of the latter, since they draw largely on common experience; but the latter, the ill-educated man, is in a poor position to understand those of the former's projects and attitudes which depend on education. His range of moral responses is consequently limited. There is even a danger of a *misplaced* sympathy: if the working man knew more about the alleged 'burdens of responsibility' which the educated managerial and professional classes bore he might often, and rightly, feel *less* sympathetic towards them. This point underscores Herbart's insistence that morality must rest on a many-sided interest, on straight forms of knowledge as well as on sympathy: insofar as an understanding of natural science or mathematics, for example, can help to shape a man's outlook and way of life, one is morally impoverished, if one lacks this understanding oneself, in entering into such points of view. Self-understanding, finally, is also important, as Herbart points out, in deepening and refining one's

sympathies. Psychology is another form of knowledge of obvious relevance here.

(2) *Sympathy with society*. We move now to fostering interest in the welfare of the whole community rather than that of individuals. As Herbart says, the pupil now has to learn to adopt something like the politician's point of view and so needs to be equipped with something like the politician's knowledge: of the complexities of larger social relationships, especially of the division of labour; of forms of compliance and non-compliance; of government and other social institutions — in contemporary terms, perhaps, of parts of social science and social history, international affairs, economics, and political theory. This branch of moral education — political education or 'citizenship' — is not so much concerned with a grasp of principles or virtues. Once again, the pupil may already be assumed to have acquired from ordinary social intercourse a basic sense of fairness, tolerance, compassion, honesty, etc. As Gauthier argues in another context, it is concerned not with the major premise of the practical syllogism, but with the minor premise, with an understanding of the *consequences* which might flow from such and such a political act — consequences which are not at all obvious to those ignorant of the politically-relevant forms of knowledge.[5] One cannot, for instance, decide whether a progressive income tax is fair or unfair without some appreciation of the consequences of either having or of not having one. Having just used the expression 'politically-relevant forms of knowledge' I must again underline the point that which forms are *not* relevant it is difficult to say.[6] Some knowledge of science, especially today, is obviously relevant; so is some mathematics. These are only two examples.

(3) *The relation of both (1) and (2) to the Highest Being*. This raises one's moral sights above the flux of ongoing social and political arrangements to the contemplation of humanity as a whole and its relation to the universe. It directs one to ultimate ponderings about the 'meaning of life', lacking which the merely political or social man seems busy without point. Herbart talks here of developing sympathy with the universal dependence of man, and the importance of reflecting on the shortness of human life. He also talks of obedience to God, of keeping the Sabbath, and of community with the Church. We do not have to accept his Christian or theistic recommendations to see the broader force of what he is saying. It has obvious connections, indeed, with Mr Blackham's 'orientation' — as also with another of Mr Blackham's interests, existentialist thought. Biology, religious studies, existentialist and other metaphysical philosophy are all clearly relevant to this third topic. But then, as usual, as soon as one begins to consider such subjects as literature, physics, and even mathematics, the rest of the curriculum, too, comes knocking for a place.

Many of these points about the three aspects of moral education are familiar and, it may be thought, do not need further reiteration. But familiar or not, they are not now woven firmly into any contemporary educational theory. Their implications point in an opposite direction to the conservative tradition, not towards diversity of objectives, but towards *common* achievements. Herbart himself had no doubts about the importance of stressing the universal rather than the particular. His comments on the place of individuality in education are instructive. Individual differences between people are important, in society as a whole, because of the division of labour, and in education because methods of instruction must be individualized so as to marry on to differences in mental equipment. But, for all this, education must leave individuality alone as far as possible. It should *protect* it, but not (as in the conservative tradition) *sharpen* it. Individual bents and preferences are likely to be one-sided rather than many-sided. In deliberately promoting them one would be in danger of producing 'a crowd of humpbacks and cripples of all kinds, tumbling wildly over each other. But this is what happens where society is composed of men of widely different modes of thought; each brags of his own individuality, and no one understands his fellows'.[7]

The brief account of selected Herbartian themes will show, I hope, their relevance to the reconstruction of an educational theory at odds with the ultra-individualistic one to which we have grown used. In this we shall no longer think of 'ME' as a *section* of the curriculum. Perhaps, indeed, we shall not think of *moral* education at all, but of education in general as planned around a predominantly moral purpose. Only 'predominantly' moral, for the general education which subserves morality also subserves the aim of equipping the individual to choose his own way of life within what is morally demanded and permissible. (This individualistic aim is different from the 'ultra-individualistic' one of sharpening individual differences: unlike the latter, it implies a common curriculum). But *predominantly* moral all the same, because the individualistic aim must find its place under the umbrella-aim of moral development. The former is only definable in terms of the latter: personal ideals, careers, ways of life are to be chosen 'within what is morally demanded and permissible', for without such a proviso, the two aims, the moral and the individualistic, would be unrelated and therefore often in conflict. An individualistic aim which sought simply to equip pupils for reflective choice of ways of life could be egoistic through and through. If the two aims were left unrelated, they could well be in competition. Suppose a pupil were taught certain intellectual disciplines — history, science, geography, maths, or whatever — so as to better his own chances in the world, it would be irrational to inject certain other content into the curriculum so as to satisfy the moral aim, since what went on in the former area would be at odds with what went on in the latter, and vice versa. Irrational it may be; but it is what goes on, I suspect, in many of our schools. Why, after all, do many of our pupils study their science, maths or history? They do so, usually, either for this instrumental reason of 'getting on', or because of its intrinsic delights, or both. But both of these reasons are individualistic. The more space in the timetable given over to individualistic purposes, the more impossible it is for any moral counterweight to tip the balance. The more difficult, too, will it be for the pupil satisfactorily to relate the demands of prudence and morality. With the weight of conventional educational wisdom pressing him to develop his potentialities to the full, or to work hard at his 'O' and 'A' levels to secure a foothold in higher education, or to select curriculum options relevant to his vocational preferences, how is he to square this with the school's more muted calls for moral and political maturity? Will he tend to ignore the latter, seeing the relatively little esteem in which the system holds them? Or will he just be in a spiritual mess?

Contemporary educational theories of all complexions have failed to stress the need properly to relate moral and individualistic aims. This is because they all tend to work within individualistic assumptions. We have mentioned the industrially-oriented individualism of the conservative tradition. Extreme child-centred theories have been equally individualistic in their plea for the maximum development of the pupil's potentialities. Moral development has often been included in this, but only as a *part* of total development: the fact that moral considerations can be at odds with the claims of personal development is overlooked. The obsession of contemporary educational psychology with Piaget's theories has breathed new life into this older child-centred tradition. Contemporary philosophers of education often tend to criticize child-centred theories, but rarely to the extent of questioning their individualistic presuppositions: in viewing education as centrally concerned with intrinsically worthwhile activities, with autonomy or with the development of the rational mind for its own sake, they do but share them. This is not to say that the philosophers have not been interested in the moral side of education. On the contrary, moral education has been a prominent topic in their writings. But the problem of squaring moral objectives with individualistic assumptions has not been faced. Most often, moral development tends to be seen, as in the child-centred tradition, as just one element, one 'form of understanding' in the growth of rationality in general: the overridingness of moral considerations, though often argued for in general in contemporary philosophy, has not been connected with the problem, itself overlooked, of deciding the relative priority of different educational aims.

What is needed, I suggest, is a new architectonic of the curriculum. Until now we have had to make do by sticking together the pieces of old traditions and mainly individualistic ones at that. We need to reorganize our curriculum content and objectives within a clear framework of priorities. Moral objectives must, for the reason given in the last paragraph, be placed at the apex, with individualistic aims properly subordinated to them. We need, too, to determine more thoroughly than ever before just which kinds of curriculum content, in both the moral and the individualistic areas, we should make common to all pupils and which can be left optional. Whether this can be done effectively without introducing some measure of state control of school curricula I am inclined to doubt: it is hard for many reasons, not least those of teacher-supply, to visualize school after school independently devising a new framework for its curriculum until the whole system is rebuilt on more coherent lines.

Would there be any place, in such a reconstruction, for ME as a separate curriculum subject? I see no reason for ruling it out *a priori*. Some elementary understanding of ethics ought, in my opinion, to be one of the common curriculum objectives for the older pupil. This would be necessary, among other things, to help him distinguish moral from prudential considerations and thus minimize the kind of spiritual confusion, mentioned just now, which can arise from their conflation. It would also help him to separate the sphere of the moral more clearly from other spheres with which it is often too closely assimilated, the aesthetic, for instance, or the religious; to reflect on the foundations of his moral beliefs to see how far they are based merely on authority or more autonomously held; to prevent his coming to have an over-rigid conception of a moral rule by bringing him to see how such rules may legitimately be broken on occasion; to preserve him from the grosser confusions of common doctrines like psychological egoism and various forms of subjectivism, relativism and determinism; to see the application of fundamental moral principles to practical problems in political and social policy. To what extent one can accomplish all this with the normal sixteen-year-old school leaver I do not know. I am only concerned here with the foothills of ethics, not with its upper slopes; but, even so, some of this material may be more suitable for some kind of continuation study beyond the school-leaving age. In an elementary way, however, — I very much agree with John Wilson on this — much of it can probably be made accessible to pupils still at school.

It does not follow, though, that whatever ethics *is* taught at school is best taught as a separate subject. The topics just mentioned could well arise in literary or political studies, for instance. Careful organization would be necessary, if so, to ensure that they were adequately woven in. If the organization required were just too complex and if the fact that the topics were all of a philosophical nature meant that it was better on balance to teach them together rather than to integrate them into other things, this would obviously support the separatist case. There are just two further points I want to underline about this case. First if there is to be a separate curriculum slot for ME, the reasons for insisting on it must be clear. It is not enough to wish vaguely to turn children into morally responsive beings: they are these to a large extent already. Neither is the more analytical approach of the Farmington research wholly satisfactory: it is possible conceptually to take apart the different components of moral agency, but nothing follows from this about what the best content of a separate ME programme should be. This is because — and this brings me to the second and final point — what the best content of a separate ME programme should be cannot be discussed in isolation from a broader look at the moral foundations of the curriculum as a whole. The job of a separate moral component is to teach what cannot easily be taught within the ordinary curriculum, perhaps elementary ethics, for example. Its job is not at all to provide the school's main counterweight to egoism.

Notes

1 PERCY, Lord E., Speech at North of England Education Conference, Liverpool, January, 6th, 1927.

2 ADAMS, J. (1897) *Herbartian Psychology*. Boston: Heath. On the popularity of Herbart's ideas in the period 1890–1910 see:

SELLECK, R.J. (1968) *The New Education: The English Background, 1870–1914*. London: Pitman.

DUNKEL, H.B. (1970) *Herbart and Herbartianism: An Educational Ghost Story*. Chicago: University Press.

3 HERBART, J.F. (1806) *The Science of Education*, translated by H.M. and E. Felkin, 1892. London: Swan Sonnenschein.

4 DEARDEN, R.F. (1967) 'Instruction and learning by discovery'. In: PETERS, R.S. (Ed.) *The Concept of Education*. London: Routledge & Kegan Paul.

5 GAUTHIER, D.P. (1971) 'Moral action and moral education'. In: BECK, C.M., CRITTENDEN, B.S. and SULLIVAN, E.V. *(Eds.) Moral Education: Interdisciplinary Approaches*. Toronto: University Press.

6 WHITE, P.A. (1971) 'Education, democracy and the public interest', *Proceedings of the Philosophy of Education Society of Great Britain*, January. Reprinted in PETERS, R.S. (Ed.) (1973). *The Philosophy of Education*. London: Oxford University Press.

7 HERBART, J.F. *op cit.* p. 142.

B. Moral Education:
Difficulties in Communication

Conditions for Dialogue in Moral Education between Teachers and Educational Philosophers

J.R. Ungoed-Thomas

Bernard Shaw once said, 'Those who can do; those who can't teach.' Like most epigrammatic statements, this was both unfair (to teachers), and thought provoking. It raised the problem of whether teaching is a creative activity in its own right, or simply consists in passing on to the young the deeds and thoughts of their predecessors. To Bernard Shaw, and perhaps to most of his generation, it seemed fairly obvious that teachers were little more than cultural transmitters. Times change however. New issues come to the fore, and new ways of looking at problems develop. Accordingly, it is perhaps time that Shaw's words were modified to take account of altered circumstances.

I would suggest that if Bernard Shaw were alive and kicking today, he might have said, 'Those who can teach; those who can't preach.' This too is of course unfair (to preachers) but it does, I think, bring into focus a critical contemporary educational problem, namely the question of the terms in which the relationship between thought and action, between thinkers and activists, between philosophers and teachers, should be defined.

It is probably fair to say that, in the field of moral education, a number of teachers are wary of those who tell them what they ought to be doing. Initial reasons why this is so can be illustrated by reference to the articles of John Wilson, J.P. White and H.J. Blackham. Advice, if it is to be of use to teachers either operationally or in their thinking, should be clearly expressed and comprehensible. The language and arguments used by Wilson, White and Blackham are not always evident even to themselves. White comments of Blackham's contribution, with reference to the issue of 'guided diversity in the curriculum', 'It is not *absolutely* clear what kind of diversity and guidance he has in mind'. While Blackham, although in sympathy with Wilson's plea for putting morality into the curriculum in regular periods of direct teaching, is not altogether happy about 'What I think he means'. And Wilson does indeed use language which on occasion might be identified as clumsy and ungrammatical. Phrases such as 'This goes against quite a lot of grain, for reasons I am not clear about', are at best not exactly crisp.

Teachers tend to object to unclear expression and argument first, on professional grounds: teachers require their pupils to work towards reasonably high standards of clarity, and therefore naturally are inclined to expect it from qualified adults in the educational field. Secondly, if there is one thing teachers have learned about modern philosophy, it is that it is above all concerned with the analysis of language, and that consequently, to quote John Wilson himself 'An important question to ask about any argument is "Is it clearly written, not confused or "waffle"?'[1] If philosophers appear to fail themselves, in the standards they set for others, not unnaturally they run the risk of forfeiting respect and attention.

A further cause of doubt in the minds of teachers concerning the value of the activities of the philosophically inclined in education is that their individual strivings to establish the truth can on occasion resemble less a mutual and co-operative enterprise, than a sort of internecine tribal warfare. Wilson, for example, launches bitter attacks on a virulent host of unnamed adversaries who suffer from the 'fantasy' that morality stands for one quality; and from the 'obsession' that 'morality has little to do with *thinking* or *learning* at all'. J.P. White not only spends his first section attacking Blackham, but goes on to argue, perhaps rather ambitiously, that 'contemporary educational theories of all complexions have failed to stress the need properly to relate moral and individualistic aims'.

Now it is not my thesis that philosophers should never disagree. As a rule, they always have, and as a rule no doubt they always will. Nor even am I arguing that philosophers should always express themselves clearly: some of the greatest, Hegel for example, are difficult in translation and just as difficult in the original. What I am suggesting is that educational philosophers who wish to establish a dialogue with teachers about curricular aims and procedures, particularly with reference to moral education, are not likely to succeed in the task which they have set themselves unless they devote some thought to the conditions which must be observed if they are not to fail in their objectives. Teachers neither respect nor pay attention to confusion, whether it is manifested as a result of low standards of self-expression, or of ill-tempered argument.

The main necessary conditions to be observed by educational philosophers if they are to establish a dialogue with teachers are that they follow first a clear and explicated definition of their functions; second, reveal operational realism; and third, display understanding of the logic of scientific research. An initial problem arises from the question of who is to undertake the philosophic functions? A distinction has to be made here between the tasks of philosophy, and the practitioners of philosophy. On the one hand, there are certain tasks which philosophy is required to perform; on the other hand, there are individuals who perform these tasks. It is easy to accept the apparently reasonable proposition the philosophic tasks should be performed by philosophers. However, in the field under discussion, this idea is subject to qualification in two respects. First, those who appear to be philosophers by virtue of teaching educational philosophy are not always philosophers in the sense that they have received a degree in philosophy or other philosophic training of substance. If philosophic tasks are to be confined to trained and professional philosophers, are such, as it were, bastardized philosophers to be refused permission to participate?

Secondly, the particular philosophic tasks to be discussed are susceptible of being performed very adequately by many who, while not being trained philosophers, do have relevant experience. Accordingly, while philosophic tasks need to be clearly defined, it seems reasonable to suggest that they may be carried out by individuals who are not necessarily themselves trained philosophers.

Those who undertake the tasks of educational philosophy in the moral field perform their labours under the handicap of a difficult heritage. The traditional task of moral philosophy has been to discuss and establish the nature of the good life: the more modest function of modern philosophy is conceptual analysis, the critical undertaking of enabling and encouraging others to think clearly. What, therefore, is the function of moral philosophy in education? In the footsteps of Kant and Aristotle, to establish what the good life is, and state how it is to be achieved? Or following the lead of Hare[2], to help us 'to think better about moral questions by exposing the logical structure of the language in which this thought is expressed'? Not infrequently, philosophers pay lip service to the modern view, while holding the traditional one, thus placing a mask of humility over features which may in reality be somewhat authoritarian. In practice, both traditions are relevant to the tasks of the moral philosopher in education. Moral education cannot be properly practised without a widespread understanding amongst teachers, parents and others concerned, of what the good life is for which pupils are being educated. In his traditional role, it is the task of the philosopher to initiate or contribute to discussion in this area. Equally, however, unless such discussion is clearly thought out, little real understanding is likely to emerge. Consequently, the philosopher in his modern role needs to promote insight by clarifying the terms of discussion. Also, although consideration of curricular design falls into the teaching rather than the philosophic domain, philosophers can assist and promote effective planning by pertinent analysis of the vocabulary and ideas employed. Finally, it is necessary to distinguish, in consideration of aims, between a generalized discussion the purpose of which is to evolve a set of aims which are acceptable in philosophic terms; and a specific discussion the purpose of which is to relate aims which can be defended philosophically, to the educational situation. The former type of discussion is primarily philosophic (although, as argued, teachers and others can, and should, participate); while the latter type of discussion cannot effectively take place unless there are contributions both from individuals performing a philosophic function (exposition and clarification of substantiated aims); and from individuals performing a teacher's function (exposition and clarification of the needs, limitations and possibilities of the school and classroom situation.)

Breakdown in teacher philosopher dialogue can be attributable either to misunderstanding of the philosopher's function, or to failure to define it adequately. For example, those who consider themselves philosophers may implicitly or explicitly exclude teachers and others from effective discussion of curricular aims in moral education, designating it as their own professional preserve: many teachers are unlikely to accept aims to the formulation of which they have not had an opportunity to contribute. Another source of breakdown can be due to an attempt by individual philosophers to impose a particular personal viewpoint upon teachers without having previously subjected it to the rigours of examination in philosophic discussion, or while it is still undergoing such discussion. Failure of communication in such instances can be caused by teachers themselves perceiving the fragility or inadequacy of arguments being proposed; or by teacher reluctance to translate into curricular terms aims which they are aware do not have widespread support. Teachers are particularly reluctant to accept aims in moral education which have not shown to be widely acceptable, not only because of any personal dislike they may have of shoddiness or going it alone, but because of the feeling of moral responsibility they have towards their pupils. Very few teachers would be prepared to educate pupils towards moral aims which subsequently turned out to be derived from inadequate argument, or not to be acceptable to a substantial proportion of parents and other teachers. Consequently, if philosophers wish to establish dialogue with teachers, they need to avoid a confusion of that function which demands that agreed aims be evolved in philosophic discussion; and the other function which demands that agreed aims, once evolved, be discussed with teachers so that they may be translated into practical terms.

Operational realism is the second main necessary condition which I have suggested needs to be accepted by philosophers if dialogue with teachers is to be established. It is simultaneously the condition which is the easiest to indicate as desirable and the least often observed in practice. What can be thought is limited only by lack of intelligence. What can be done is limited not only by lack of intelligence, but by circumstances as well. Philosophers, even those in the educational field, are predisposed to overemphasize the significance of intelligence, and underestimate the importance of actuality. Consequently, philosophers are inclined to consider that a set of practices derived from agreed aims (and which they accordingly consider constitute a valid 'ought') can easily be transmuted into an operational 'is'. If their 'ought' does not become an 'is' they tend to look for the cause of the failure in the stupidity of teachers, rather than in the intractability of circumstances, or, to put it another way, in the irrelevance of their ideas.

If philosophers in moral education are to establish dialogue with teachers, they have to accept a certain circumscription of their philosophic activity; this limitation requires that their thinking be operationally directed. Any aims which cannot be translated into practice are of little use to the teacher; any proposed methods which cannot be employed simply cause annoyance in the staff room; any proposed materials which are rejected by pupils are no more and no less than the cause of a disciplinary problem in the classroom. Now, it may seem to many philosophers that any philosophic activity which must be limited by concrete situational demands, is a sort of second class philosophy hardly worth undertaking: They may possibly be correct. But whether or not they are correct, if that is how they feel and think, then the educational world is not for them; they should either become pure philosophers, or, if that is not satisfactory for them, take up some other form of occupation. What should be self-evident is that education is not a field designed to offer a living for academics who have no sympathy with the demands which the nature of teaching make upon their work as philosophers.

As well as accepting a necessary limitation upon the nature of their intellectual activities, educational philosophers need to acquire a new dimension of professional expertise. In order to understand the operational situation with which they are confronted, they must have acquired practical insight into that situation. For the great majority of people, insight into actual situations can only come through personal experience. Educational philosophers, therefore, need to have in general, experience of working in schools and in particular experience of working in schools which are not atypical. So, it is very unlikely that an educational philosopher who has never taught will be able to establish a dialogue with teachers; it is also unlikely that a philosopher who has taught for example only in independent schools with their idiosyncratic organizations, will have much which is relevant to say to teachers in local education authority schools, in which the vast majority of children are educated; finally, it is not very likely that a philosopher who has taught only for a limited period, or many years ago, will have much understanding of the situation facing teachers today. Few teachers will be prepared to hold a dialogue with a person who shows ignorance of the circumstances in which they work, but who nevertheless has the temerity to propose aims and procedures which it is suggested teachers should translate into practice. A philosopher who is to contribute more than a monologue in the field of moral education has to be capable of putting himself in the teacher's shoes, and that is not an easy task for anybody to undertake successfully.

The final condition to be observed by philosophers is that they display an understanding of the logic of scientific research, and particularly of research in the social sciences. I have so far concentrated, for purposes of identifying and discussing a particular set of communication problems, upon the teacher philosopher relationship, and treated it as if it were lineal, involving as in a conventional marriage, only two parties. However, fortunately or not, depending upon one's view point, there is a third party (thus creating a triangular relationship) whose presence cannot be entirely overlooked.

The educational researcher is not always a welcome presence to either teacher or philosopher: both are inclined to believe that research raises more problems than it solves. However, while it is possible in the present discussion to avoid analysing the terms of dialogue particular to the teacher and researcher (which I have considered elsewhere)[3] and those particular to the philosopher and researcher, there is one issue which, while central to the way in which the researcher relates to philosopher and teacher, also inescapably influences the teacher philosopher dialogue.

The problem in question relates to the procedures by which recommended curricular methods are arrived at. From the teacher's point of view, it can appear either as a result of their own observations or as a result of what they are told, that to use broad categories, they have a choice between methods evolved as a result of deductive procedures and methods evolved as a result of inductive procedures. The former are characteristically associated with philosophy, the latter with research. For example, John Wilson has proposed an outline list of moral components, which he discusses as follows 'What is important, at this stage of our work, is to be clear about its logical status and function. It amounts to little more than a brief explication or enlargement of the various ways in which moral thought and action can be rational or irrational . . . . . . These components are, then, merely a first hesitant step towards bridging the gulf between our criteria of rationality and any specific recommendation that might eventually be made for moral education. It is important to realise just how wide this gulf is.'[4] Despite John Wilson's own misgivings about the reliability of his components, and despite the fact that only one of his moral components (Phil) has been the subject of research, and in this the results obtained were not conclusive[5], he nevertheless recommends that 'the teacher is given some coherent material on "moral methodology", that is, those concepts, types of reasons, abilities and so on which are basic to the subject. I should expect these to look not much unlike the list of "moral components" which I and my research colleagues have publicized elsewhere.'

It could be argued that the type of procedure described is deductive at two levels: first, the moral components proposed are reached as a result of deductive reasoning; secondly, the materials proposed are to be deduced from the moral components. On the other hand, it could appear to teachers that methods proposed as a result of research are the outcome of inductive procedures. For example, the methods and materials published by Peter McPhail and the team of the Schools Council Moral Education Project as part of the *Lifeline* programme were derived from research. And of this work, the authors have written, contrasting their approach with the allegedly deductive procedures of philosophers, 'We must preserve our empirical zeal and continue to identify problems and find solutions by asking questions and studying the answers.'[6]

Accordingly, in contradistinction to the philosophic approach it could be argued that the research approach is inductive at two levels: first, theory is derived inductively and secondly, recommended materials and methods are derived inductively. This establishment of two apparently hostile camps, the decutive philosophers and the inductive researchers, undermines not only the researcher philosopher relationship, but also the teacher philosopher dialogue, since it raises the natural suspicion in teachers' minds that if one camp may be right, then the other may be wrong, and that perhaps they should wait and see who wins before establishing dialogue with either.

Since the root of the problem over inductive and deductive methodology is logical, and since logic comes firmly within the province of philosophers, it is upon them that the main responsibility rests to indicate if the apparent conflict is real, and if it is not, how the two parties may be reconciled. While I do not intend to trespass upon the philosopher's domain, it does seem to me possibile to indicate the general context within which the particular problems of moral education can be considered in detail by reference to work which is fundamental not only to philosophy but also to scientific research.

The inductive/deductive problem currently raising hackles in moral education is of ancient lineage, and well-known as a source of friction and confusion. It was authoritatively and conclusively dealt with by Karl Popper in *The Logic of Scientific Discovery*. This work provides a framework within which the apparently conflicting inductive and deductive approaches can be reconciled, in that it can be demonstrated, by reference to Popper, that in moral education philosophy and research are not undertaking identical aspects of the same task in different ways; but are attacking different aspects of the same task in different ways. The task itself may be broadly defined as the establishment of a theory of, to quote John Wilson, 'moral thought and action'. The first step in such a task is to distinguish between the conception of a theory and its testing. The process by which a theory is conceived falls in the province of the psychology of knowledge: the process by which it is tested in the province of the logic of knowledge. The former deals with empirical facts, the latter with logical relations. Any ideographic or descriptive research (such as the critical incident technique employed by Peter McPhail and the Schools Council Moral Education Project team) is part of the process by which theory is conceived. It is admissable to call such a process inductive. Equally, insofar as John Wilson's components are a description of observed facts (even though such observations were made on a chance rather than controlled basis) they could be described as inductively, or perhaps intuitively, reached.

However, once a theory has been postulated, possibly as a result of inductive procedures, it can only be tested deductively. Such deductive testing takes place through examination of the internal consistency of any system of ideas proposed, through comparison with other theories, and through empirical application of conclusions derived from the theory. The crucial points, as Popper points out, are first that it is not logically admissable to 'argue from the truth of singular statements to the truth of theories'; and secondly, that 'belief in inductive logic is largely due to a confusion of psychological problems with epistemological ones'.

In fact, neither researchers, of whom I have taken Peter McPhail and the Schools Council Moral Education Project team as an example, nor philosophers, of whom I have taken John Wilson as an example, have denied that theories must be deductively tested. What has perhaps occurred however is a no doubt unintentional failure to make sufficiently plain the fact that, inevitably, theories of moral thought and action relevant to curriculum planning are still in comparatively early stages of formulation and testing. John Wilson's components have not been fully tested; and although the theory of adolescent moral and social learning formulated by Peter McPhail has been tested,[8] the research was carried out with a comparatively limited sample. There has also perhaps been a tendency to commit the error identified by Popper of confusing psychological and epistemological problems. However, the difficulties, I would argue, arise from lack of definition rather than genuine conflict. Consequently, provided philosophers are prepared to investigate, discuss and explicate the logic of scientific research, there is little reason why their dialogue with teachers should be obscured by interference from the sounds of misunderstanding and conflict between researchers and philosophers.

I have tried to define the conditions in which dialogue between teachers and philosophers can take place because it seems to me premature to attempt to enter upon such a dialogue prior to considering the circumstances in which it can occur. That the framework of teacher philosopher communication in the field of moral education has not previously been analysed, although perhaps at first sight strange, may be attributed to the fact that moral education, although a traditional interest of education, has only recently become a matter of contemporary concern; while educational philosophers, although now both numerous and vocal, are very new arrivals on the educational scene. Further, that this is a task worth undertaking seems to me self-evident and indisputable. Although teachers and philosophers separately have their own contributions to make to education, the effectiveness of such activities must surely be enhanced if each can benefit from the experience and ideas of the other. Effective curriculum planning and design in moral education must be considerably hindered in the absence of effective teacher-philosopher dialogue.

Finally, it may seem to educational philosophers that I have concentrated, perhaps somewhat critically, upon their role, while possibly having rather less to say about teachers. If this is so, I would justify it on two counts. Of books and articles telling teachers what to do, there is no end, but of books and articles assessing the contribution of educational philosophers there are few indeed. It is only just and reasonable that something should be done to correct the balance in favour of teachers. My second point is more serious. Philosophers have either put themselves, or been put, in to the magisterial position of critics and evaluators of the educational world: they analyse what is being done, they discuss aims, they relate all of the many parts into one whole. It is of course excellent that such a job should be carried out. The educational world which is the philosopher's oyster, is undeniably a better place for their existence and activities. But their very success raises a problem. In the words of Juvenal's old Latin tag 'Quis custodiet ipsos custodes?' The answer surely must be that all those with whose educational activities philosophers concern themselves should have not merely a right of reply but the same freedom to discuss the role of educational philosophers which those philosophers claim *vis-a-vis* others. Only if this occurs can genuine dialogue between teachers and educational philosophers take place. Much is talked and written of a more democratic education: one contribution to such an education might be the development in the field of moral education and curriculum planning of an open and constructive dialogue between teachers and educational philosophers in which there was equality of respect and esteem.

Notes

1 WILSON, J., (1970) *Moral Thinking*. London: Heinemann. p 86.

2 HARE, R.M., (1963). *Freedom and Reason*. London: Oxford University Press p.*v*.

3 UNGOED-THOMAS, J.R. (i) 'Educational research and curriculum development', *Journal of Moral Education*, 2,2. February, 1973.

      (ii) 'Dissemination, process and training' *Cambridge Journal of Education*, 4,2. Easter Term, 1974.

4 WILSON, J., WILLIAMS, N., SUGARMAN, B. (1967) *Introduction to Moral Education*, Harmondsworth: Penguin, p. 195.

5 SUGARMAN, B. (1973) 'Altruistic attitudes in school', *Journal of Moral Education*, 2,2. February.

6 McPHAIL, P., UNGOED-THOMAS, J.R., CHAPMAN, H. (1972) *Moral Education in the Secondary School*. London: Longman, p.24.

7 POPPER, K.R. (1967) (2nd English edn) *The Logic of Scientific Discovery*. London: Hutchinson.

8 MCPHAIL, P., *et al., op cit.*, p. 54.

Establishing a Dialectic in Moral Education

John Wilson

I very much welcome Jasper Ungoed-Thomas' remarks, not only for the comparative moderateness of their tone, but because they focus on an area of the utmost importance: that is, problems of communication between different disciplines and between 'academics' and practising teachers. What follows here is intended less as a 'reply' than as a continuation of a dialogue which he evidently takes to be as important as I do.

'Public relations'

The points that Ungoed-Thomas makes here (if I may put them under this rather commercial-sounding heading) seem to me absolutely right. They amount to the need for mutual trust. In dialogues with teachers, even a philosopher like myself — though concentrating (perhaps pardonably) more on whether what is said is true than on the various 'images' of the people saying it — cannot help noticing that attitudes change if, for example, I happen to let slip that I spent a year teaching deprived children in Port Said. Of course this fact is probably irrelevant to whatever is being discussed; but it is not irrelevant to the problem of personal acceptability. I shall not easily forget a lady in the USA beginning with a virulent 'You rich upper class Oxford academics . . .', learning (over a few drinks) that I was a poor son of a humble parson, and rapidly switching to 'Ah, you too, then, have suffered'.

We have to remember that there are faults on both sides here. A man with bad breath may still talk sense: he should try to do something about the bad breath, but his hearers should try to listen to the sense and forget the bad breath. Moral education is too important for us to argue or react *ad hominem*. Various images, no doubt including those incorporated in words like 'philosopher', 'academic', 'Oxford', 'theory', and so on, may (for some) be counter-productive; certainly philosophers should do all that Ungoed-Thomas says they should in order to improve trust — be clear, not be virulent, arrogant, ivory-towerish, and so on. But we should all try very hard to forget about any images, and concentrate only on what is true and false. Otherwise what we do will look more like politics or advertising than education.

The philosopher's difficulty

The problems of communication for the 'philosopher' (if we must talk in such terms) lie somewhere in this area. In particular, he is supposed to have some expertise or practice in certain kinds of questions and problems which many people find it hard even to identify: thus, the main problem in teaching philosophy is simply to get students to understand what it *is*, without which one can hardly start. It is not just 'getting clear about words' or 'sharpening up definitions', and it is certainly not laying down 'aims' and 'values' for other people in some dictatorial way. It is about the conceptual problems that arise in almost any educational area and, regrettably, 'conceptual' will not mean much to anyone who has not taken the trouble to understand what philosophers actually do.

Clearly, if we are working as educators — and I mean *we*, not just 'philosophers' — in some area called, say, 'moral education', 'RE', 'science' or almost anything else, we have to know as clearly and precisely as possible what we are talking about. What *is it to be* 'morally educated'? What is to *count as* 'educated in religion', 'good at science', and so on? This has nothing to do with facts about schools, teachers' experiences, 'scientific' or 'inductive theories', or anything of that kind. It is just an attempt to get clear, in detail, what we are going to count as *success* in these areas. Unless we do this, it is hard to see how we can guide any educational research or practice: for we would not know in what direction to guide it.

Now this should be, as Ungoed-Thomas says, a joint enterprise. If 'philosophers' are more expert in it than others, at least they are not being paid for nothing, but for the enterprise to succeed we must jointly agree, or at least jointly understand, what is to count as (in this case) 'educated in morality'. But — and I think it is very important that this be recognized, otherwise we cannot really face the problem at all — the enterprise is not only difficult in itself, but for various reasons unpopular and always liable to be evaded. In 1967 the Farmington Trust sent a questionnaire to almost all countries in the world asking 'What, in your view, could reasonably be meant by "a morally educated person"?' We got replies ranging from 'a good Catholic', 'a good Party member', etc. to 'a democratic and hygienic person' and (incredible but true) 'someone who helps the national economy and is prepared to invade land when necessary'. Few if any replies suggested that the respondents had taken the *words seriously*; they were too anxious to sell some line of their own.

Some possible evasions of this — obviously necessary — task include: (1) the idea that we can do it by counting heads, or accepting some sort of 'social consensus' or what is 'acceptable' — as if 'educated in morality' (or any other phrase) meant what most people thought it meant; so that if, say, a consensus in Nazi Germany thought it meant 'being indoctrinated to obey the Führer', that would be all right; (2) the idea that giving any account must involve things called 'value-judgements', which are ultimately indefensible and which researchers and/or educators should not make; (3) the idea that we do it by asking the consumers, e.g. if pupils say that the most important moral values are such-and-such, then we can accept that as satisfactory (this sometimes seems to be the basis of McPhail's work, but perhaps I misunderstand him;[1] (4) the idea that the task is impossible, because (I suppose) no account of what 'educated in morality' means can be any more or less adequate than another; and (5) the idea that any such account must be a 'theory' to be tested by 'the facts'. Ungoed-Thomas, 'John Wilson's components have not been fully tested' flirts with this idea).

I hope that it is clear why these are evasions, and what they are evasions of: that is, of the common-sense (not grandly 'philosophical') task of first getting clear what we are talking about. This is a long and arduous business, inevitably to do with taking words, concepts and distinctions seriously; and it is not surprising that it is unpopular. (Think of what happened to Socrates.) 'Philosophy', if we must call it that, can perhaps only cut real ice when and where there is enough trust, patience, and desire for this kind of truth or clarity. It involves a great deal of close-knit dialogue, impersonal but crisp, and the initial willingness to admit that we *are* unclear and need to get clearer. In morality especially ('RE' is another case), most of us have vested interests — some of which, I think, it is fair to describe as fantasies or compulsions — which prevent us from even really wanting to be clear.

Some steps forward

I hope that the above will do something to dispel the idea of 'teachers', 'philosophers' and others sitting in different armed camps. The idea is difficult to get away from: even Ungoed-Thomas talks constantly of 'philosophers' and 'researchers' as if they did not overlap, and it is important to see that 'philosophy' — the task of getting clear in the way I have described — precisely *is* a large and important *part of* 'research'. Questions about meaning and questions about empirical facts intertwine in a way which makes it impossible, as I have tried to show elsewhere,[2] to do much serious educational research without 'philosophical' assistance of a very close-knit or built-in kind.

This is just another way of saying that we — all of us — have to conduct this operation with as much assistance as we can get. To use a parallel: obviously we are in a muddle about what to do under the heading 'religious education'. Now little is gained either (1) by philosophers of religion and education just *telling* us what to do — first, because the rest of us have to understand and see the point for ourselves (not just, as it were, obey orders); and second, because when it comes to practical action we have to combine the knowledge of psychologists, practising teachers and others with philosophical clarity; or (2) by simply shirking the task of answering the question 'What fairly *counts as* "being educated in religion"?', and (having shirked it) being driven by fashion, social or political pressure, consumer demand, our own personal preferences, or just what seems easiest. The crucial move is to *face the question*, and answer it adequately — and it is at least to be hoped that professional philosophers will be able to help us.

How can we help each other to take this task seriously? A few points may be worth making here:

(a) The communication has to be plentiful and close-knit. Unless those engaged in educational research and practice engage in many man-hours philosophical debate, and bring those most skilled in confronting such tasks into close alliance with themselves, their work is likely to be autistic. Here I cannot forbear to say that — tiresome though philosophers may be — most educational researchers and developers are somewhat less than eager to ask for their advice and criticism. Perhaps they fear endless arguments 'about words', and want to get on with 'their thing'; perhaps they are short of time; perhaps they are over-anxious to turn out some 'practical' end-product. But *if* — a big 'if' — they have grasped the nature of the task and its importance, they should naturally want as much hard argument at close quarters as possible. An occasional conference or seminar is nothing like enough: the gulfs are too wide. And in a book (like this one) there is insufficient flexibility to allow a close dialectic. The result is that the gulfs remain wide.[3] Some philosophers, at least, are anxious to help, and should be used and worked as hard as possible.

(b) So far as possible, we have to keep ourselves free from political or quasi-political pressures. I mean simply that we have to address ourselves to what is *true* or *correct*; not to what the DES, or the Schools Council, or 'society', or teachers, or pupils, or anybody else finds acceptable or popular. This is a hard saying (particularly if one is financed by this or that body); but it is not only economic facts that cause the trouble. In moral education, we have (rightly) abandoned the idea that all we need is some authority telling us the answers, but (wrongly) fallen into talking as if there were no such things as true or correct answers, quite independently of whether 'society', or pupils, or teachers think there to be. Over and above any 'democratic' interplay of ideas, beliefs, 'values', and so on, there stands the notion of what is actually reasonable or right; if it did not, we could not educate at all — we could only influence pupils' attitudes in various fashionable directions for which we had no final justification. This is why it is so important to grasp such justifications and (in this case) to establish a detailed concept of 'being morally educated' which is free from cultural pressures.

(c) It is not to be expected that all or even many teachers and empirical researchers will have time or inclination (or need) to learn very much philosophy, any more than to learn very much science. But it is to be expected (or hoped) that they will get some idea of what philosophy — the task of getting clear — actually *is*, and see its relevance to their work; just as non-scientists at least know what a scientific question is, and will call expert scientists in when necessary. Speaking not only as a philosopher but as someone very much concerned with practical education, I should die happy if educators could achieve this much; that they should have read Hegel and Kant (let alone Peters and Wilson) is less important, and might even be counter-productive. Just as philosophers must naturally defer to practising teachers, psychologists and other experts in certain matters, so — to put it as mildly as I can — there must be *some* kind of respect for philosophy as a discipline and as part of educational enterprises. Philosophers may be wrong, like anyone else; but the task remains.

I must add here that, if we do take the task seriously and reach some clear understanding of what it *means* to be 'morally educated' — what counts as being reasonable, or competent, or a good performer in this area — then it is hard to see how we could *not* put this 'in the curriculum': at least in the sense that we would *tell* the pupils of our conclusions and get them to practise this methodology. In something like the same way, if we are reasonably clear what it means to be 'good at (educated in, competent at, etc.) science', we can make the pupils aware of what is necessary here and give them practice at it — not, of course, forcing it down their throats, and giving plenty of opportunity for argument even about these basic principles, but not leaving them in a total vacuum. This can be attempted without the benefit of any 'theory' of moral education, indeed just by virtue of the teacher's own clarity plus a common-sense knowledge of his pupils. If we do not attempt it, the implication is that we are not serious in our desire to educate or, more probably, that we have not reached any clear understanding.

Let me end by stressing what seems to be the most important practical point in all this. I have been glad to add to Ungoed-Thomas' remarks here in print, and have tried in various publications to make certain points about moral education as clear as I can. But it is obvious that (whether I or anyone else is right or wrong on any particular issue) this sort of communication is too long-range and, as it were, lumpish or large-scale. Much more interesting and 'real' would be the tape-recorded results of a really intense and sustained face-to-face dialogue, in which I (and, I am sure, many other 'philosophers') would be very willing to take part. We could then record, inspect, play back and make public the actual issues involved — issues which, as Jasper Ungoed-Thomas has well brought out, underlie (and impede) a great deal of what is said and thought about moral education. Indeed, the unreality and autistic quality of many books about education in general is perhaps largely due to this need for much closer and longer communication — the dialectic of a seminar, not the sweeping debates of politicians and those who have axes to grind. It is devoutly to be hoped that such dialectic will in fact occur.

Notes

1 See Ch. 2 of MCPHAIL P., UNGOED-THOMAS, J.R. and CHAPMAN, H. (1972) *Moral Education in the Secondary School.* London: Longman.

2 *Philosophy and Educational Research.* Slough: NFER, (1972).

3 Compare for instance, Richard Peters' review of *Moral Education in the Secondary School* by P. MCPHAIL, J. UNGOED-THOMAS and H. CHAPMAN (*Journal of Moral Education* (1973), 3, 1) with the reply of Peter McPhail and J.R. Ungoed-Thomas (*Journal of Moral Education*, 1974, 3, 2).

The Role of the Teacher in Formulating A Course in Moral Education

An edited taped discussion between John Rose and Michelle York

J.R. We must begin by airing our views on what actually happens in the classroom where moral education is concerned. To do this properly requires layout, effort, logical sequencing of concepts and a great knowledge of the children. The knowledge of the children that I am thinking about is more in terms of motivation. What motivates the child at a particular age? What are his interests, his hobbies, what are his aspirations? These are, of course, dependent upon his experience, his environment, the group he plays with, and it's this sort of knowledge of the child that the teacher ought to have. And not only that, he ought also to be aware of how far the child has gone in understanding the process of reasoning. This involves the child putting forward his own views on situations, and having these views altered by discussion, or modified by further evidence or additional views in terms of facts about other people's interests, i.e the idea of fairness and respect for persons presented by the teacher. All this knowledge is relevant if the teacher is to enable the children to go further in developing their perception and reasoning.

  Where moral education is concerned the haphazard kind of approach — any subject can be treated this way — and the same applies to religious education, is not, I think, a viable one. If the thing is going to be done it must be done, I think, on its own, with a developmental framework that any other subject would want to have. The difference here is that whereas subjects like history, or English or geography have a definite factual content that is distinctly historic, geographic or to do with the English language, moral education does not necessarily have such clear-cut areas of fact, areas of knowledge.

M.Y.   Isn't this due partly to the fact that it's so much more personal.
       You can't change the facts of history, but people's moral out-
       looks can and do change, and this will be reflected in the way
       they teach. Very few people are prepared to teach moral edu-
       cation. You ask the average teacher, perhaps in a middle school,
       if he will step in and teach history for a couple of weeks because
       someone is away, he probably wouldn't mind, but you ask him to
       teach moral education and he might not be so enthusiastic, because
       he is putting forward a personal point of view and very often people
       aren't prepared to do this. They like to retain a certain amount of
       their personal opinion, there is a certain holding back, and in teac-
       hing moral education you are opening yourself to the children far
       more than in any other subject.

J.R.   The difficulty lies in the body of knowledge, its structure and
       methodology. Moral education is further complicated because it is
       inherent in history, in geography and in English. All those subjects
       contain attitudes, values, and the sort of criteria against which
       pupils are expected to judge the merits of actions, and, indeed, their
       own actions.

M.Y.   Moral education is, then, an umbrella overall of them, isn't it? It
       comes into all of them.

J.R.   And religious education in some degree? You couldn't have
       history without some reference to religion, could you, especially
       if you talk of religion in terms of ultimate ideas, and questions
       that concern man? Questions like, 'Who am I?' 'What am I here
       for?' 'What do I want to do with my life and why do I want to do
       it?' 'How am I going to live?'.

M.Y.   'Am I going to drift along with the crowd, because it is so easy to
       drift along with the crowd?' This is particularly so of the fourteen-
       to fifteen-year-old who, naturally, wants to gain recognition
       amongst his peers and the only way to do this is to drift along
       with them. He's afraid to stop and think because he's afraid of
       being left behind.

J.R.   He isn't being given the opportunity in school, you see.

M.Y.   He's not really being given the opportunity anywhere. Other
       people's opinions are constantly inflicted upon him through
       television, radio, the 'pop-culture', and yet it is only through
       moral education that one can point out the way in which you

should stop and think — the importance of stopping and thinking, or slowing down and thinking.

J.R.   It's a bit of both moral and religious education; some might say that those questions are religious, but the two are so intertwined when you're dealing with value judgements. For some people 'Religion' will mean things about commitments, values, etc. and so is inextricably linked with morals. So in morals, there are questions that the pupil has to come to terms with and is not coming to terms with in those other school subjects. So the school needs a specialist person, who is skilled and trained in dealing with the ideas which pupils want and need to come to terms with.

M.Y.   And don't know how to.

J.R.   In training the specialist moral educator I think it is important that he has a basic understanding of his pupil's moral development from Heteronomy, through Socionomy to Autonomy. Added to this basic understanding of what a child's moral outlook is likely to be at any one time must then be the kind of training which enables him to give the child material which allows him to develop perceptive abilities, to understand and apply his understanding to a wider area of living than he could previously, and to deepen his understanding so that he is better able to strengthen the foundations for his own philosophy of life. It would further be necessary for the teacher to understand different philosophies of living, involving necessarily belief and faith, which provide the motivation for a whole range of human endeavour and activity. The student teacher should be able to refer to anthropology and sociology, the study of other civilizations, other cultures. He would need also to make references to history and be able to point to situations which add a further shade of meaning to a child's understanding. He would need to know a certain amount of psychology since the children would also require some knowledge of basic psychology to understand themselves and to understand others. With this whole range of training the teacher would then come equipped to widen and deepen the child's understanding.

M.Y.   What about the position of philosophers in the teaching of moral education? I don't think teachers have time to sit and read the material. It might stimulate thought, but it may also lead to confusion because of the difficulty involved. In my experience, in the primary age range I can't think of anyone who has read widely in moral education, and yet they are teaching it implicitly and explicitly every day.

J.R.   I think there is a vast gulf between theory in university and practice in school. The theory tends to deal with a lot of generalities, is very well thought out in terms of aims, but less well thought out in terms of practical application, of stimulating material. For example, I feel that some of the latest material intended for moral education in the secondary school would be laughed out of my school. The cartoons are badly drawn and the presentation in general is very badly done. I think that if you are dealing with real-life situations then real-life situations ought to be contained within the material that you are using. Photographs, and to a certain extent representative, impressionistic drawings and paintings are valuable to get a point across, but I think this use of cartoons has perhaps gone too far, although there may be a small place for them (pupils could even create their own to illustrate a viewpoint) but this should be limited so that people laugh *with* rather than *at* the material.

M.Y.   I agree, they can reduce the situation to a comic level, and the children would not take it seriously at all. It reduces moral education to the level of the comics they read. It takes away the seriousness of a situation; for example, if you showed a photograph of a starving woman or a leper there is far more impact than a series of cartoon strips even though they might be about someone like Father Damien. Also, the materials available mostly seem to apply to the secondary age range. Do you think that development is aimed more in the direction of the secondary school than in the primary /middle? If it is, its starting at the wrong end!

J.R.   Well I wonder if its happening at all, at least to any great extent.

M.Y.   In the lower age range, before the age of ten for example, most children are not as socially aware as children of ten plus.

J.R.   I think this is very true, but I would say that a child of primary school age would certainly have values, mainly obtained from his parents, and would be very vehement in what he considered to be right. He would say, for example, that harming animals was very wrong.

M.Y.   Primary school children, for instance, probably feel more strongly about the practical, day-to-day existence as it affects them personally and this is how one must tackle moral education with them.

J.R.   I think that teachers, if given the opportunity, can understand the language of the philosopher and the language of the psychologist; these may even shed light on areas of confusion and help to get straight about what our approach is to be with different age and ability groups.

M.Y.   I agree, but I don't think they have sufficient opportunity.

J.R.   Well they have in some of the in-service courses that are being run in colleges and universities for teachers.

M.Y.   But not everyone has the opportunity, this is the trouble, moral and religious education is very important and through no fault of anyone, more for financial reasons, every teacher can't be given the opportunity to sit back, to read and think about their ideas.

J.R.   There is a lot of concern amongst teachers for a framework. As we mentioned earlier, if they're going to teach moral/religious education then they've got to have a framework of knowledge to which they can constantly refer. I think that there is a demand amongst teachers for this framework, as is shown by the support for these courses run in colleges and universities. What is required is that philosophers and psychologists do meet practising teachers and get down to the nitty-gritty: going into the classroom, getting together with teachers and putting these laudable, excellent aims that are being thought out and expressed by philosophers and psychologists into classroom language. In other words, translating them into lessons, giving their meaning and their theories a practical application.

Obviously it is necessary to have much discussion between philosophers, researchers and teachers on how to structure the individual lessons so that a particular concept or proposition is taught and grasped by the pupils. Concepts and propositions are taught, discovered, put forward, and knocked about and reshaped, by the testing of hypotheses through decision making and problem solving. Reshaping also occurs in inductive concept learning, that is, showing a number of positive examples and also negative instances to reinforce deeper concepts. In addition, hypothetical deductive learning enables us to describe propositions which can then be applied by the pupil to a particular situation and further tested by this reference. There are various ways in which the children can become involved in learning; role-play — imagine yourself in a situation, drama, discussion, creative writing, reading and learning about similar cultures/societies where comparable situations exist which illustrate that particular concept or similar ones, debating etc.

Research material contains marvellous aims and objectives, contains valid and highly laudable questions, pointers, guidelines to classroom development, but researchers aren't actually getting into the thick of things and trying them out.

M.Y. The dissemination is poor. Teachers must be floundering, wondering what to do. I know they are because I have taught with people who say they don't do any moral education because they just don't know what to do. Moral (religious) education is only covered in many teacher training colleges by perhaps a year of lectures on 'contemporary thought' — that doesn't really help anyone.

J.R. Yes, I think that is a point that must be brought out, the colleges of education must take a greater hand in covering moral and religious education if it is going to be taught in school. But I think we must go back to schools to find out how it is going to be done. Working parties would be of use here, philosophers, psychologists, researchers and teachers actually criticising each others' work. Some of the practical work that has been produced on a commercial scale in humanities has been of value but there are parts of these projects which need criticizing, need working at. So what we require is more dialogue between those people who are writing the theory, formulating the theory, advancing the objectives, not merely to write to a teacher in the school and get his views, but to go in there and talk to him and perhaps even see him in action.

M.Y. Yes, because so many of these schemes are worked out, tried, found to be satisfactory and then just left in the air for teachers to cull out from them what they can, if they have time for this analysis. There's no work done on the backwash, so to speak.

J.R. If philosophers were to actually go into school, not only to talk with the teacher, but to see the implementation of their ideas then there would perhaps also be this cross-fertilization that would be enormously valuable. Researchers are doing this already but sufficient reference isn't being made to the experts in moral education and in the associated disciplines.

We must get clear about the aims and then we can do all the development/practical work required. Philosophers/theorists should, obviously, be of most help with clarifying aims, though of course their understanding and contribution to the development/practical work will also be vital.

We can gain several hints from programme learning, in that

the material for use with pupils mustn't be too advanced or too simple, it must stimulate interest yet not produce any over-reaction. It mustn't be boring, but must contain an element of 'slog', in that anything learnt requires effort. If people are brilliant they can understand quickly, they can move onto more difficult questions and decisions. This leads me to suggest that some form of sequencing in dealing with questions of value is going to be rather important, since what you want to do is to enable a person to become more able to understand the basis for his own actions and thoughts. He can gain more ability by moving on to more difficult and abstract considerations.

M.Y. So what is needed is for the philosopher and psychologist not to sit in their ivory towers and send out their minions to do research from which they can draw their conclusions, but to set up working parties to work among the people who need the help — the teachers. It is no good just churning out papers on this and papers on that without following up with a great deal of discussion which can lead to a synthesis of ideas.

J.R. What moral education really needs is empirical feet. Yes, going into school, as you say, and really establishing the sequential, developmental, conceptual learning framework that is required.

M.Y. We are going to be concerned with concrete situations that people react to in different ways, particularly in very personal ways. Something terrible in the news (bombings, kidnappings, etc.) prompts immediate personal involvement and leads us to consider the concept of justice for example. And what I deem to be just other people may not.

J.R. Well I think that this is a particular reason for talking about the question of justice and seeing where one actually does stand.

M.Y. This is what I am trying to say — these are things which teachers are afraid to tackle.

J.R. I don't agree I think they are not necessarily afraid, they just haven't got anything to go on.

M.Y. Isn't this why they are afraid?

J.R. I don't think they are afraid.

M.Y. They are afraid of losing control of the situation because they haven't got enough confidence in their own convictions to allow a group of children to have a discussion without having a tight rein.

J.R. I wouldn't talk of it in terms of fear because I think that teachers are responsible, professional people who simply want to tackle teaching in a responsible, professional way and they can't do that at the moment to any great degree in moral education because there are not substantial professional guidelines in terms of the nature and content of the things to be tackled.

M.Y. Yes, I agree. You have said what I was trying to say. Teachers haven't the confidence because they haven't the back up material which states what is necessary, material which they could read and say, 'I agree with that, that's exactly how I feel'. But because there is little such material they lack the confidence to tackle these questions.

J.R. Carrying that on, I think that the work of philosophers and psychologists does have a lot to say, and a lot to give to the classroom situation but it has got to be translated in terms that children can understand, in terms that teachers can teach. Work has been started but there is a great deal more to do.

M.Y. And it must be in terms that teachers can understand and grasp quickly without having to wade through reams and reams of theory.

J.R. Teachers are willing to try new areas of discovery if professional guidelines are adhered to — school standards must not drop because of some airy question that has been thought of in some remote ivory tower. If there are committees of teachers working together, and pupils, philosophers and psychologists, who are willing to get their toes burnt — because it will inevitably involve that — many of the desired solutions to these problems could be found.

M.Y. I think that it is most important that you involve the pupils, because in formulating schemes one must know what their problems are. After all it is the pupils that one is trying to help.

Section Two
Neutrality and the Teacher

' "Do you understand why he says why he
has to be neutral?"
"Well, I think because we've always been
used to doing what the teacher says, and if
he's going to give his point of view, we're
going to follow it . . . ".'

' "And the teacher doesn't say what's
right or what's wrong. She let's you say what
you want."
"She's just there, not exactly to put you
right because you've got your own opinion. She
doesn't give her opinion one way or the other.
She just sits and listens and gives out these
slips for us to talk over and it just goes on
into conversation. Sometimes it goes off into
other things but . . . ".'

'How pupils view neutral
chairmanship', from *Towards
Judgement*, Hamingson, D.,
(Ed.) 1973, CARE Occasional
Publications No.1, p.184 and
pp.188-9.

The Neutral Teacher[1]

May Warnock

Those who advocate neutrality in teachers do so, in my experience, with great passion. There appear to be two major grounds for their advocacy, which are not, however, totally distinct from each other. The first ground is the desire to avoid turning teaching into indoctrination. The second is the desire that pupils may learn whatever they do learn by discovering through experiment, trial and error and genuine argument; that they may have the pleasure of coming independently to their own conclusions, with the teacher simply as chairman of their meetings.

I want briefly to consider the indoctrination argument first, but this will not take long, since it will be clear already how this argument shades off into the second. It is worth considering the *word* 'indoctrination', however, since it is rather a vogue word just at the moment. Indoctrination means the imposing upon a captive child the body of doctrines held by the teacher (or supposed to be held by him). The essence of the situation is that what the teacher says is true is to be accepted by the child uncritically. The bad feature of indoctrination therefore (and the word is obviously pejorative) is precisely in the docile and uncritical state of mind which it produces in the pupil. The concept of indoctrination certainly has some use; but there are great difficulties in marking off its limits exactly. For instance, if the teacher is a charismatic person it may well be that his pupils are disinclined to doubt what he says, even in areas where doubt is perfectly reasonable. If he is the opposite, whatever he says may seem dubious or at least unmemorable to his pupils. Again, it is not clear whether the word

1 This paper was originally presented at a conference on 'Philosophy of Education', sponsored by the Royal Institute of Philosophy in 1973, and is included together with replies by Richard Norman and Alan Montefiore in the proceedings of that conference, *Philosophers Discuss Education*, Ed. S.C. Brown, Macmillan, forthcoming.

'indoctrinate' means 'to induce uncritical belief deliberately' or not. If I am an absolutely convinced believer in the single authorship of the *Iliad* and the *Odyssey*, such that I have never even raised the question whether Homer was one author or several, then I may teach my class that the *Iliad* and the *Odyssey* were written by one Greek whose name was Homer, and they may go through the rest of their lives believing this, especially if they do not develop any particular interest in Greek poetry. It may become simply part of the seldom-examined furniture of their minds. Have they then been indoctrinated? I certainly did not *mean* to indoctrinate them. I simply meant to tell them what I took to be the truth. I did not even know that it was controversial. But it may be asked, does anyone ever set out deliberately to indoctrinate another? Do we not always attempt simply to teach them the truth? Perhaps sometimes, in cases where there is a received body of dogma which hangs together, and belief in which is thought to be particularly desirable in its effects, a teacher may say, like the Jesuits, I will catch him young, and ensure that he accepts it all, lock stock and barrel. But when you come to think of it this is a pretty rare phenomenon. For most teachers the question whether or not to indoctrinate in this narrow sense of the word hardly ever arises. Apart then from 'indoctrination' in the narrow sense, the word seems mostly to be used of other people, when we ourselves disapprove either of the content of their teaching, or of their methods. As such it is perhaps not a very useful word to analyse further.

Let us move on, therefore, to consider the second ground for holding that a teacher should be neutral. This is the desire that pupils should learn by discovering things for themselves rather than by being told; and this course of discovery will include, among other items, the discovery that it is possible to hold different views about a vast number of subjects, between which views he will have to choose. Thus, the neutral teacher will present to his pupil the different views that exist, will put him in the way of evidence, or other considerations, which might favour the different views, and will then sit back and allow him to make up his own mind. Now it will be obvious at once that this kind of description of the teacher's role applies only to certain kinds of material, if at all. There are some sorts of teaching situations in which the question of the pupil deciding something for himself does not really arise, and this even where the material is, in a sense, controversial. Let us suppose, for example, that I am trying to teach someone to do something. In the very simple kind of case, such as where I may try to teach you to ride a bicycle, there will be very little theoretical content to my teaching; I will merely guide your efforts with advice and physical support. If I am trying to teach you, on the other hand, to drive a car or play the French horn, there may be a good deal of theory involved. But nonetheless my aim in teaching is to get you to be able to do something. And when you can do it reasonably efficiently, then you can perfect your technique by practice, rejecting some of my teaching if you find it better to do so, that is, if you find it more efficient. The question of neutrality can hardly be made to bear on such cases at all. A great deal of what one teaches at school is in fact of this kind, disagreeable though it may be for some theorists to accept this. Reading and writing are indeed often spoken of as 'skills' and it is acknowledged that in teaching them we are teaching children how to do something. But a great deal of mathematics must also be learned as a matter of skill or technique; and in the case of languages, the aim is also to teach people how to talk, write, or translate. Of course a teacher may get things wrong. He may simply teach his pupils to write bad French, or give them a cumbersome or confusing method for solving equations. But this again has virtually nothing to do with whether he is neutral or not. It is a matter of whether he is intelligent and understands his subject matter. I mention these cases only to show that there is a vast area of very important teaching, (though somewhat neglected in the writings of educationists) which is the teaching of techniques or skills, and where it does not enter our heads to demand the neutrality of the teacher. The question of whether he is neutral or not just does not arise.

But obviously, embedded in these techniques and subjects there generally lies a core of fact and of theory. I teach someone to read Latin, and teach him in doing so *that* Cicero uses the subjunctive in relative clauses to convey this or that nuance. This is taught as a fact, which can be verified by appeal to the texts. And behind this fact lies a theory, or at least a system, which enables me to split up written words (in this case) into sentences, and sentences into clauses, to distinguish nouns from verbs, and to distinguish, within the class of verbs, those which are indicative from those which are subjunctive in mood. And so on. At last we may begin to see some of the difficulties. How are we to distinguish, in what lies behind the taught technique, between fact and theory? Are we to teach the theory as well as the fact? Must we preface all our teaching of Latin syntax (to stick to this example) with the words 'This is a subjunctive verb *according to our present classification*; but of course there could be other classifications?' How much do such provisos actually add to a pupil's understanding? Do we want him to be thinking all the time about alternative geometries, or do we first want him to learn a bit about Euclidean geometry, and then contemplate alternatives? One thing is certain. In teaching such subjects as Latin syntax, a teacher cannot simply act as a chairman. His duty is to provide positive information, which he must make intelligible by as many examples as he can. No child can be expected to discover Latin syntax unaided from the ancient texts. In such a case the teacher must actually teach — that is pass on information and understanding which he has and his pupil, so far, has not. Whether or not he wishes to preface all his teaching with remarks of the form 'things being as they are' or 'using the syntactical classification as we do', he must at some stage actually assert what is the case. I think that, empirically speaking, it would create endless confusion if he always put in the covering clause; and no sensible teacher who actually wanted to get his pupils to learn something would think of doing so.

We have come upon a case then, (and there are very many such) where although it is logically possible to regard the matter in a wholly different light, yet the teacher is justified in teaching certain facts as facts, as an aid to teaching certain skills. He need not continually point out that someone else might deny that what he had taught was a fact. If he wishes he may suggest that there could be a different frame of reference within which things would look different, but to point this out is most of the time irrelevant to his purpose. A teacher who never pointed this out, who either did not believe it, or had never thought about it one way or another, need not be described as doctrinaire, nor need his teaching be described as indoctrinating. A man who accepts some facts as such, and passes on his knowledge of them is not failing to be neutral.

However, up till now, we have been dealing with the easy cases. We have looked only at cases where the pupil has little scope either for discovering facts for himself or making up his own mind between conflicting accounts. But we have only to think of a few more lessons in the school day to come upon subjects where the distinction between what is a fact and what is not is much harder to draw. In the discussion of history and geography (as they used to be called), indeed of the social sciences generally, it is frequently claimed that it is absolutely impossible to distinguish between facts and non-facts, and the notion of a fact is dangerously misleading, and that teachers must not deceive or bully their pupils by telling them things on the assumption that this distinction can be made. I want now to examine this claim a little further.

In the first place, it will be agreed that in the teaching of, for example, history, there has to be considerable selection of material, even if a teacher himself does not do it, but relies on a text book or syllabus maker to do it for him. Selection, notoriously, may be biased or one sided. The good teacher will do his best to supplement material which he feels is inadequate in this sort of respect; but he would find it very hard radically to change the assumptions of our whole culture about what is worth discussing and what is not. The main historical issues to be examined will remain the same changing only gradually, for many generations. The teacher cannot aspire to a god-like status as far as selecting material goes. If he chooses, he may preface all his remarks with the warning that he is looking at the thing from the standpoint of a twentieth century historian. But this warning, like the general warnings we looked at before, turns out to be empty, because he cannot specify at all exactly what alternatives there may one day be. He *is* after all a twentieth-century historian. That he will be teaching from largely pre-selected material, then, is necessarily true, and need not be taken to impair his neutrality, nor need it be taken to undermine the whole concept of the fact. But this is not the whole story. In most branches of the social sciences, the main purpose of the teacher is not only to impart information, but to give to his pupils a sense of evidence, of what does and what does not count as an argument, so that they may, if they wish, go on with the subject by themselves. It is in this area that the demand for neutrality is likely to become insistent. A teacher must present evidence fairly; he must not conceal evidence, nor exaggerate that which is favourable to one side or the other. His pupils must weigh the evidence, and decide on the truth. Is the teacher thus put, whether he likes it or not, into the chair? Is chairmanship enough?

Let us take a concrete example. Suppose a class to be discussing the history of Mary Queen of Scots. They have arrived at the stage of the murder of Darnley. The question arises: 'Was Mary or was she not implicated in this murder?'. Now one thing is certain. Pupils in an ordinary school class cannot examine any fresh evidence on this point. They cannot even read the secondary sources in detail, still less can they go back to contemporary sources. They must use evidence which is merely described to them, rather than presented in detail. The teacher must tell them what the sources are, and must tell them, for example, that Buchanan's history was specifically designed to incriminate Mary, that it contains inconsistencies, and cannot be taken as true or unbiased. The teacher must help his pupils to reconstruct the probable course of events, relying on his own knowledge of the period, and his own common sense and experience of how people in general behave. But in helping his pupils, is he not to tell them what he thinks is the most likely account? Of course in a case like this no one cares very much one way or the other, and no one is likely to attack the teacher for non-neutrality. But the case is worth considering, since the principles governing the teacher's behaviour in this case are general and apply equally to cases in which the passsions are likely to be involved. I would argue that unless the teacher comes out into the open, and says in what direction he believes that the evidence points he will have failed in his duty as a teacher. For what his pupils have to learn is not only, in an abstract way, what counts as evidence, but *how people draw conclusions from evidence*. The whole notion of evidence independent of any probable conclusion is meaningless. Of course there may be cases where the teacher thinks the evidence is genuinely inconclusive, and in this case he must say that there is really no ground for coming down on one side or the other. But such cases are rare. If all evidence were inconclusive, then the concept of evidence itself would be, if not empty, at least radically different. Thus the teacher must, if he is to teach his pupils to assess evidence fairly, give them actual examples of how he does this himself. His pupils may disagree with him. The more adult they become, and the better their earlier experience of arguments, the more capable they will be of weighing the probabilities differently. But unless they see before them the spectacle of a rational man drawing conclusions rationally, they will never learn what rational probabilities are. Obviously, all kinds of factors personal to the teacher come in here. If he is dynamic and likeable his views may tend to be uncritically accepted. If he is despised, they may be uncritically opposed. But all the same, to see that the teacher is committed to a view which he thinks rationally follows from the evidence is of tremendous value in itself, whether his pupils follow him or not. The teacher must be a *leader* in argument if he is to teach argument. And a leader cannot sit on the fence for ever.

So far I have been treating only of facts, albeit selected and dubious facts. In this area I hope I have suggested that uncommitted neutrality in the teacher, in so far as it is possible, is not desirable. I want now to consider whether this conclusion has any bearing on the real question, the problem that all the fuss is about, namely the question whether or not a teacher should be neutral when the subject of the class is a matter of values. I do not wish to embark here on the problem of distinguishing facts from values. It is sometimes argued that as there is no such thing as a pure fact, no proper distinction can be drawn between fact and value. If so, then perhaps we could take a short way with the subject and say that what has been said about facts ought to be said about values, since they cannot be distinguished. But this would not be convincing. I would rather assume that we can all of us give examples of what in non-philosophical moments we should be prepared to call statements of fact. An example would be that Mary Queen of Scots knew that Darnley was to be murdered on February 9th 1567, or that she did not know. (The fact that many people would be inclined to condemn her for conniving at the murder of her husband, however unsatisfactory, is neither here nor there. The factual question is, 'Did she know about it or did she not?'.) We can, I shall assume, all of us produce instances of obviously evaluative statements, such as that the publications of pornography ought to be severely restricted by law. It is to the second kind of statement, and the arguments which may take place in class about them, that I want now to turn.

Now it is a truism that matters of fact may be relevant to the drawing of evaluative conclusions, though they may not entail these conclusions. That being so (and especially since relevance is one of the main lessons he has to teach), it follows that all the duties a teacher may have with respect to evidence in the historical example already considered will be equally incumbent upon him in the evaluative case. And of course many of the historical cases may also be evaluative. But the collection and presentation of evidence is likely to be fraught with difficulties in the evaluative cases. Notoriously, for example, it is hard to discover what the effect of pornography is upon its willing consumers, even if an agreed starting definition of pornography can be arrived at. It is perhaps still harder to discover its effects upon those who have to consume it whether they like it or not. All evidence of the form 'people in general do or suffer x' is extraordinarily hard to collect or present fairly. Still worse is evidence of the form 'people suffer harm if x is done to them'. For it is not only the scope of the generalization which causes difficulties, but the conceptual content as well. What is to count as harm? Such difficulties as these must be faced by the teacher who is trying to present the material on which his pupils are to base their judgement of whether or not pornography ought to be radically and further restricted by law. But he must be neither daunted nor deflected by this. He must plough his way on as best he can, making it absolutely clear what he is doing, where he is assuming something that he cannot prove, and what he is preparing them to do. He must use the material, as far as he is able to collect it, as *grounds* upon which to found a judgement. But now what happens? Does he jib at forming a judgement himself, and simply demand that his pupils make one? Or does he state, as I have maintained that he should in the relatively 'pure' historical case, his own view? Once again, I have no doubt whatever that he should state his own view, and thus demonstrate to his pupils the whole process of basing a judgement on an interpretation of the facts. Insofar as the argument we are supposing is just an argument, the very same considerations apply to it as applied to the argument about Mary Queen of Scots. A pupil cannot understand the relevance of factual considerations to conclusions without experience of the conclusions being actually drawn. But in the evaluative case there are other and more important considerations as well.

First, as will be obvious from a consideration of the foregoing example, the facts cannot be absolutely determined. Interpretation is going to enter into the presentation of the grounds right from the start. It is therefore virtually impossible to separate a conclusion from its grounds. The conclusion as it were enters into the presentation of the grounds. But even if such separation were possible in practice, other objections would remain. There is a psychological objection to the spectacle of someone remaining neutral in a highly charged dispute about a subject which is supposed to affect everyone and therefore be everyone's concern. The neutral man cannot but seem uninterested, and however much he claims to be *putting aside* his own beliefs in order to act the part of neutral chairman, this does not prevent his seeming either alarmingly remote, or positively scornful or patronizing, if he will not join in the dispute. There is a kind of nightmare in which one is in danger or pain or in some state of emotional tension of a painful kind, and all the time on the sidelines, there is a perfectly impassive observer, taking no steps to help or comfort, or even to acknowledge the existence of a crisis. It is the nightmare of the knitters at the guillotine, or of the absolutely rational parent observing a child's tantrum and letting him simply go on screaming. Something of this nightmarish sense is conveyed to pupils whose teacher will not take part in a debate, or attest his own moral view.

It may be argued that this is a neurotic, or at any rate an exaggerated reaction. Any such disagreeable effects are far outweighed by the desirability of getting pupils to see both sides of any question so as to ensure that they judge, when they do, rationally and without prejudice. Since a teacher has, it is argued, no right to impose his own prejudices on his pupils, he had better not voice them. He cannot expect his pupils to eliminate prejudice from their minds if he is seen to be guilty of prejudice himself. So runs the argument for neutrality. The weakness of the argument lies, self-evidently, in the word 'prejudice'. I wish to distinguish between a prejudice and a moral belief, and thus to conclude that if a teacher states clearly his own moral belief, he is not displaying prejudice. He has not *pre*judged anything. In the case supposed, he has examined and assessed the significance of what facts he has been able to assemble and then made his moral judgement of what ought to occur. Very well, it may be said, let him express his moral belief, provided that he both shows how he has arrived at it, and is careful to say that it is simply *his opinion*. Let him by no means seek to impose this opinion on his pupils. If he cannot keep his mouth shut, or if he feels that he must state his own conclusion in order to demonstrate the drawing of a conclusion, let him at least clearly show that he realizes that other opinions are just as good (or as people prefer to say, as valid).

But, alas, this is impossible in the nature of the case. And here we have come upon the real nature of evaluative judgements. It is strictly impossible at one and the same time to say 'this is wrong' and 'but you need not think so'. Although we all know perfectly well that values are relative to our society and our culture (or even to our little bit of society or culture) yet it is impossible to assert this truth *and* in the same breath seriously to assert a value judgement. We are inevitably and for ever divided in our minds. Either we make no value judgements, and are content to stand outside the making of them, or, if we do make them, we must for the time being put on one side our anthropological spectacles through which we survey the conflicting opinions of the human race. Moreover, if we have come to our moral judgement by the route of serious thought and a consideration of the evidence as fair as we can make it, then we cannot think that an opposite judgement follows equally 'validly' from this same evidence. If we have concluded that something is wrong, we *must* think that everyone ought to hold it wrong, even though we know that they do not and that we must put up with this. Now this feature of evaluative judgements is something that at some time or other pupils must learn to recognize, and, if possible, understand; and they can start to understand it from the expression of genuine moral conviction by their teacher. They will learn that someone who sincerely holds a moral conviction does not, and cannot, feel that any other conviction is *just as good*. That is the nature of the case. Moral relativism may be a fact; but it is not a fact that we feel while we are forming moral judgements. If we really believed that any moral view was as good and worthy to be adopted as any other, then we would of course make no moral judgements at all. And the same is true of all other, non-moral evaluations. We cannot evaluate and accept another evaluation at the same time as equally sound. Moral views, then, are not prejudices; but they are also totally distinct from matters of opinion.

One may of course raise the question, 'What is the point of getting people at school to discuss such topics as whether or not the legislation about pornography should be changed?' Part of the point, as has been suggested already, is to teach them to judge fairly on the evidence, and to understand the arguments both for and against the proposition. But part of the point is also thought to be actually to get them to think about right and wrong, good and evil, to think, that is to say, about morals. If this is accepted as part of their education, then they must not be deprived of the spectacle of a teacher who holds and clearly expresses moral views. There is nothing but benefit in the contemplation of a man of principle. A man without moral views is after all a monster, and it is hard for pupils, especially if they are quite young to realize that the neutral teacher is only play-acting. Moreover, if they do realize this, they resent it. Practically speaking, one of the things one learns from teaching children is that play-acting is despicable. The first rule of teaching is sincerity, even if one's sincerity is dotty or eccentric. A man ought to have, and to express, moral beliefs, and this entails that as a teacher he cannot remain neutral. For, holding a moral belief is in some respects like having a vision. It is in a sense an imaginative vision of how things ought to be, though they are not. Expressing a moral belief is thus attempting to share a vision or way of looking, and this cannot be done without in some sense attempting to get your interlocutor to see things as you do, if only for a time. A pupil may discover, in the course of discussion what he himself thinks, what moral views he holds. But he cannot do this without exercising his imagination, to see in the material under discussion a moral issue. He must see it as a starting off point from which he may envisage a world in which such things do not happen, or do happen freely. The teacher must help him to exercise his imagination; it is indeed his only serious function, and thus he must help him to see the material as morally significant. This he can do only by demonstrating that it appears so to him. If a teacher, by the attractiveness of his personality, causes his pupils for the most part to share his vision, aesthetic or moral or of whatever other sort, the passage of time will remedy this, if remedy is needed. To have been conscious at some stage of one's life how someone else, a grown-up, actually saw the world is far from harmful, even if later the viewpoint is totally abandoned. I conclude therefore that in the sphere of the evaluative, as of the factual, the teacher has a positive obligation, if he is to teach well, to be non-neutral; and that this is necessary because of the nature of moral and other evaluative judgements.

It will be noted that in the foregoing argument I have seemed to assume that the teacher is older than the pupil, more knowledgeable and more rational, and also possessed of more experience, common sense and imagination. I make this assumption knowingly. I realize that there are teachers who are in all these respects (except generally that of age) the inferior of their pupils. Nevertheless, the teacher's essential role is to be in all these respects his pupil's superior, and this is the role he must try to fill, necessarily. It is the role which creates the teaching situation, with all its intrinsic authority, and it is this role, not any particular occupier of it which has been the subject of discussion. In such a role, I have maintained, the teacher will fail if he attempts to remain neutral.

Teaching and Neutrality

John Wilson

I don't want to dispute Mary Warnock's admirable essay in detail, since I agree with almost all of it. My feeling is roughly 'Well, if *that's* what "those who advocate neutrality" are advocating, then they're mistaken' for very much the kind of reasons that she gives. But it may be that something can be advocated under the title of 'neutrality' which is not so silly; which may indeed be extremely obvious, and yet worth remembering; and which needs to be carefully distinguished from some current educational theories or fantasies.

I'm encouraged here by the fact that Mary Warnock seems to take it for granted that we know what 'neutrality' *is*. If 'being neutral' is opposed to such notions as 'teaching skills', 'stating facts', 'holding and declaring moral opinions' and 'drawing conclusions from arguments', then of course no teacher could 'be neutral' and still teach: there would be nothing for him to do. And indeed much modern educational practice, like the 'neutral chairmanship' idea, suggests a concept of neutrality which has to do with being *inactive* in certain obviously unsatisfactory ways; thus if we are concerned, not just with giving pupils a shop window tour of various moral or religious opinions, but with pursuing the question of which of them may be *correct* or *mistaken* (and how we are to determine this), then we need more than a chairman. We need a teacher — and, perhaps (I shall discuss this later), what Mary Warnock calls a 'leader in argument' who does not 'sit on the fence'. Without this, the message that the pupils are likely to receive is that there is *no such thing as* being 'correct' or 'mistaken' ('right', 'wrong', etc.) in these areas; a message at least as disastrous as most forms of 'indoctrination' or 'authoritarian styles of teaching' (whatever this may mean).

But in fact 'neutral' is not normally used like this. Its opposite is not 'active' but something like 'partisan'. What it means to be neutral is strictly relative to particular contexts: one may be neutral as between X and Y, but at the same time passionately concerned about Z and extremely active in promoting it. Switzerland may be neutral as between particular combatants in a war, yet active in trying to reduce suffering and patch up a peace. Judges and arbitrators are concerned with their jobs, whilst at the same time being 'neutral' (or 'impartial') as regards contending barristers or disputants. Indeed it is part of their job that they should be neutral in this way, that they should not be partisan.

Whilst of course teachers are not judges (nor chairmen), it is utterly clear how this notion applies to many kinds of teaching. If I am marking a history essay, I am likely to mark it on whether the pupil has a good grasp of the facts and has used the evidence intelligently; not on whether I agree with his particular conclusions — nor even on whether the conclusions are right (in such cases as it makes sense to say this). In assessing work in science, or even in mathematics (where 'right answers' are plainly possible), I may judge more by the 'working' than the answer. I am, in a clear if boring sense, neutral or indifferent to the answers, but I am not neutral as regards the grasp of fact, the deployment of the evidence, and so on. Even more obviously, if what I am trying to assess is someone's debating skill, I am neutral as regards whether he is making out a case for the Labour Party or the Conservative Party, except of course insofar as that affects the merits of his speech and argument as a whole (a brilliant speech showing all the faults of the Labour Party would not hang together with a conclusion that one ought to vote Labour).

If one were to go on to quote particular cases of this kind, I doubt whether we should meet with much disagreement; and indeed this may account for the fact that we should hardly want to use the term 'neutral' at all — we should more naturally talk in terms of 'impartiality', or 'bias', or perhaps 'relevance' (a person's particular political leanings just aren't *relevant* to his debating skill). So it's even more baffling to be confronted with demands that 'the teacher' should or should not be 'neutral' *in general*. What could this *mean*? How could one reply if one was asked 'Do you think doctors (parents, engineers, bus conductors, unmarried mothers) should be neutral?'It would mean nothing unless related to a particular context of being neutral as between X and Y.

I mention these tedious and obvious points because there seems to me a serious danger of playing into the hands of those who live off educational fashion and fantasy, if we take sides in such matters. 'Should teaching be "child-centred"', 'Should the curriculum be "relevant"?', 'Should we "integrate" or **"segregate"**?', 'Should "motivation" be "intrinsic" or can it sometimes be **"extrinsic"**?' — none of these are questions to which any serious person could conceivably give answers. And when we get down to particular cases, either the questions have obvious answers ('Can you advocate a case and still be neutral about whether it's true?' — of course you can't), or else we need to know more facts ('Do more children learn more mathematics if you use such-and-such methods?' — we don't know).

So what does one do here? Well, one can try to identify certain general fears or fantasies (Mary Warnock kindly calls them 'grounds . . . for advocacy') which may underlie a prevailing fashion or 'movement' in education, bring these out into the open, and try to show why they are unreasonable. The difficulty here is that they are hard to identify and the 'grounds' may always be switched. Alternatively one can refuse to play in these broad terms at all, but insist philosophically upon clear meanings (for terms like 'neutrality', 'child-centred', etc.) before even starting to discuss but then most educationalists are too impatient to play *that* game. A third possibility, which I shall adopt here (though without much optimism), is to discuss things in terms of a reasonably clear notion of what it is to *educate* people, which needs hanging on to at all costs.[1]

In teaching children to do history, or science, or mathematics well, there are two things I am *not* doing. I am not saying to them (1) 'You must arrive at the right answers, which are as follows . . . ' with the implication that it doesn't matter how they get there. Nor am I saying (2) 'It doesn't matter what answers you arrive at'; that would make nonsense of any subject, for it implies that conclusions don't follow from evidence. What I am saying is something more like 'Examine this question in the light of the evidence, which will of course suggest conclusions to you'. These conclusions are not 'mine' or 'theirs'; their worth is no more nor less than the evidence behind them. I am trying to cut personalities out of it: to introduce them into forms of knowledge and understanding which are (necessarily) impersonal.

It is here, I think, that fears of 'indoctrination' come in. Amid the wealth of literature on indoctrination is the point (originally made by Flew) that the word is not happy where there is no question of a *doctrine* being implanted. It is certainly odd to talk of 'indoctrination' in respect of such things as, for instance, the multiplication tables, or the dates of English kings, irrespective of whether these are or are not true (or 'facts'). I think this oddity arises from the fact that in some areas of knowledge there are methodologies which can fairly be said to be accepted by all rational and informed people — most obviously, in mathematics, science and perhaps history. In these cases we only talk of 'doctrines' (if we talk of them at all) in reference to very disputable, high-level opinions: perhaps those of Toynbee or certain cosmologists may be fair examples. It is in cases where the methodology is not clear, or not accepted, that we get worried: most obviously in the areas of morality and religion.

In these areas, what should worry the educator is not so much that people or societies have lost faith in their ordinary ground-level moral and religious opinions; for some at least of these may never have been derived from rational consideration of the evidence in the first place, and in any case the educator is not just concerned to pass these opinions on to pupils — he wants the pupils to see how any opinions follow from evidence. What should worry him is that there is no higher-level methodology to serve as a background against which conclusions can be drawn; or, at least, none which commands assent and which can itself be seen as rational. It is at just this point that he may retreat into inactivity, in effect throwing in the sponge: as if he were saying 'We don't have any idea how to get "right answers", or how to make progress, in these areas, so we'll just "stimulate" you and encourage you to discuss and give you various "experiences" so that you can make up your own minds' — and this itself is now a pointless task, since there is no purpose in discussion and 'experiences' unless the pupils can thereby *get better at* whatever 'morals' and 'religion' may be about.

In fact we do, surely, have *some* idea of what counts as 'getting better at' these areas of human thought and life; and hence something like a methodology or at least a set of attributes which are relevant to these areas and which we want pupils to possess, so that this view is unnecessarily bankrupt.[2] My point is, however, that without something like this it would be equally absurd either to sit back as a 'neutral chairman', or to advocate particular moral and religious opinions. For, without it, we have no criteria of rationality to attend to, and hence no aims of education in respect to these two areas. Both being 'neutral' and being 'committed' would be a waste of time. (This is why, in my view, there might be very little to choose between those who take children on shop-window tours of various religions and those who try to inculcate one particular creed: neither seem interested in establishing criteria and methods whereby pupils can determine the truth or reasonableness of religious opinions. Without such interest we cannot do much that can seriously be described as 'education in religion'.)

Mary Warnock, however, plainly believes (as I do) that there is such a thing as 'getting better at' morality, or 'making progress' in this area of thought, as surely do most sane people. It is a pity that she does not say anything about what this consists of, because the issue of 'neutrality' might then be clearer. But let us suppose (*pace* the vast volume of philosophical literature on the topic) that we do, at some stage, get some kind of clear agreement on some points about how to make up one's mind on moral issues; we might say, though not forgetting all the practical implications (or the 'affective' side) of morality, about how to 'do the subject' — in the same sort of way that we are now fairly clear about how to do mathematics, or science, or history. Suppose, for instance, that we were clear that moral reasons must relate in some way to human needs and interests — that 'reasons' like 'Because I feel like it', or 'Because Hitler says so', or 'Because all my friends do', were not good reasons or perhaps not reasons at all. Suppose we have some such outline elements of a methodology. What now will distinguish the 'neutral' from the 'partisan' teacher?

Obviously, as Mary Warnock says, the teacher cannot be 'neutral' if this means that he must not select evidence, must not at times take certain things as 'given', must not draw conclusions, must not present his own views (if only for discussion), and so on. If he did not do these things, he could not teach the methodology at all. But then — given something like an established methodology — only a lunatic would use 'neutral' in this way. The good teacher would have the methodology, the 'subject' together with its requirements of reason, as his main aim; he could not be 'neutral' about *that*. But the question arises, could he be neutral about particular moral views and opinions, or is he entitled to be 'partisan'?

I maintain that the case here is very much on all fours with other forms of thought. Roughly, if we are talking about *aims*, then these are given by the methodology. We want to produce competent moralists, not moralists who think as we do (whether or not these overlap); just as we want to produce competent historians, scientists, and so on. If we are talking about *methods* or techniques — and I think this is what Mary Warnock is talking about for most of the time towards the last part of her essay — then the question seems to me largely an empirical one, to be determined by experiment. Largely, but not entirely, for there are some things which the aims logically require. They logically require, as she says, that pupils have the experience of someone drawing conclusions from evidence; of expressing moral opinions with sincerity and force; of holding and defending a distinct and deeply-felt point of view. But whether the *teacher* must do this, or how much time he should spend doing it (one might argue that pupils get enough experiences of this kind anyway) seems an open question. Perhaps the good teacher would bring in 'committed' moralists and believers, and himself subsequently act in the capacity of one who helps the children to work out how much sense and nonsense there is in what such people say. After all, to *teach* morals — again, remembering that we have something like a methodology — isn't primarily to *display* moral opinions, but rather to see how they measure up to the methodology.

Perhaps the importance of the existence of a methodology may be made a bit clearer if we take an analogous form of education: the appreciation of literature or music. Here too we might say with Mary Warnock that the teacher can and indeed should get his pupils to 'share a vision': he is aware and enamoured of the world of Shakespeare or Beethoven or whatever, and how *could* he elicit appreciation and enthusiasm from the pupils without this? Yet (we also want to say) his *aim* mustn't be that the pupils end up feeling just the same way about Shakespeare and Beethoven as he does — with his likes and dislikes of particular writers and composers. The apparent *impasse* is resolved when we remember that what he is trying to do can be put more generally: he is trying to get the pupils to do such things as read a play intelligently and sensitively, to pay due attention to certain features of musical form, to avoid imposing their own prejudices or egocentricities on poetry and music, and so on. Now these general aims might not merit the title of 'methodology' (though we would include a lot of 'tips', suggestions, etc. — 'play the record several times over', 'you need to see the play on stage', and so on): but it is because they exist that we can acquit the good teacher of 'indoctrination' (or whatever word is appropriate).

If we now ask 'How far should the teacher bring his own aesthetic preferences to the fore?' — and this is now a question about *methods* — what can we reply? Obviously real enthusiasm, 'striking sparks', etc. may count a lot, but also a fairly hard-headed refusal to lyricize and a stern insistence that the pupils do a lot of the work for themselves may also be useful. (He may even want them to spend some time looking at *bad* works of art, so that they can come to see why they are bad.) It seems clear that there is a pretty stringent limit on how far we can generalize here, since very much will depend on the kind of pupils and the kind of conditions which the teacher faces.

In this light, some of Mary Warnock's generalizations strike me as a bit wholesale. One particular example is important, not only as an instance of this: when she talks of 'the spectacle of someone remaining neutral in a highly-charged situation' and hence seeming 'either alarmingly remote, or positively scornful or patronizing'. Interestingly enough, this is just the impression normally created by philosophers in many contexts, from Socrates onwards. In a sense, they 'join in the dispute', but in another sense they are often neutral: that is, as one might roughly put it, they do not take sides (perhaps they think that both sides are confused), but are anxious to promote truth and rationality in a more general way. Now we don't want to say that one should *never* do this (even if people sometimes get annoyed); any more than we want to say that parents should *never* let the child 'simply go on screaming', or that it is *never* right for psychotherapists to be 'non-directive'. But the question arises of how far, or when, or under what conditions, it is desirable.

I take this to be a particularly important question for 'neutrality', because it connects once more with the existence or non-existence of a methodology which is accepted: itself, I believe, connected with the immense power of passion and fantasy in the areas of morality and religion. It is partly if not primarily because we cling to fantasies that we do not accept rational methodologies, and the result is that what are described as moral *beliefs* or *judgements* would not, on closer inspection, be seen to deserve such titles. Very often they are hopes, fears, desires, guilt-feelings and so on loosely bound together in a fantasy-picture, and masquerading as evidence-derived assertions or claims to knowledge and truth.

In this situation (it applies even more obviously to religions and other highly generalized outlooks and emotional investments) what teachers can do or ought to do at once runs up against general problems which apply to educational contexts (as they may fairly be called) outside the classroom as well as inside: to psychotherapy or social work, for instance. How 'directive' or 'non-directive' one should be, when one should intervene and when one should not; how much 'seriousness' or 'maturity' one can expect from different people; all these are questions which need much more investigation – and even then, there may be very few generalized answers we can give.

What we can do helpfully, perhaps, is at least to distinguish clearly between the different sorts of things we are trying to do with pupils. Thus we can distinguish between giving them 'moral support' (being on their side, loving them); giving them enthusiasm and imagination in morality; giving them a grasp of the appropriate methodology, and so on. The disastrous thing is to think that some *one* aim, or some *one* general method or 'approach', is 'the answer'. On any account, 'being educated in morality' will involve a large number of very *different* attributes (skills, types of knowledge, aptitudes, etc.). The danger with views to the effect that the teacher should (or should not) be 'neutral' is that no across-the-board views in such terms have much hope of being sensible.

But equally we cannot dismiss particular methods as *always* inappropriate. Suppose we knew (I don't think we do, but suppose) that children at a certain 'stage of development' regard morality only as a set of commands flowing from adults in general (including teachers); and suppose that, if we are to have any hope of getting them to make further progress, we have to present them with at least one adult who refuses to issue any commands. That is, suppose it could be shown that this was, in point of empirical fact, the only way – at that particular point in time – of handling the situation. Then the 'neutral chairman' idea seems plausible. One could run a similar supposition about the equal importance of firm order-and-obedience contexts for children at certain points, and for certain purposes. In fact the likelihood is that children need something like a *mixture* of these (and other contexts); so that our first task is to get clear about the differences between these contexts and their effects, as related to a detailed list of the aims of moral education. What I am saying here is simply that we *know* very little about all this, and that generalizations (or, worse, fashions in educational practice) are not much good.

Here again the question of a methodology is crucial for teachers: for whatever else teachers may be called upon to do (e.g., act as psychotherapists, strong father-figures, 'neutral chairmen', drill sergeants, etc.) they must be centrally concerned with *teaching*. How much time, in some schools today, teachers *can* in fact spend on teaching (as against, for instance, 'crowd control' or 'custodial care') is another matter. But if their title of 'teachers' means anything, or insofar as it means anything, they will have to make acceptable educational sense of the notion of 'teaching morals', 'teaching religion', and so on. In trying to determine what contexts, what types of 'neutrality' or 'non-neutrality' suit what children, we could at least begin by judging these in the light of those particular goods that can reasonably come under the notions of 'learning' or 'education'. Quite a few goods — for instance, keeping children happy, producing greater social mobility, generating self-confidence and many others — do not fall under these notions: they represent 'social' or 'mental health' aims rather than strictly educational aims. But if we are (at least for part of the time) interested in the latter, then we want to know what contexts, what attitudes on the part of the teacher, etc. help pupils to *learn* more about **morality**, or religion, or whatever form of thought we are dealing with; and the methodology — that is, a detailed breakdown of *what it is* to be a competent moralist — must be our sole guide to the merits or demerits of particular contexts.

Besides the need for empirical research, then, questions about 'neutrality' require also a proper classification of logically different types of 'aims' or 'goods'. For instance, the 'neutral chairmanship' idea *might* (but we don't know) be a total failure on the educational front — that is, the children might not *learn* anything much about **morality** but it might be a very good context for generating self-confidence, or making pupils less frightened of authority, or something of the kind. How — even when the facts are known — we are to weigh or balance 'educational' goods against other kinds of goods seem to me an extremely difficult question, though crucially important for most substantive questions in educational practice. There are also difficulties, or at least the need for sensible decisions, in making the initial classification: Are we going to count processes which 'inspire', 'strengthen', 'strike sparks', etc. as 'educational', or only processes which in themselves develop understanding? (Mary Warnock's 'sharing a vision' would need a closer look in this light.)

Yet another point at which the methodological background crops up is when we consider the importance of initiating pupils into a particular *tradition*. In the case of subjects about which we are reasonably clear, we have a public, interpersonal tradition of thought within which all but the most lunatic educationalists are happy to bring up our pupils. We initiate them into standard ways of doing mathematics (even if we sometimes take time off to show them how one might work to other bases than base ten); we show them how to conduct a scientific experiment, rather than encouraging them to waste time in trying to transmute things to gold or consult the stars, and so on. Even in the thorny area of aesthetics there is substantial and rational agreement on a broad front about what works of art are, on the whole, worth looking at, and how one goes about trying to appreciate them. Notions of 'neutrality' here, if they arose at all, would in practice be settled fairly quickly by common sense, in reference to the established traditions.

But if we now say, as surely we must, that pupils will have little hope of being properly educated in morality or religion unless they are initiated into some kind of moral or religious tradition — some form of life in which morals and religion are taken seriously and practised seriously — we have a right to be more worried. Again, it is not so much that people differ in their ground-level moral or religious views; that could be catered for, if we had a tradition of discussing and settling such differences against a common background. It might, for instance, make little difference if one pupil were brought up in a Catholic household and another in a Communist one, provided both households also had a tradition of mutual discussion and truth-seeking based on some kind of common methodological ground. The difficulty is rather that, in many cases, even this seems to be lacking. What would a satisfactory moral or religious 'tradition', or form of life, or 'home background' *look like*? How would one distinguish such a thing from something we might prefer to describe as a kind of institutionalized fantasy or mass psychosis (as with the Nazis or perhaps Babylonian astrology)? This is where the temptation arises to do nothing at all for fear of doing the wrong thing.

Even without a methodology, we have some idea of what it is to be *serious* about these disputed areas. 'Serious' here does not mean 'earnest', but something more like 'rationally enthusiastic' or 'fantasy-free'. I agree with Mary Warnock chiefly because she seems to share this view. The kind of moves or interventions on the part of the teacher which she defends against the 'neutral chairman' notion may or may not be effective (and, where ineffective or even harmful, might be criticized by saying that it would be better, in this or that case, if the teacher were 'neutral' as regards something or other); but at least the idea behind them is to encourage seriousness in the pupils. It would be nicer if the content of this 'seriousness' were spelled out more fully; but at least it is clearly contrasted with notions according to which opinions are 'a matter of taste', a 'toss-up', 'just a question of how you've been brought up to think', 'all relative', and so on. This is a contrast which, in the present educational climate, needs a great deal of emphasis.

Notes

1 Of course this notion is disputable, and not much is gained by pressing the *words* 'educate', 'educated', etc. But Professors Peters and Hirst have at least outlined *a* tolerably clear concept fairly marked by 'education' which is important in itself, and delimits *one* class of 'goods' or set of 'aims' which needs to be constantly borne in mind. See e.g., their corporate work *The Logic of Education*, (1970), London: Routledge & Kegan Paul. Ch. 2; also my *Philosophy and Educational Research*, (1972), Slough: NFER, Ch. 1.

2 Indeed I think we can go a great deal further than that. See my *Education in Religion and the Emotions*, (1971), London: Heinemann. Chs. 6 and 10, and *The Assessment of Morality*, (1973) Slough: NFER.

Neutrality as a Criterion in Teaching: The Work of the Humanities Curriculum Project

Lawrence Stenhouse

Although the notion of a neutral chairman is common enough in the context of committees and arbitration panels, it entered educational discourse in this country through the Humanities Curriculum Project (1967 — 1972). That Project, of which the present writer was Director, was a major research effort with a budget of a quarter of a million pounds over five years and its work is rather well documented (Aston 1971: Bagley and Verma, 1972: Dhand and Wilson, 1971; Elliott, 1969; 1970; 1971; 1972; 1973a; 1973; 1975a. 1975b; Elliott and Humble 1972; Fordham, 1974; Hamingson, 1973; Humanities Curriculum Project, 1970; MacDonald, 1971; MacDonald and Ruddock, 1971; Parkinson and MacDonald, 1972; Rudduck, 1973; Simons, 1971; Stenhouse 1968; 1969; 1970a, 1970b; 1971; 1972; 1973; Verma and Bagley, 1973; Verma and MacDonald, 1973).

It is apparent both from lack of citation and from the content of their papers that both Mary Warnock and John Wilson have overlooked the existence of this Project, which is the major research in the field. Indeed, John Wilson actually calls for empirical research while failing to notice that it is there. This lack of scholarship in the two papers on which I am asked to comment gives me little base on which to work, and I propose therefore to make a minimum reference to them.

The Humanities Project was funded in anticipation of the raising of the school leaving age. It was asked to provide for teachers who were for the first time facing a full age group in the fifth year of secondary schooling *stimulus, support and materials*. Another phrase used by the Schools Council in setting it up was that it should *extend the range of choice open to teachers*. Our commission suggested to us that we should attempt to follow a line of inquiry and development which might make accessible to teachers some teaching strategy which would extend their professional resources. It is worth mentioning that although it is clearly the task of such a project to set out its premises and the lines of argument it has followed and to report its results, it is not appropriate that it should advocate a particular course of action. Our claim has always been *You may find this useful*, never *You ought to do this*.

At the time the Project was set up there was much talk of relevance in the classroom, and the concept of relevance was being criticized on the grounds that the criterion of worthwhileness should be over-riding. We asked whether any topics might claim to be both relevant and worthwhile and arrived at the idea of *human issues of universal concern*. Such issues might lie in such topic areas as War and Society; Education; the Family; Relations between the Sexes; People and Work; Poverty; Law and Order; and Living in Cities. These were in fact the topics we developed. Others could be added.

It appeared that such topics were in a particular sense controversial. We adopted a definition proposed by Dorothy Fraser (1963):

A controversial issue involves a problem about which different individuals and groups urge conflicting courses of action. It is an issue for which society has not found a solution that can be universally or almost universally accepted. It is an issue of sufficient significance that each of the proposed ways of dealing with it is objectionable to some section of the citizenry and arouses protest . . . When a course of action is formulated that virtually all sectors of society accept, the issue is no longer controversial.

It is important that this is an empirical, not an epistemological, definition of controversiality. We took the view that some teachers would regard themselves as answerable to the citizenry to the extent that they would wish to be able to claim that they had done what they could within the skills available to them to avoid the accusation that they had used their position of authority in the classroom to promote their own beliefs.

We carefully avoided the use of the word indoctrination. If such a term be used to describe a teaching strategy, its referent must be clear, and it is not. There is no necessary implication in the Project that teachers can in fact promote their own beliefs. It is enough that there should be uneasiness in the face of the possibility that they may be able to do so. Given that, some would wish to be able to claim that they had been at pains to avoid the possibility.

Five major premises of the Project were stated. There was no assertion that the premises were *correct*. The intention was to state a position clearly enough for teachers to know whether they were interested in exploring its implications.

The premises were:

1. that controversial issues should be handled in the classroom with adolescents;
2. that the teacher accepts the need to submit his teaching in controversial areas to the criterion of neutrality at this stage of education; i.e. that he regards it as part of his responsibility not to promote his own view;
3. that the mode of inquiry in controversial areas should have discussion, rather than instruction, as its core;
4. that the discussion should protect divergence of view among participants, rather than attempt to achieve consensus;
5. that the teacher as chairman of the discussion should have responsibility for quality and standards in learning.

(Humanities Curriculum Project, 1970, p..1.)

I shall comment on the last three of these before turning to point 2. In adopting discussion as the key mode of teaching in this area the Project was of course associating itself with a long tradition stemming from ancient Greek philosophy. It was also offering to investigate a teaching method not generally covered in teacher training and quite inadequately researched. This looked a promising line.

Most groups engaged in discussion naturally adopt the style of striving for consensus which is typical of decision-making, rather than of educational, groups. The protection of divergence might be justified on the basis of the teacher's concern to avoid the accusation of promoting his own views or on the basis of a concern to avoid peer-group pressures or because the full exploration of divergent views is important in understanding controversiality. In any case, little research had been done on discussion work which did not aim at consensus.

In suggesting that the teacher should be responsible for standards and quality we were making it clear that we assumed the teacher would wish to develop a style such that he could accept a degree of accountability for the standards attained. Chairing a discussion was not simply a cop-out.

In the matter of neutrality the important point to stress is that it is a criterion by which to criticize the teacher's performance. Of course, no teacher can be neutral. There are no perfect performances. No teaching of philosophy is perfectly philosophical. When one talks of a *neutral chairman*, one means a chairman working to certain criteria.

In practice, it proved important that the teacher spell out to the students the criteria to which he was working, and why. Students are then able to criticize the teacher's performance. 'He's a communist, but he's a good chairman.' 'You had difficulty hanging on to your neutrality this morning.' This readiness of the teacher to work to *public* criteria seems to have been important.

It is also necessary to add that neutral chairmanship only makes sense if the teacher *qua* person is not neutral. It is a role based upon the acceptance of a discipline and not an attribute of the person filling the role. To take an extreme case, Catholic priests have acted as neutral chairmen.

At the beginning of the Project no teacher knew what neutral chairmanship implied in practice, nor did members of the Project team. A two-year experiment was mounted in schools. Teachers developed a role in response to the position I have just set out in this paper. They tape-recorded their work. The Project team studied the tapes in order to define the role empirically.

Certainly a characteristic role emerged; but we have no way of knowing whether an alternative role could have developed in response to the same criteria nor do we know whether an observer studying the performance of a teacher skilled in that role would be likely to use the word *neutral* if he had not encountered it through Project theory. The main aspects of the role as it emerged are spelled out in the Project's introductory handbook *(Humanities Curriculum Project, 1970)*.

Initially it was suggested to the teachers that in their work they attempt to promote an *understanding* of controversial issues. This was intended to imply that they would take on to their agenda the question: 'What constitutes an understanding of such issues?' just as a history teacher might be concerned as to what constitutes an understanding of history. It is assumed that the teacher's answer to such a question will be under continuous development.

Later on when we came to write the handbook we proposed as a teaching aim *to develop an understanding of human acts and social situations and of the controversial value issues which they raise.* This was a bad formulation in two respects. It might appear to imply that *value* issues are *necessarily* controversial, a position not intended. It might also imply that controversy in discussion is always about values. Not so. The fact was that we had outgrown the political justification implied in Dorothy Fraser's definition, but had failed to register this. In discussion an issue is controversial if it divides the group: It need not arouse the citizenry as value issues tend to do. There is much controversy in the interpretation of evidence.

And indeed the interpretation of evidence lay at the heart of Project work. For the topics were pursued through the discussion of evidence bearing on issues under discussion. The problem of the nature of such evidence is as interesting as that of neutrality, but is not to our purpose here.

It is worth trying to capture here the flavour of an HCP discussion (when things are going well). A group are discussing the Hitler bomb plot. Among the issues explored are the possible range of attitudes Hitler might have had to himself. Then the discussion moves to a consideration of the motives of the plotters. Someone suggests that they were motiviated by the feeling that Hitler was ruining Germany. Another suggests that they would be likely to have mixed motives. The rewards of success would be so great that it would be difficult to exclude entirely the motive of ambition which Hitler attributed to them. The picture that emerges is not too unlike Shakespeare's interpretation of the conspiracy against Caesar.

I give this example to make it clear that discussion is not necessarily or often at the level of abstract principles. It is frequently about the interpretation of human situations: How does it feel to work to a pace determined by a moving production line? Or it is about problems of action: What could be done to help the down and outs in a Salvation Army home? When higher order principles are at stake they often emerge from the consideration of cases. For example, faced with the proposal that children should be rescued from chaotic slum homes and brought up by the state or foster parents, a boy says 'But who do children belong to − the state or their parents? − that's a moral issue.'

It is, of course, not possible here to do justice to all the issues and insights produced by five years of research by a team of twelve. But three further points are worth making before I turn to consider the effects of neutral chairmanship.

First, the Project attempted to find a line of research which did not treat school leavers as special sort of people − Newsom children. The circumstances of our schools are such that HCP work is often confined to leavers' classes. However, a considerable number of schools now work with HCP across the entire ability range. It is also used in sixth forms and has been used in adult education (Fordham, 1974). Both methods and materials have been used in prisons and approved schools. And one member of the team has found much of relevance in her later work on small-group teaching in universities. It could be claimed therefore that we found a productive line for research.

Second, one of the reasons why the line has been so productive is that the neutrality criterion throws into relief crucial problems of authority in teaching. The role of neutral chairman placed in the context of the teacher's other roles provides a laboratory situation in which he may explore the nature of his authority both in relation to students and in relation to knowledge.

Third, it is worth mentioning that on average schools spend four to six hours a week on humanities discussions. It is true to say that many teachers claim that the experience has affected and developed their teaching in other areas. Nevertheless, it is important to stress that HCP has not been proposed as a total curriculum. It was hoped that it would provide for the school leaver an experience equivalent to that offered to sixth formers by the best sort of sixth-form general studies.

In turning to consider the effects of the attempt to implement neutral chairmanship and students' reactions to it, I rely heavily on the work of the evaluation unit attached to the Project which was directed by Barry MacDonald. Quotations are from Hamingson (1973). The evaluation design is explained in MacDonald (1971). It combined case study with a large measurement programme, the final results of which are still being processed.

First to the experience of teachers.

Teachers find the role of neutral chairman difficult to learn and extraordinarily demanding.

'One teacher, who was thinking of joining the HCP team in his school, made the following remark after a spell of classroom observations:

'It seemed to be stretching the staff in all sorts of ways. Had they gone into a class to teach their ordinary subject and been so put about one would say they were incompetent or they've only done three months on the job. But in fact . . . he is an experienced teacher as well as a competent teacher, as are the others. None of these people have the signs of being green or incompetent yet this was suddenly standing them on their ears. They had problems which I couldn't understand.'

(Hamingson, 1973, p.91)

This observation tends to be confirmed by the measurement programme. A series of statistically significant shifts were recorded on a number of variables. These shifts did not occur in the control groups. They occurred in HCP schools where teachers had had access to training. *They did not occur in HCP schools where teachers did not have access to training*. These went the way of the control groups. This suggests a difficult task of unlearning and relearning in which training support is required.

The Project divides teachers. Some find it congenial, others uncongenial. We have no evidence on the variables which contribute to this reaction.

The Project has led to teachers taking up a critical attitude towards their own teaching and often to examining their own teaching with colleagues by means of audio tape or video tape.

Neutrality is the crucial problem for teachers. Perhaps because the teaching is so difficult, it sometimes tends to become the *guiding light* or the *dragon* responsible for all the problems. There is some problem in the development of a cult of neutral chairmanship from time to time.

There is some evidence from teacher interviews of transfer of skills from HCP to other areas of teaching.

There is much more that could be said, but it would need to be said at length. I conclude here that neutral chairmanship is controversial, and that it is difficult to learn, but that a reasonably large number of teachers find it a rewarding skill. It can lead to self-study and group study and to the development of research attitudes to one's teaching; and it can become a cult. The reaction of students is also mixed. No doubt it is often determined by the performance of the teacher, but this is of course a given. Students commonly attempt to force the teacher back into his familiar role. Once this stage is passed through, some students regard the style of work very highly, others are sceptical or even disaffected. There is no evidence of serious insecurity of the kind feared by Mary Warnock, but this does not prove that it never occurs.

Hamingson (1973) supplies transcript evidence from student interviews in order to illustrate a range of response. One student says: 'Giving you responsibility, this is a shock. Speaking your own words in class and speaking to each other and not to the teacher, this is a shock.' Most of the reactions can be construed as responses to that shock or to the half-recognized incompetence of a teacher struggling with only partial success to meet new criteria through a new role.

In the measurement results, the most striking (confirmed in further processing) are increased in reading ability as measured by the Manchester Reading Test, vocabulary as measured by the Mill Hill Vocabulary Test and increases in pupil self-esteem as measured by the Coopersmith Questionnaire and by a Sentence Completion Test constructed by G.K. Verma of the Project Evaluation Unit. These results seem to me to indicate that the role of *neutral chairmanship* is favourable to verbal achievement as conventionally judged when used with 14- to 16-year-old school leavers, and that these effects may well be related to the tendency of neutral chairmanship to increase self-esteem.

There is also some evidence of a shift upward in intelligence scores and in academic motivation. The latter finding is confirmed in interview material. Other shifts recorded more fitfully were from obedient towards assertive, from expedient towards conscientious, from shy towards adventurous, **from group dependent towards self-sufficient,** from conservative to liberal attitude, from low self-reliance to high self-reliance, from poor awareness of social issues to strong awareness of social issues, from rejecting view of adults towards accepting view of adults, and from low evaluation of traditional moral virtues to high evaluation of traditional moral virtues. The last of these could lend credence to the charge that the Project tends to endorse the *status quo*, but the tests need to be examined in detail and in context before conclusions are drawn.

In fact, of course, the generalizations of the testing programme mask the variability of unique classroom situations. They cannot be taken as predictive of the effects of attempting to implement the neutral chairman role. Rather they must be regarded as indicating the potential without predicting that the potential will be reached in any given case.

Naturally, having been involved in the Project, I have scrutinized the results carefully and tried to interpret them. My own conclusion is — put crudely — that we are on to something of considerable significance and importance for both attitudes and attainment. It is quite clear from the lack of shifts in the control groups that conventional teaching is not working with the population under study.

What seems to me difficult to judge is whether the role of neutral chairman is capable of development in other directions.

It is this problem that Mary Warnock throws up when she associates it with the role of the teacher in discovery and inquiry teaching in *academic* subjects. She obscures the issue by discussing areas like skills and languages where discovery and inquiry teaching is clearly irrelevant. What is at stake is the teacher's stance in relation to his students in the face of public knowledge having logical structure which is not merely conventional. It would seem that the stance of neutrality has something to offer here; and a detailed study of discovery and inquiry teaching which draws on the experience gained in the Humanities Project is in progress at present. (Elliott and Adelman 1973a, 1973b, 1973c; Cooper and Ebbutt 1974).

In general, I do not think that it is worthwhile to tackle in detail the points made by Mary Warnock or John Wilson. Had we been able to start on the common base of discussing the research findings it would have been a different matter. I am bound to say that I find nothing new in either paper. There are no points — even the absurd ones — which have not been considered by the Humanities Project team.

What does seem clear is that both protagonists are prepared to settle the question of the potential of a teaching stance disciplined by the criterion of neutrality without allowing their minds to be clouded by looking at the available evidence. I have not done justice to that evidence — space has not allowed it — but I have at least supplied the references through which the reader can follow it up.

References

ASTON, A.E. (1971) *The Humanities Curriculum Project*. London: Inner London Education Authority. NEDAL Occasional Paper No. 6, October.

BAGLEY, C. and VERMA, G.K. (1972) 'Some effects of teaching designed to promote understanding of racial issues in adolescents', *J. of Moral Educ.* **1**, 3, 231–8.

COOPER, D. and EBBUTT, D. (1974) 'Participation in action-research as an in-service experience', *Cambridge J. of Educ.*, **4**, 2, 65–71.

DHAND, H. and WILSON, B. (1971) 'Handling of controversial issues in the classroom', *Nova Scotia Soc. Studs. Rev.*, May.

ELLIOTT, J. (1969) 'The role of the humanities in vocational education', *Studs. in Educ. and Craft*, **2**, 1.

ELLIOTT, J. (1970) 'Learning through discussion', *Times Educ. Supp.*, 13th November.

ELLIOTT, J. (1971) 'The concept of the neutral teacher', *Cambridge J. of Educ.*, **2**, 60–7.

ELLIOTT, J. (1973(a)) 'Neutrality, rationality and the role of the teacher', *Proceedings of the Philosophy of Educ. Soc. of Great Britain*. **7**, 36–65.

ELLIOTT, J. (1973(b)) 'The Humanities Project on "People and Work" and the concept of "Vocational Guidance"', *The Careers Teacher*, Spring. 21–31.

ELLIOTT, J. (1975a) 'The values of the neutral teacher.' In: BRIDGES, D. and SCRIMSHAW, P. (Eds), *Values in Education*. London: University of London Press.

ELLIOTT, J. (1975b) 'The Humanities Project on "People and Work" and the concept of vocational guidance'. In: ELLIOTT, J. and PRING, R. (Eds), *Social Education and Social Understanding*, London: University of London Press.

ELLIOTT, J. and ADELMAN, C. (1973(a)) 'Inquiry and discovery teaching: a new Ford Teaching Project', *New Era*, **54**, 5, 115–17.

ELLIOTT, J. and ADELMAN, C. (1973(b)) 'Reflecting where the action is: the design of the Ford Teaching Project', *Educ. for Teaching*, November 8–20.

ELLIOTT, J. and ADELMAN, C. (1973(c)) 'Teachers as evaluators', *New Era*, **54**, 9, 210–18.

ELLIOTT, J. and HUMBLE, S. (1972) *Humanities Curriculum Project: An Introduction to Discussion*. A compilation of video tape recordings of discussion work in classrooms together with extracts from interviews with the teachers and pupils concerned. Centre for Applied Research in Education Humanities Project Evaluation Unit.

FORDHAM, P. (1974) 'The Humanities Curriculum Project in an adult class', *Studs. in Adult Educ.*, published by the National Institute of Adult Education, **6**, 1.

FRASER, D. (1973) *Deciding What to Teach.* Washington DC: National Education Association.

HAMINGSON, D. (Ed.) (1973) *Towards Judgement: The Publications of the Evaluation Unit of the Humanities Curriculum Project 1970–1972.* CARE Occasional Publications No. 1. Norwich: Centre for Applied Research in Education, University of East Anglia.

HUMANITIES CURRICULUM PROJECT, *(1970) The Humanities Project: An Introduction* London: Heinemann Educational Books.

MACDONALD, B. 'Briefing decision-makers – the evaluation of the Humanities Curriculum Project', Paper from the Humanities Project Evaluation Unit, March, 1971.

Also published in HOUSE, E.R. (Ed.) (1973), *School Evaluation: The Politics and Process*, 174–88. and under the title 'Humanities Curriculum Project' in *Evaluation in Curriculum Development: Twelve Case Studies*. Schools Council Research Studies. London: MacMillan, 1973, 80–91, and in *Towards Judgement: The Publications of the Evaluation Unit of the Humanities Curriculum Project 1970–1972*. CARE Occasional Publications No. 1 Norwich: Centre for Applied Research in Education, University of East Anglia, 12–36.

MACDONALD, B. and RUDDUCK, J. (1971) 'Curriculum research and development projects: barriers to success', *Brit. J. of Educational Psychol.* **41**, 2.

PARKINSON, J.P. and MACDONALD, B. 'Teaching race neutrally', *Race* **13**, 3, 299–313.

RUDDUCK, J. (1973) 'Dissemination in practice: an account of the dissemination programme of the Humanities Curriculum Project', *Cambridge J. of Educ.* **3**, 3, Michaelmas, 143–58.

SIMONS, H. (1971) 'Innovation and the case-study of schools', *Cambridge J. of Educ.*

STENHOUSE, L. (1968) 'The Humanities Curriculum Project', *J. of Curriculum Studs.*, **1**, 1, 26–33.

STENHOUSE, L. (1969) 'Open-minded teaching', *New Society.* 24th July.

STENHOUSE, L. (1970(a)) 'Pupils into students?', *Dialogue* No. 5, 10–12.

STENHOUSE, L. (1970(b)) 'Controversial issues in the classroom', *Values and the Curriculum.* A report of the Fourth International Curriculum Conference. Washington DC: National Education Association, Centre for the Study of Instruction, 103–15.

STENHOUSE, L. (1971) 'The Humanities Curriculum Project: the rationale', *Theory into Practice*, **10**, 3, 154–62.

STENHOUSE, L. (1972) 'Teaching through small-group discussion: formality, rules and authority'. *Cambridge J. of Educ.*, 18–24.

STENHOUSE, L. (1973). 'The Humanities Curriculum Project'. In: BUTCHER' H. J. and PONT, H.B. (Eds) *Educational Research in Britain 3* London: University of London Press, 149—67.

VERMA, G.K. and BAGLEY, C. (1971). 'Changing racial attitudes in adolescents: an experimental English study'. *International J. of Psychol.* **8**, 1, 55—8.

VERMA, G.K. and MACDONALD, B. (1971). 'Teaching race in schools: some effects on the attitudinal and sociometric patterns of adolescents', *Race.* **12**, 187—202.

Neutrality in School

Celia Dusoir

The first point of interest arising out of the previous three papers is the varied interpretations of the concept of neutrality. While this is not too worrying if the writer makes clear exactly what he is going to mean by the term, it can lead to a frustrating lack of communication. This is to some extent the situation here. John Wilson, while agreeing with most of Mary Warnock's paper, is of the opinion that she has spent much of the time discussing a concept of neutrality which no sane person would dispute **and** which anyway is not normally used. Lawrence Stenhouse does not think fit to discuss the concepts in the previous papers, nor does he give a clear account of his own concept of neutrality. He displays some antagonism at what he calls the 'lack of scholarship' in the papers, feeling that they should have started 'on the common base of discussing the research findings'.[1]

This lack of communication is very obvious and somewhat disquieting. Clearly there is much more to be said, at a philosophical level, about neutrality and related concepts (impartiality, bias, judiciousness, fairness and others);[2] **clearly, too**, such discussion must be related as closely as possible to practical work done by Stenhouse and others, rather than dissevered from it. Such relation requires better conditions of communication than are perhaps possible from a number of discrete papers.

My reaction to Stenhouse, at least, is to say 'Yes, of course get together on common ground, but why assume others should choose just your narrow strip?' It is narrow on two counts:

(i) It deals with research on a very selective section of the educational system — the school-leavers and upwards;

(ii) It dismisses as irrelevant or unworthy of comment the part that philosophy plays in elucidating educational concepts.

On (i): Stenhouse may wonder whether his Project is applicable to younger age-groups, but (a) this still does not take account of neutrality as understood *now* by teachers of, say, 5–13 year-olds, and (b) anyway he might well find that much of what worries him is absent in many primary school systems. So often in educational writings the author deals with a topic at secondary school level, while giving the impression that there is nothing to be said with regard to other levels. While Stenhouse is perhaps aware that there are relevant comments to be made about neutrality in teaching other age-groups, he makes me suspicious when he accuses Mary Warnock and John Wilson of not considering 'the' (*sc.* his) research findings. The Humanities Curriculum Project deals almost exclusively with the notion of a 'neutral chairman' for older children, which it may properly claim to have introduced into education in 1967; but as the previous papers show, the concept of neutrality is broader and of interest to a wider band of teachers. On the other hand, Mary Warnock and John Wilson do not even mention the Project, and it would surely have been courteous to have done so, if only to disagree with it.

On (ii): Again, this is a worry that occurs on reading much educational material. Getting clear as to what is being discussed, often heatedly, appears not to bother many writers. Yet how can one understand or comment seriously on something that is muddled or unclear? According to J. Elliott,[3] the Project has been much misunderstood. He admits that philosophers would say that the problem was due to 'conceptual confusion' and yet sees this as the fault of others: it is they, the critics, who have 'misconceptions of neutrality'. Since however the same 'old chestnuts' apparently continue to crop up in argument against the Project, it should surely make him think that perhaps the Project is at fault for not making itself clearer.

This, with respect, is what I feel about parts of Lawrence Stenhouse's paper. I suspect the trouble lies to some extent in the area mentioned earlier: lack of understanding between different sections of education. He, on the one hand, has been dealing with his Project for many years, and is completely familiar with its terminology. I, on the other, am a teacher who has not taught the Project, and am not wholly conversant with the various terms used. Yet presumably the paper is written not just for the converted. I, and others like me, would wish to understand it without necessarily reading anything else or speaking to teachers who do use the Project. The paper should surely stand on its own, and not contain assumptions that perhaps arise from thinking 'they *must* know what that means', or even perhaps from not thinking at all. I sympathize with the fact that this leads inevitably to spelling the same things out again and again, but this needs to be done.

To give some examples of what is unclear:

(a) On what grounds were the five major premises of the Project chosen if they were not seen as 'correct'?[4] Surely in some sense they must have been regarded as such, otherwise why not five different ones?

(b) Why should the teacher 'protect divergence of view among participants' of a discussion rather than, for instance, sensible or correct views? I realize, firstly, that the notion of there being correct views in controversial areas is disputable; and, secondly, I cannot imagine Stenhouse to mean that just *anything*, however idiotic, can be said and 'protected'; but nothing is mentioned to cover these points. As regards the second, the need to cover it is more real than might appear — some educational theory in the past few years has given the impression that, provided what is said and done by a child is his own thought or action, all is splendid.[5]

(c) I gather from the short paragraph on the fourth premise[6] that the main concern is to avoid coming down on one side of the argument rather than another; and this may clearly be important — provided, I should want to add, that there are good reasons for doing so. An example might be when supporters of one view are arguing on the basis of the 'greatest happiness' principle, and others on that of the 'sacredness of the individual'. This, however, is a very difficult and sophisticated level of argument. There are many times in discussion between children when views *are* wrong or right, because based on a lack of evidence or false reasoning. While the Project may allow for this, Stenhouse does not mention it; and I do not regard the phrase, 'the teacher . . . should have responsibility for quality and standards in learning', as he explains it, to cover the point adequately. To have concern for the development of a 'style' of discussing in ordinary English would cover only the *manner* of expressing a thought. This might prevent a child from being rude, or develop in him a sense of the dramatic, but it would not govern the *content* of his thought.

I have read and received conflicting information as to whether a teacher as neutral chairman *does* point out a child's erroneous views. Some argue that above all the teacher must not influence what is said, and if he so much as gives a hint as to the direction in which he thinks it right to go, the children will alter their ideas accordingly. But if a child's views are mistaken or illogical, and not just different, surely a teacher ought to point this out *in order to* alter what he thinks. If he does not, he is not teaching, nor is it in an important sense a 'discussion'. And some proponents of the Project would agree with this.

II

I want now to give some examples of what the notion of neutrality can mean to the teacher of the younger child.

(i) *Teaching morals as a subject*

In teaching subjects like mathematics, science, history, etc. Mary Warnock has shown that neutrality **is no more relevant** than, say, the ability to knit. Elliott also says[7] that where there are 'standards of reasoning' agreed upon in a subject-area, then neutrality is not an issue. But Mary Warnock wants to go further and say that issues in the *moral* area demand a similar view because moral *beliefs* logically entail the idea of right and wrong; and John Wilson makes the point that insofar as teachers are concerned with moral *education*, then, as with science, there must be standards of reasoning to apply. It is true that the standards are not as agreed and established socially (like science in earlier times), but this does not prevent the teacher from helping to get them established, e.g. he should teach the child that characteristically lying and stealing are wrong. Of course I agree with Lawrence Stenhouse that there are issues where it is not so plain, but this does not mean that many 'controversial' (and what is to be called 'controversial' is itself disputable) issues are not capable of being settled, or at least getting as near as one can to a settlement. Stenhouse thinks that a controversial issue in discussion should not lead to a decision; but this creates a wide gap between timetabled discussion-groups and the general teaching of morals that must go on in the day-to-day running of the school, and this surely will create confusion. For instance, suppose some children were reading a magazine labelled 'pornographic' by some people, and a teacher sees them reading it. Either (a) he says 'No, you can't read that for the following reasons . . . ', or (b) he allows them to; in each case he has made a decision. If however, ten minutes earlier, he had had a discussion-group on pornography, in which he had not let his beliefs be known, the children might reasonably feel cheated (if he did (a)) and also want to know why he had not told Billy (who held opposite views to those now known to be held by the teacher) why his were wrong. Stenhouse says that the teacher's beliefs, if voiced, would influence the children's in an undesirable way, but to have a belief *is* to think it *right* for certain reasons.

In primary schools, on the whole, this gap does not exist, because discussion of controversial issues takes place quite often as a result of something that has actually happened, and the teacher uses this to get across what is important in this area. For instance, Bobby, Terry and Joe steal some money from some teachers. They have a system worked out: **one** stands guard outside the staffroom door, one is the lookout-man, one takes the money; all three know they are going against the code of the school. When found out, the discussion brings to light that Bobby at least does not regard the school's code as his own. At home, in fact, his father encourages him to steal from 'them'. Here the teacher's job as educator must surely be:

(a) To get the children to see the facts: e.g. teachers are people like themselves, able to feel pain, etc.

(b) To get them to **realize** that school rules, even if different from dad's, must be obeyed *in school*. The discussion here should entail what rules, sanctions, contracts, etc. mean.

(c) Lead the talk on to the idea of a moral code about stealing in general. Given that we live in a society, it must be right not to steal because otherwise no one could call anything his own — not even, it must be emphasized, the food Bobby is about to eat for school lunch or the nose on 'his' face. Unless the teacher guided the situation on these lines, one would surely be inclined to say that he was not seriously concerned with moral education at all.

One point about discussion in general can be mentioned here. The teacher as chairman of discussion in primary schools has in practice been around a long time. In many schools much of the teaching uses this method. Often classrooms are either arranged in bays (number, art, science, etc.) or there are no classrooms as such but a large open-plan area. Children move about freely and the teacher goes round listening, talking and asking questions. If secondary schools adopted this kind of approach, perhaps Stenhouse's worries about the teacher's role would disappear (though others would no doubt arise). Certainly in my own experience the worry is not so much about encouraging children to discuss and air their own views, but about how to make them stop for just one minute — teacher too has something to say. With this age-range (5 to 13) much of the discussion, particularly in groups, is often spent in getting the child to really *listen* to another child's point of view, rather than just give a monologue. The point here is simply that, in a large number of primary schools, the emphasis has in fact for many years been on 'discussion' rather than just 'telling'.

(ii) *The teacher as judge*

John Wilson's idea of a neutral person is of someone impartial but active, like a judge. And in spite of his saying 'teachers are not judges', their neutrality often *is* to be seen when they are playing the part of a judge. For example, a teacher is supervising the children in the playground, and two children (aged 8) come running up. Billy claims Simon has bitten him on the chest, and shows the marks to prove it. Simon claims Billy bit him on the ear and also shows marks. Billy is tearful, Simon on the defensive; but (the teacher discovers) this is because Billy inevitably *is* tearful and Simon defensive when making accusations, and not for any other reason. Questions then have to be asked:

(a) Why did they bite each other? Nine out of ten times the answer will be 'Because *he* did'.

(b) Who bit first? Each claims the other did.

(c) A few more questions as to whether anyone else was involved (no), or whether anything else happened ('Simon punched me').

(d) Why did Simon punch? 'Because Billy called me names'.

(e) Why did Billy call him names? (1001 reasons).

And so one gets to the sequence of events:

> B called S names
> S punched B
> B bit S
> S bit B — and the children now come to the teacher to judge the issue.

The teacher has to explain the respective gravity of each of the actions; when this is done, depending on (a) whether it is the first (second, third) time they have called names (bit, etc.), and (b) whether they have therefore been told what is acceptable behaviour in school, and what the rules are, the teacher either reprimands them or gives some form of appropriate punishment which the school recognizes.

All this of course has to take place in a matter of minutes, because in a playground a teacher has perhaps 150 or more children to attend to. In this situation, he must (a) show that he is impartial between the two children on all relevant counts; that Billy has a runny nose and is disliked by other children is not relevant, that he has been told that he must not bite, is relevant, (b) take some kind of action without which (in my experience) no child will be happy. The kind of action to take is quite often a problem, but it is not a problem about neutrality, that is, it is not a question of deciding whether to be impartial or to take action at all, but of deciding what is to be done for each child. Whether the children themselves or the teacher do the deciding is also irrelevant — granted that any group of people must have rules, then there must also be sanctions if these rules are broken (otherwise they would not be rules).

These, then, are some of the points that arise out of the previous papers. No doubt teachers with different experiences from my own would wish to modify or expand various points. Perhaps the most important one, in the long run, with which most would agree is the need to communicate better amongst ourselves as well as with children.

NOTES

1 See Stenhouse's preceding article, p. 124.

2 A recent book by A. Montefiore deals with this: MONTEFIORE, A. (1975). *Neutrality and Impartiality — The University and Political Commitment*, Cambridge: Cambridge University Press.

3 ELLIOTT, J. (1973) 'Neutrality, Rationality and the Role of the Teacher', in *Proceedings of the Philosophy of Education Society of Great Britain*, **VII**, 1, Jan.

4 STENHOUSE, *op cit*, p. 124.

5 This is mainly the case at primary school level, but nevertheless such views are generally insidious.

6 STENHOUSE, *op. cit.* p. 125.

7 ELLIOTT, *op. cit.*

Section Three
Discipline in School and Society

'In one week — (the week before last) I
had to deal with an irate mother; two boys
stealing — including £1.00 from a teacher's
purse in lesson time; a boy stealing from the
Co-op; a boy stealing a watch from a friend's
house; a weeping student; a very rebellious
2nd year boy; a bomb scare so that we had to
evacuate the school on a Friday and then a minor
one on the following Monday.'

Headmaster of a junior school
in a rural town

Discipline: a Psychological Perspective

Derek Wright

It is difficult to say anything new on the topic of discipline in schools. Both as a practical issue and as a topic of debate it has existed as long as schools have. By now most approaches to the problem have been argued and tried out. Yet, positions are as entrenched and dogmatic as ever. What is urgently needed is a cool and dispassionate look at the matter.

A single chapter can do no more than touch on selected aspects. I propose to do three things. First I shall take a brief look at what we mean by discipline, the current debate about it, and the social situation in which we have to make our decisions. Then I shall offer a summary account of what psychological research has to say that is relevant. Finally, I want to take up the practical aspect of discipline in schools where it has become a problem.

1. The general question of discipline

Whatever else it may imply, discipline is about doing what you do not want to do and not doing what you want to do. Obligation is pitted against desire, and in the disciplined person usually wins. This does not at all mean that the battle is necessarily dramatic; on the contrary, obligation can establish such an habitual ascendancy over desire that subjectively felt conflict is rare. Discipline is very largely a matter of the kind of habits you have acquired. Moreover there are those happy occasions when desire and obligation coincide. But in our normal usage of the term, discipline implies some measure of sacrifice. When someone says 'I ought to do this' we interpret his remark as implying that he does not want to do it (or wants to do something else) but is anxious or fearful about not doing it.

So discipline is the control of behaviour in the interests of some value which is held to be more important than whatever else is immediately desired. It is therefore always instrumental to the achievement of some valued end. It is the acting out of a relatively long term plan in the face of distracting attractions and deterrents. It implies consistency, effort and reliability; the undisciplined person is self-indulgent and disorderly.

Discipline is connected with effectiveness and success rather than with moral goodness. Success at burglary, fraud or terrorism requires discipline. By general consent the hallmark of moral goodness is compassionate love. This can never be the fruit of discipline, though its constructive expression may demand discipline. Love, faith and hope, like hate and fear, give birth to plans that discipline can serve but they cannot themselves be its goals.

Leaving aside those plans and purposes which most of us would regard as undesirable, there are broadly three kinds of values which are worth distinguishing. First, there are those concerned with making a productive contribution to society through work, through earning a living, making things, organizing and running institutions, providing services, and so on. School work, in this sense, consists in preparing to make such a contribution later on. Then there are those values associated with becoming a certain sort of person. They may include physical and mental health, expertise and skill, personal development, and even perhaps sanctity or enlightenment. Finally, we have for our own good as well as that of others to fit in with other people both personally and through institutional roles. We must take account of other people's points of view, be concerned for their welfare, and have some sense of justice. Each of these tasks and their associated values require discipline for their successful achievement. The point is that of all social institutions the school is perhaps most explicitly concerned with all three, and for all children.

This brings us to the central questions to be asked about discipline. Who chooses the values and goals in the interests of which behaviour is controlled, and what are the actual values and goals? And who exercises the control and how is it exercised? When the individual chooses his own values and goals and exercises his own control over his behaviour we call him self-disciplined, as distinct from being disciplined by others. On the actual nature of the values and the manner of control hinges the question whether or not the discipline will be successful, and, if successful, whether or not it will be pathological.

Clearly the distinction between being self-disciplined and being disciplined by others is a relative one. On the one hand we live and work in society and cannot escape the controlling influence of others through social institutions which, in greater or lesser degree, are hierarchical (if only because they necessarily involve differentiation of role and function). On the other hand, it is a characteristic of the human system that under normal conditions it develops in the direction of autonomy, self-direction and self-regulation. Nevertheless it is part of our understanding of the term that the more self-disciplined a person is the less susceptible he will be to the disciplinary influence of others. Neither the relatively self-disciplined person nor the relatively undisciplined person is easily controlled by others. Moreover, as we shall see in the next section the socializing conditions which encourage self-discipline are not necessarily the same as those which produce someone who is highly amenable to externally imposed discipline.

The characteristics which in relatively extreme form go with high susceptibility to the discipline of others include respect for those in authority (or for collective opinion), dependence upon their approval, a readiness to accept that 'they know best', a habit of obedience to them, and a corresponding anxiety about disobeying. The more autonomous individual, who works out his own values and regulates his life according to them is much less impressed by people in authority and much less psychologically dependent upon them. He has to make his adjustment to institutionalized authority but this is in his way, on his terms, and for his purposes.

Whether the primary locus of control is internal or external, discipline begins to take on a pathological character when the values and goals it serves are unrealistic and when control of behaviour is inflexible and continuous. Clinical psychologists like Abraham Maslow (1970) have long argued that an essential ingredient in the growth and maturity of the personality is the capacity for fun and enjoyment, the ability to be happily idle. Discipline is not an end in itself, and it is questionable whether there is any value which justifies the frustration of fundamental human needs and which twists and distorts personal growth. It is of course difficult to talk of this in general terms. The range and extent of individual difference in temperament and ability is such that a discipline which one person takes in his stride is crippling for another. Without the discipline necessary for the realization of the values listed earlier, personal development will suffer; it will suffer as much if not more if the pursuit of those values involves a kind of psychological amputation.

In education today, as in the past, two rival voices can be heard on the topic of discipline, both well established. For convenience I will call them the 'traditional' and the 'progressive'. Though both would approve of self-discipline as the goal of education, the former stresses the need for externally imposed discipline in school and respect for authority whereas the latter urges the need for 'freedom' and self-direction for children. It is no easy task disentangling the roots of this conflict of view, but it does seem that underlying it is a difference in the way human development is conceived.

Traditionalists appear to emphasize what might be called the 'original sin' view of human nature. If children are left to 'do what they like' they will grow up wild, uncontrolled and unhappy. Hence teachers and parents must move in early and establish authoritarian control over them. Throughout school life they must be trained and disciplined more or less strictly so that they will later on fit smoothly into society. Progressive educationalists emphasize the 'original virtue' point of view. Children are living, growing organisms, and nature knows best what they should be like. Training and discipline as the traditionalist understands them can only distort this growth producing neurosis or rebellion.

It would seem to the interested observer that both sides have a point. The question is then one of balance. One of the considerations brought in by each side is the current state of society. The traditionalist's account is all too familiar. In its heated-up form, it consists of such statements as that 'society is falling apart', there is a 'catastrophic decline of the national morality', and 'civilisation is in danger'. Sometimes these assertions are given a political flavour when the supposed corruption in our society is attributed, at least partly, to left wing, atheist teachers and psychologists. There is an amusing irony about this when we remember that, as far as it is possible to compare societies, it is precisely such socialist states as China and Russia which exhibit in the greatest degree the kind of externally imposed discipline of which the traditionalists judge our country to be at present in need. The progressives also regard our society as sick, but for them the sickness lies in the corrupt values and institutions of the establishment and they conclude that what is needed is new people who are autonomous and independent and who will create a more just and loving community.

If we try to take a detached look at current social changes it seems to me that there are certain features which stand out clearly and which are relevant to discipline in schools. It is obvious that we cannot escape a concern for the values that others in our society live by. If any society is to survive there must be an area of shared values and an area where it is agreed that individual differences are not only permitted but desirable. What appears to be happening in our society is that consensual values, the ones we must all in some measure acknowledge, are changing in emphasis, and the hazy and muddled line between public, shared values and private ones is being somewhat redrawn.

What is surely indisputable is that the last hundred years or so has seen a sharply increased sensitivity to those values associated with the political, social and economic rights of the individual. It is difficult to deny the massive moral advance this implies. We no longer tolerate injustices that were once taken for granted. Two consequences have followed. The first is intrinsic to such a change. It is that respect for and obedience to institutionalized authority has faded. The second is not a necessary concomittant. With increased emphasis upon the rights of the individual has come a weakened sense of accountability to the community as a whole, of our all being in the same boat.

If this is true, then we can safely expect that children in school will reflect these social changes. As educators we are then faced with the decision of working with them or against them. If we work with them, as I believe we should, then at least two consequences follow. First we must encourage self-discipline in children to a greater extent than ever before. Second we must do all we can to foster in adolescents moral growth beyond the stage of concern for their own rights and their loyalty to particular people and groups to the level of commitment to general principles. It becomes important to an unprecedented degree that individuals so expand their awareness that they have an informed concern for society as a whole which balances and on occasion takes priority **over their own rights and parochial loyalties** and obligations. The research of Kohlberg and his associates in the United States (1969) has shown that this is not only possible but represents the natural direction of development in late adolescence.

Still within the area of consensual values there are two very common assertions made **about** our society. The first is that respect for the property of others has declined. The difficulty here is that on the one hand so much property is today collectively owned, and so many institutions are not the property of those who run them, and on the other hand concern for economic justice has rendered problematic the right to certain kinds of ownership. It is not obvious that respect for the personal possessions of others in the narrow sense has declined. The second assertion is that our society is much more physically violent than it was. However, in the light of the social history of the last hundred and fifty years, of the number of crimes of violence known to the police in any one year in relation to the size of the population, and of the level of violence in other countries, it is frankly astonishing that intelligent people can say this. None of which is to deny that theft, vandalism and violence are serious problems, and that they only have to occur to be too much.

Little need be said about the changing boundary between what may be called the private and public sectors of value. Suffice it to say that the individual can no longer exercise power over others and exploit them economically to the extent to which he could in the past; and at the same time the religious, sexual, and leisure time aspects of his life are recognized as much more fully his own business. In the private sector **it is** clearly the task of the school to help the individual work out his own value code in the light of his own temperament and situation and in the light of that principle of justice and concern for others which is basic to all creative relationship to others.

II Psychological research and discipline

The bearing of psychological research upon teaching is not simple. Certainly it is not a simple matter of straightforward deduction from research to practice. This is so for at least two reasons. Research always deals with a limited aspect of a problem under more or less controlled conditions; and teaching is not a technology but an art in which the teacher's unique personality and ability are key factors. Nevertheless research is relevant, and practice is likely to be that more effective if it takes account of it.

Within psychology there are two theoretical perspectives which have inspired most of the research relevant to discipline. To some extent they echo the traditional and progressive points of view discussed earlier. The first is social learning theory which is concerned in great detail with the ways in which the child's behaviour is shaped and controlled by others. The second is cognitive-developmental theory, of which Piaget is the main architect, which focuses upon the ways in which self-directive and self-regulative processes develop in children and how this development may be facilitated. Though there are points of conflict between the two perspectives it is quite clear that they are to a great extent complementary. It is obviously not possible to give an adequate review of these theories and the associated research here. An account will be found in Wright (1971; 1972). I shall simply mention some of the main outcomes.

Research stemming from social learning theory does much to illuminate the conditions under which externally imposed discipline can be most effective. Here an important distinction has to be made. There is first the problem teachers face in establishing control over the children who are actually in front of them. This will be taken up in the third section of this chapter. The question which will concern us now is how the teacher can so influence the child that his behaviour is shaped in the direction the teacher wants in a relatively permanent way, and when the teacher is not around to supervise. The fact that adult-imposed discipline may result in the child conforming to adult — specified rules when he is alone and outside immediate adult control is sometimes taken as evidence that it results in self-discipline. Traditionalists sometimes use this fact to defend the importance of externally imposed discipline. But such conformity to rules is not true self-discipline for the decision as to how the child should behave is not taken by the child himself but by the adult. Children can be trained, much as domestic animals are, to behave 'correctly' when unsupervised, but when this is done, again like domestic animals, they have no hand in deciding what is correct. Of course such training may serve a useful function in laying a foundation of habit upon which the child's later self-discipline can build, but it does not directly encourage such self-discipline. Such training may therefore be most valuable in the early stages of development, and it is significant that most of the relevant research has been conducted upon young children.

The main factors involved in such influence will now be discussed.

1. Though social learning theory has not yet been extended to accommodate the fact adequately, research has shown that a crucial condition for the effectiveness of adult training, as defined, is that the child is attached to the adult. The point is so fundamental it can be generalized into a kind of law: **a teacher** will not have any long-term positive influence upon the values and behaviour of his pupils unless they like him and in some way he counts or matters to them. It may seem so obvious as to be trivial, yet it is still not given the attention it deserves. Much could be said about the conditions under which such attachment comes about, but only two can be mentioned here. First, the pupils must see the teacher as liking them and being interested in them individually, and second he must have skills, knowledge and personal qualities that they can value and depend upon.

2. The feature of adult influence most usually associated with discipline is punishment. It is also the most controversial. Traditionalists regard it as essential, progressives as unnecessary and a sign of failure. It is important therefore to be clear on a number of points (see Wright, 1972). Firstly, in the broadest sense of the term punishment is inescapable in human relationships. The technical term 'negative reinforcement' is perhaps better for this broad usage. In this sense, implicit or explicit disapproval, momentary irritation, the withholding of praise, and even such trivial things as forgetting the child's name can be as negatively reinforcing or 'punishing' as conscious and deliberate acts of punishment. Secondly, whatever the motivation that leads a teacher to punish its effectiveness must be judged in relation to the purpose it is intended to serve. Apart from such things as relieving the teacher's feelings, it can be intended to produce either ordered behaviour here and now or long term changes. For understandable reasons teachers seem preoccupied with the former, but it is the latter which concerns us at the moment. Thirdly, if punishment is to have long-term effects the child must in some sense be on the side of the teacher; that is he must like and value the teacher and see the justification for his sanctions. Fourthly the purpose of punishment is to inhibit behaviour. There are basically two emotional responses to punishment, aggression which is disinhibiting and anxiety which is

inhibiting, and of course both may occur together. Clearly therefore the more punishment evokes aggression, the less it will lead to subsequent inhibition of behaviour, and the more it evokes anxiety the more it will. Characteristically sanctions which are physically or psychologically aggressive and which are felt as unjust and humiliating will maximize the aggressive response. Anxiety is most strongly evoked when the child values his relationship with the teacher and therefore the teacher's good opinion of him and the teacher's response to the child's behaviour is obvious but non-aggressive disapproval. Fifthly, punishment always results in increased arousal. The more aroused someone is the less able he is to learn complex discrimination, to think clearly and reasonably. Hence it follows that if the teacher wishes the child to understand why his actions are wrong at the time he is being punished, the greater the severity of the punishment the more the teacher will defeat his own ends. Sixthly, if punishment is to have long-term effects it must be accompanied by explanation at the child's level of understanding. The function of such explanation is to help the child see the justice of the sanction or disapproval (if the disapproval is in fact unjust then the teacher is likely to have to face up to this injustice in trying to explain its justice!), and to enable the child to generalize from the particular situation to others when the teacher is not about. Of course the explanation must be designed to do these things; the 'because I say so' explanation is manifestly inadequate. Lastly experiments have shown that seeing someone else punished can inhibit a child when he is on his own afterwards, but the conditions under which this occurs have not yet been fully explored.

3. Punishment for undesirable behaviour will never be effective without encouragement and praise for desirable behaviour. It is obvious, though some teachers seem to forget it. But there can be few teachers who have not observed the astonishing effects that praise and success can have on a much punished, 'naughty' child. Approval and praise not only sustain the attachment crucial for all effective discipline but they build the child's self-esteem. There is good reason for thinking that much of the behaviour of which teachers disapprove springs from damaged self-esteem, and of course punishment may damage it further. The child who feels he has worth and value and that this worth is recognized and supported by the teacher is of all children least likely to be hostile and uncooperative towards him. This issue is far more important than its brief mention here might suggest, and is a key factor in the development of self-discipline. Clearly the kinds of behaviour that are rewarded and punished are important. The only point to be made here is that what the teacher thinks is being rewarded and punished may not coincide with what from the child's point of view is

actually being rewarded and punished. Is protest against felt injustice punished? Are honesty and integrity being punished? Is hypocrisy, time-serving and lying being rewarded?

4. Finally, research has amply vindicated the commonsense idea that children are powerfully influenced by the example of adults. Children tend to adopt the values of the adults that surround them without these values ever being explicitly stated, and this is more likely to happen the more attached they are to them. If the adults are self-disciplined, they will tend to become self-disciplined. It does not follow that teachers should be continually and self-consciously aware of the example they are setting; that way they will end up setting an example of someone setting an example. It is enough that they be reasonably civilized, compassionate and human people. But there is a problem which all people in authority face but which is professionally the concern of teachers if the long-term moral development of children is part of their responsibility. We all know that power corrupts, but are disinclined to think that it happens to us because the beginnings of this corruption are so imperceptible. The reason is simple. When we have power and authority we can and do control the way others respond to us and thereby encapsulate ourselves from the kind of feedback which would make us more fully aware of what we are really doing. For example, the command 'take that smile off your face', if successful, obliterates for the teacher an important cue indicating that for the moment his conduct is seen as somewhat ridiculous. More seriously, when such feedback is hidden from the teacher by virtue of his power and the nature of his role as he conceives it, the slide into self-indulgence can be irresistable. Thus a teacher may end up presenting an image of cynicism and gross discourtesy whilst expecting the opposite from his pupils. Consider, too, what happens when a teacher physically punishes a child for bullying; for in exerting his superior power and strength to inflict physical pain, he is giving an example of the very behaviour which, in the child he is punishing at the moment at which he is telling the child that the child's behaviour is wrong. There is no easy solution to this general problem. But it must lie in a continuing sensitivity on the teacher's part to its nature, and the effort to create relationships with pupils within which the teacher can safely support the expression on the child's part of the way he sees the teacher's behaviour towards him.

Social influences remain operative throughout life for all people, but the person being influenced changes, especially during the period of childhood and adolescence. As the person changes so the strength and nature of these social influences will be modified. From our present point of view the most important development during childhood and adolescence is the emergence of the ego. By the ego is meant that central, organizing part of the living human system which plans, reasons, thinks, knows, chooses, decides, values, intends and acts. It is that complex structure located in the brain which processes· information from inside and outside of the system and directs and controls operations on the environment. It is the seat of intelligence and consciousness, and is the primary 'organ' of adaptation. A strong ego structure is one which, relatively speaking, integrates the individual's varying needs, desires and plans into some measure of consistency and stability, which clearly and accurately differentiates self from the rest of the world, and which is relatively independent of social pressures. Such an ego structure implies a shadowy, implicit and inarticulate kind of underlying philosophy which holds together the various aspects of the individual's life into a relatively coherent meaning. The greater an individual's ego-strength the more he is influenced by others to modify his behaviour only when they provide him with new information and reasons which he finds convincing. Moreover, when we approach someone in this manner, respecting his decisions and expecting him to make them for himself, we tend to sustain and even increase his ego-strength.

The cognitive developmental perspective is directly concerned with how ego-functioning matures and with how interaction with others fosters this development. It is Kohlberg (1969) who has made the major contribution so far to our understanding of this development in the area of moral thinking and decision. He has found evidence that young people tend to pass through an invariant sequence of stages in their moral thinking, though many may not reach the later stages. Each stage represents a characteristic way of thinking, or type of logic. In the earliest stages the salient considerations in moral decision making are whether or not an action is rewarded or punished, whether it will have pleasant or unpleasant consequences for the self. At the next stages the primary consideration is whether an action meets the approval of others or of an authority. At the highest stages, moral decision making is guided by a sense of contractual obligation to others of a symmetrical and reciprocal kind, and finally by relatively abstract and general principles among which that of justice is paramount. It is important to stress that Kohlberg is not so much interested in what the child says, in the superficial sense, but in the underlying structure of his thought, for it is at this level that thought and action are one. Self-discipline is most clearly manifest when the underlying thought structures have matured to the highest levels.

The educational task, then, is to encourage development to these levels. It is Kohlberg's claim that stages cannot be skipped. It follows that the teacher's job is to tune in to the wavelength the child is currently on and help him to move on to the next in his own time. To develop, the child must realize that his present mode of thinking is not adequate to cope with the contingencies he has to face, that it breaks down. The teacher helps this realization by the way he acts towards the child and by discussion with him. The reason why some teachers give up discussion and conclude that 'you can't reason' with some children is either because the level at which they themselves reason with the child is so far beyond the child's level that he cannot understand it, or because the relationship between teacher and pupil is such that genuinely influential dialogue is not possible.

There are at least three kinds of talk that can go on between teacher and pupil. First there is talk which is a form of punishment, such as threats, sarcasm and abuse. Then there is the kind of explanation mentioned earlier in connection with social learning theory. Here the teacher points out what is right and what is wrong and gives his own reasoned justification. Both could be described as forms of authoritative, asymmetrical talk, for it is the adult who does the thinking and speaking, and its success depends upon the child listening, understanding, and passively accepting it. The third kind is much more democratic and symmetrical. It is the child, now, who does most of the thinking. With the teacher's encouragement he tries to articulate his present thoughts in relation to the moral issues he faces. The teacher's role is to support this thinking and raise discreetly the difficulties which stimulate the child into thinking afresh. This implies in the teacher an awareness of how children's thinking develops, and even more a readiness to listen at length.

There are other implications. Whether or not the kind of discussion described is possible depends upon the teacher's whole style of relating to his pupils. It becomes questionable whether, except perhaps in the very early stages or under special circumstances, the teacher ever really needs to 'assert his authority'. At one stage the child will naturally see the teacher as an authority, and later it is the teacher's job to help the child think through and out of deference to his own authority.

Teachers can sometimes be heard saying, for instance of a young adolescent, that 'all he understands is a good hiding'. Doubtless the diagnosis is correct. What it means, among other things, is that the boy is grossly retarded in his moral thinking, and the reason is most probably that adults have consistently confirmed him at this level through their actions towards him. To give him a 'good hiding' would confirm him yet more. What he needs is a much more imaginative response which will perplex him a bit and the kind of meeting of minds that will stimulate him into thinking in a different way. That this demands considerable skill from a teacher goes without saying.

If a teacher wishes to foster self-discipline, then, his goal must be to support, strengthen and stimulate the growth of the pupil's underlying thought structures, the construing, reasoning and planning processes which shape behaviour and speech. He does this through a style of relating to his pupils which makes possible interaction that is characterized by mutual respect and symmetry and through an interest in and sensitivity to their own way of thinking.

III The 'problem of discipline' in the classroom

Whether his goal is to produce adults amenable to externally imposed discipline or to foster self-discipline, the teacher must count in the eyes of his pupils, he must be able to guide and direct activities in the classroom, and he must be valued and liked. The way in which he is liked and the things for which he is valued will vary; but *that* he counts and is valued is essential if he is to have any real influence. The 'problem of discipline' arises when the teacher does not count and is not valued.

Discipline in this sense is always highly individual. But there are situations which all teachers find difficult. In their extreme form they occur when the pupils in a class or school are mostly wild and uncontrollable, when they reject school and teachers as irrelevant or as enemies, and when they are bandied together into more or less cohesive gangs with antisocial norms and values. The teacher is caught between on the one hand a society who pays him and holds him responsible for educating his pupils together with the norms of a profession which regards lack of discipline as a sign of failure, and on the other hand the pupils themselves who refuse to cooperate and actively try to make his task more difficult.

I want to focus upon this extreme situation, for it is apt to precipitate a personal crisis for the teacher. Some break down in it and some have to break out of it to preserve their sanity. Indeed the first thing to be said is that the teacher's primary duty is to himself. If he cannot find some measure of creative fulfilment in such a situation and if his temperament and personality are not suited to coping with it he should move out of it as soon as possible. However, if he can rise to, and struggle with, the challenge the personal gains for him may be considerable. That statement, it should be said, is based upon my own limited experience of facing such situations and my observations of others in them. That the learning experience is painful cannot be denied by anyone who has crept home daily with a bruised and trampled ego and who finds himself looking enviously at people in less stressful occupations.

The simplest way of coping is to meet the foe head-on. The basic equipment for doing this appears to be a fierce, relentless will, an intelligent, acid tongue that can point up with cutting clarity the deficiencies of offending and disobedient pupils, and perhaps also dominating muscular strength. I have seen how successful this can be. It is surprising how much a tough young thug can be cowed by a biting tongue that knows precisely the vulnerable points to attack and which can speak within a frame of reference the pupil understands. At the level of verbal attack he is hopelessly outplayed and at a loss to cope. Once his ascendancy is established, and his tongue feared, the teacher can begin to win his pupils over by showing he also likes them, by his humour, and by being interested in them.

But if that is not your style, and it was not mine, then the task takes longer. The teacher's main assets are his resilience and his intelligence. His goal is to win the war by enlisting the enemy on his side; the outcome of particular conflicts is unimportant beside this. In planning his campaign, for it needs planning, there are some general points worth considering.

It is a useful working hypothesis, or act of faith, that behind the leathery face a pupil presents to his teacher (and to everyone else) is a soft centre, lonely, anxious and a bit bewildered. The problem then is to get in touch with it. This means relaxed, informal and individual contact. If the school organization does not help you have to make the opportunities for yourself. It is always possible. The point is that private and personal lines of communication with individuals in a class sap enthusiasm for collective resistance to the teacher's direction. And it is strategically sensible to start with the group leaders.

A common characteristic of antisocial youths is a manipulative attitude towards adults. Throughout a history of distrust and hostility they have come to learn the strings that make adult puppets jump, and to use this knowledge for their own purposes. Collectively in the classroom the purpose is often to have a ball at the teacher's expense by pulling the strings that make him angry, incoherent or embarrassed. Of course if they unleash a tiger in the teacher they may quickly learn to leave those strings well alone. But a more effective solution, and one more educative for the pupils, is when the teacher learns the art of jumping in unexpected directions when the strings are pulled. As George Lyward used to say, 'insert the question mark', and at least for a while you have their attention. If you do not fit their preconception they are for the moment unsure and at a loss. This is, of course, a difficult art, and it is unlikely to be successful if it is forced and unnatural. But unless I am much mistaken it begins to flow naturally when the teacher's insight into his pupils moves beyond that which most adults have previously shown them, and beyond their insight into themselves. If the teacher actually perceives them as unhappy and as problems to themselves as much as to him (they will not all be of course) and that their hostility to him is less personal than against what he represents, then he will be less trapped within his own feelings and more free to act imaginatively. Donald Winnicott once said that all antisocial action is an expression of hope. This may be extreme, but it has this degree of plausibility, that when antisocial behaviour is a form of protest (it is not always so; sometimes it is just excited 'fun') then it necessarily implies hope; for people who have given up hope do not protest. The general point is that when the teacher construes antisocial behaviour in this kind of way it is easier for him to respond creatively rather than punitively, and he is less likely to be drawn into conflict with his pupils at their level and in their terms. Of course you cannot put a particular construction on their behaviour simply to change your own feelings. What it implies is a continuing desire to understand and a refusal to be stuck with easy formulae. Such understanding is certainly helped by a knowledge of the theories and research on antisocial behaviour, but much more important it comes from listening to what the pupils themselves have to say.

It is sometimes said that disciplinary problems are generated by the fact that middle class teachers try to impose on pupils from a working class background values that are alien to them. This is easy to say but it is much more difficult to establish how true and important it is. Certainly Kohlberg has found that the developmental sequence of stages in moral thinking is independent of class difference and there are certain general values like justice and reciprocal obligation which are essential for all stable community living. What is important in the situation we are concerned with is that the teacher focus upon his primary target and avoid clashes over less important issues. Matters like 'bad language' or 'rude manners' are insignificant beside the central task of establishing influential communication with pupils. Part of the learning experience for a middle class teacher is that it forces him to distinguish what is important from what is not.

Among adolescents in particular admiration and affection for a teacher are most likely to come when two conditions are fulfilled. The first is when the teacher clearly shows he is good at something the pupils would like to be good at and when through his help they become better at it. What it is can vary widely, including such things as skill at sport, knowledge about cars, insight into people, and even telling good jokes. But the most obvious thing is the skills and knowledge the teacher is teaching when these are so designed as to fit in with the pupils' own aspirations for themselves. The second condition is the counterbalancing reciprocal of the first. It is when the pupils can display superior knowledge or skill to the teacher and the latter can appreciate and learn from them. Few things knit a pupil to his teacher more than the opportunity to teach the teacher something he values learning when the teacher is himself recognized as being good at something.

Pupils can be won over, even if grudgingly, to a respect and liking for a teacher through the sheer fact that he refuses to give up trying to educate them in spite of their concerted efforts to drive him off. It can seem to them proof that he must like them. Obviously this effect is much strengthened if they can see other evidence that though he may disapprove of much of what they do he nevertheless approves of them. Faced with an unruly mob it is all too easy for most of the teacher's communications to be of a negative, disapproving kind. Yet approval and praise, especially of the most difficult pupils, has an important function from the start; and it is always possible to find opportunities for this. However trivial the occasion may be to the teacher the psychological impact of praise can be considerable.

A complaint commonly made by teachers struggling with disciplinary problems is that they do not get support from the rest of the staff and in particular the head. Often this complaint seems justified. It is observable that sometimes the teacher with disciplinary problems becomes a kind of leper in the staff room. In subtle ways other staff keep their distance. The motives for this are doubtless mixed but they may include a sense of helplessness to help, a fear of being associated with a 'failure', and even, sad to say, a sense of satisfaction, for the presence of a failure can confirm their feeling that they are successful. Head teachers are sometimes remote and authoritarian, and treat their staff much like senior pupils. The fact that his future career depends upon such a head's reference can be a considerable additional source of stress. Moreover the problems a particular teacher faces cannot be separated from the general discipline of a school. He can both gain and lose from the way other teachers treat their pupils.

However it is not too obvious how the rest of the staff can help. The struggling teacher is apt to want a system of rules and sanctions automatically administered by the head that he can use and lean on. He wants someone else to punish for him. But the value of this is strictly limited. No class or school can function without the active cooperation of the pupils and relatively impersonal sanctions do not bring this about. Homespun tips and advice also have only a limited value. I was once advised by a weatherbeaten teacher to 'pick on the ring leader and belt him so hard that he will never forget', when such an action was temperamentally impossible to me.

The heart of the problem is the isolation a teacher may feel, of not being a member of a team with a common purpose and strategy. It is surely the head's responsibility to create such a sense of unity. Unfortunately heads often do not possess the personal skills. In the technical jargon they are appointed as task leaders, not socioemotional leaders.

It seems to me that if a school is faced with continuing disciplinary problems, and the head and educational authorities are really concerned, they should take some imaginative steps to improve the situation. One such step would be to create an opportunity for all the staff of a school to meet, on neutral ground, for a fairly prolonged period of time and with skilled outside help. The purpose would be first to create the conditions under which individuals can honestly ventilate their anxieties, frustrations, hopes and pains, and then to weld them into a mutually supportive group with common plans and strategies. This means exploring what they are really up to, what experimental changes in organization and structure might be tried out, and how support can be given to those who most need it.

It is no use expecting that the occasional, **after-school** staff meeting and chat in the staff room at lunch time will do this. Nothing short of several weekends at a country house will make any impact. There are risks, especially for those experienced teachers whose self-esteem depends upon a firmly structured set of hierarchical relations with their colleagues. But with the help and guidance of people skilled in group relations who are aware of the problems teachers face the outcome could be very creative. Furthermore, it might even make teachers feel that undisciplined and rebellious pupils are more interesting and stimulating than the passive and obedient variety found in 'well disciplined' schools.

References

KOHLBERG, L. (1969) 'Stage and sequence: the cognitive-developmental approach to socialisation' In: GOSLIN, D.A. (Ed.) *Handbook of Socialization Theory and Research*. Chicago: Rand McNally & Co.

MASLOW, A.H. (1970) *Motivation and Personality*. Second Edition. New York: Harper & Row.

WRIGHT, D. (1971) *The Psychology of Moral Behaviour*. Harmondsworth: Penguin.

WRIGHT, D. (1972) 'The punishment of children: a review of experimental studies', *Journal of Moral Education* 1, 3.

Educative Discipline

Judy A. Kyle

What is interesting about the concept of discipline is that it can be considered 'empty'. That is not to say that it is without meaning — for any concept of discipline implies minimal components of order and/or restriction. But it is 'empty' in the sense that how *much* or what *kind* of order and/or restriction is left to be specified by people in actual situations. This explains why there seem to be almost as many meanings of discipline as there are people who apply it. But further it suggests that we can be less concerned with whether we are applying the 'right' concept of discipline and can focus instead on the process of determining the appropriate application of discipline for a particular situation. People determine the specific meaning of discipline in a given situation — and whether or not they do so *reasonably* is the point.

By drawing from actual experience, I will consider some of the practical problems which face educators whose task it is to determine the appropriate form of discipline for a particular secondary school situation. I will try to show what it is to think reasonably in this area and will suggest some practical measures which can be applied in order to translate the theory into action. It will then be up to practising educators to decide whether or not these measures are applicable to their situations.

Discipline is not unique as an 'empty' concept. For example, consider the following: Since people in a school form a community, then rules are logically necessary. What rules, or how many rules, however, are not specified. If rules, then sanctions. But what sort of sanctions or how severe they should be is not specified. If rules and sanctions, then who is to make and enforce them? The question of student participation arises. Since school is, by definition, an 'educational' institution, it is reasonable to assume that as much as possible of what goes on — not just in classrooms but in the whole school —

should be 'educative'. And because there is much to learn during the processes of making and enforcing rules, student participation is logically required. Still, what sort and how much student participation is not specified. Here we have met three crucial 'empty' concepts (rules, sanctions, and student participation), all of which are 'logically required' by the nature, function, and purpose of schools insofar as they are to be 'educational' institutions.

Faced with all these 'empty' concepts to 'fill in', it is not surprising if the head's mind boggles. He would have to be a person of infinite wisdom to come up with all the right commandments, not to mention the magic formulae for their successful implementation and enforcement. It is a formidable task and he may well wonder if it should be all his.

He need not deny the *responsibility* for school discipline — clearly that *is* his. He must see that there is discipline and that it is enforced — but that is different from saying he must do it all himself. He is justified in shrinking from the task, in fact, since for him to determine the discipline alone is in an important sense to be authoritarian. The rules of the school would be rules because he said so and this is a connection to avoid if possible. Also, it is customary — and not logically implied by the concepts of discipline, order, or restriction — that discipline usually comes from the top in schools, ie. head to staff to students. Somehow he must find a way to fulfil his responsibility by sharing the task of determining the actual form of discipline for his school.

The head whose aim it is that students *learn* discipline, will not settle for having appropriate authorities 'wield' it at them; nor will he expect discipline to somehow incidentally rub off on the students as a result of academic study. Rather he will find ways to teach discipline in its own right. He will see a) that 'student participation' is an important feature of his school and b) that students not only submit to discipline in subjects and conduct, but that they also learn *about* discipline in a practical way. He can do this by being prepared to expose the school's existing discipline-pattern to rigorous scrutiny in a way which will not result either in casting aside all existing rules or in lapsing into a state of no discipline at all.

Before introducing any new measures, however, the head is wise to take into account the students' position within the traditional hierarchical structure of influence which exists within school communities. Generally there is a vertical relationship with perhaps a Board of Management or Education Authority at the top which influences the head who influences the staff who influence the students. Parents figure in the structure as well but their position varies from one school to another depending on degree of interest. Students invariably occupy the lowest position whether they like it or not if for no other reason than that they have the misfortune to be younger than everyone else. This need not mean, however, that they are the least influential. Rather theirs is simply the most difficult influence to exert. Nevertheless, whatever measures the head adopts should realistically reflect this situation.

One way to begin would be to set up a working group the function of which would be to subject the current discipline pattern to cross-examination. It could be called the 'Critical Review Board' (CRB) and would be different from and in addition to existing clubs and committees. The CRB should be representative of the school community as it is at present by including one member from each class and interest group. Teachers should be represented in proportion to their numbers despite the fact that they would be outnumbered by students. Each member should be elected by the group he represents and should have a stand-in in case of necessity to be absent. Elected members should each have a vote and the chairman should only vote in the event of a tie. All meetings should be open to 'auditors' who would have the right to contribute to discussion but not to vote. This would enable those who are interested (but not elected) to participate as well. Meetings should happen weekly (for the sake of continuity) and should have a specific time limit. And finally, to enable work to proceed without delay, the CRB should be provisionally chaired by the head. In due course this could be changed, but at this stage it is important that the head not only express an interest but that he participate. It would be an inaccurate reflection of the community for him to occupy any other position.

For the CRB to function effectively, a procedural mechanism for change which would operate school-wide is needed (Wilson, 1972). The following is a possible procedure which actively recognizes the credibility of the student group and at the same time reflects the students' position in the vertical influence-structure outlined earlier. Also this procedure acknowledges that staff decisions supersede student decisions. This 'Appeal Procedure' should apply to any change introduced from whatever source and could function as follows:

1. *Student initiated change*
Students shall 'make a case' for the change by applying to the staff in writing and/or in person (at a staff meeting) stating reasons for the change.

The staff, having read/heard the student appeal, are obliged to discuss the proposal in detail and to either reject, accept, or accept it with qualification. The staff must respond formally to the students **including giving reasons for their decision.**

2. Staff initiated change

The staff shall 'make a case for' the proposed change in writing and in person to the students by making a presentation to the CRB.

Students, having heard/read the staff proposal, shall have the time to discuss it in detail and prepare a formal response. This response may be either an 'appeal' or an assent.

3. Any change introduced without following this procedure shall be considered only temporarily in force and shall have a declared time limit.

4. All final decisions shall be publicly announced both orally and in writing. Written announcements must bear the signatures of both staff and student representatives to indicate that the procedure has been duly followed.

Although the staff are required, by this mechanism, to listen, discuss, and respond with justification to student appeals, they are not required to accept student proposals. Although the students have no guarantee that they will get their way in every case, this mechanism does guarantee them 'an official voice'. Only if the staff are extremely authoritarian or anti-student will it be the case that students never win appeals.

The 'educative' value of such a mechanism should be obvious. The situations which arise are 'real' and have practical point for both students and staff. Reasoned arguments for or against proposals are crucial and it is a prime opportunity for the staff to initiate students into the techniques of reasonable argument and of justification.

The 'disciplinary' value of such a mechanism should also be obvious. Order and restriction are important elements of the procedure and the purpose of having them is both clear and constructive. It is interesting to note that in this case the order and restriction apply (perhaps not equally, but *apply* nevertheless) to both staff and students.

A final point about the procedure is that it can be self-correcting. By using the mechanism, staff and/or students may propose changes to it as well. Meanwhile it should prove to be an effective device for clarifying tricky areas of school life.

At the first meeting of the CRB, the chairman should explain the value of having a specific pattern of procedure for meetings and he should describe some of the important principles. For example, he should make it clear that meetings will have fixed starting and ending times so that people are clear about their 'time commitment', and that there will be a visible agenda for each meeting. Also, details of discussion procedures including how to 'get the floor', how to make proposals, and the mechanics of voting, should be carefully explained. Because people will most willingly and effectively participate if they can 'see' that something is being accomplished, agendas and clear procedures are useful and, if used well, can be extremely important. Actual practice of this sort should show students conclusively that disciplinary measures have positive aspects.

Once details of the meeting procedure are understood, the CRB can immediately tackle the review of school rules. It could begin by setting up a committee to produce a list of all the school rules thought to exist and members could contribute by consulting their groups. Future meetings would then consist of a critical review of each of the rules on the compiled list. Any which the CRB wishes to challenge could be put through the Appeal Procedure and eventually a final revised list of school rules would be decided on, signed by staff and student representatives, and publicized. It is likely to be a long, tedious process and hard work, but, that **too** is a lesson worth learning. It is up to the educators to see that the CRB keeps at it.

Another problem for the CRB to consider is that of enforcing the rules. It is not enough merely to state the rules for there will always be some who will challenge by contravening. The problem of enforcement has two **important aspects**: a) what sanctions, penalties, or forms of punishment are to be used, and b) who are to be the agents of enforcement. While the CRB is at work, it is still primarily the head's responsibility to enforce the rules and until the CRB can come up with a justified alternative, he should act in the usual manner and continue to require teachers and existing student 'officials' such as prefects to act as enforcers.

At this point it is worthwhile to be clear about sanctions, penalties, and punishment. It is a confusing but crucial area and can support or sabotage all other attempts at discipline.

The first distinction to be made is between two types of 'wrong' for it is only when a person is seen to have done 'wrong' that he is in line for punishment. One concept of 'wrong' is opposed to 'right' in a moral sense. That is, an action can be somehow intrinsically right or wrong in a good/bad sense. Another concept of 'wrong' is the opposite of 'to get it right' as one would get a maths question right by following appropriate rules and procedures. Both senses have application in school situations but we must distinguish with the students which is which.

School rules are there for a specific practical purpose and must be followed if they are to have any point at all. However it is not necessary to claim that they are morally good rules (Wilson, 1972). They happen to be the ones chosen to enable teachers and students to get on with the job. They simply are *the* rules. To break a rule is therefore 'to get it wrong' and is not necessarily to 'be wrong' in any moral sense. This is where a lot of trouble starts. Students, often understandably, don't see the point of certain rules and can even make a strong case for their being 'wrong' in a moral sense, e.g. rules which stifle individuality. Assuming that the rules they attack are defective in the way they say, and ought, strictly speaking, to be changed, then the students can be considered morally 'right' to break the rules but 'wrong' in the second sense just the same. All this points to the importance of the Appeal Procedure as a device for a) ensuring that the school rules do have point, or b) changing them if they don't. Reasonable students will not object if the rules make sense; they will if there is an unjustified moral claim *about* the rules. It is an educative task for the staff to see that the Appeal Procedure functions and that students learn to reason legitimately in this area.

In deciding about sanctions, whether or not there should *be* any is not in question since it is easily shown that without sanctions, the rules simply would not stand. The question is rather what kinds of sanctions to have. This can only be answered with reference to the purpose of having sanctions — which is to uphold the rules.

A point to clear up is whether or not it is the purpose of sanctions to act as deterrents. This is often claimed but is partly mistaken. When arguing that sanctions should or do deter, it is important to specify what it is people are being deterred *from*. A close look shows that those who are deterred from committing a particular wrong act because of a particular sanction are in fact deterred from the *sanction* and only indirectly (if at all) from the wrong act. It is the unpleasantness they wish to avoid and so they conform. Mistakenly we take this conformity to mean they have 'learned' to act rightly and we miss the point altogether. Sanctions as deterrents are short-cuts to acceptable conduct. We get the desired conduct all right, but for all the wrong reasons. As educators we should be alarmed — not satisfied.

It is important to be sure that the sanctions are there to uphold the rules and that that is all they are there for. Although we may not intend sanctions to act as deterrents, it is true that they will for some. But this is not a connection we need to emphasize or even encourage. We want to focus on the act itself, and particularly on the reasons why the act is right or wrong. We miss the target if we focus instead on the penalty *for* the act.

Before thinking of specific sanctions, it is well to consider how the concept of 'punishment' fits in here. Too often punishment is equated with discipline, deterrents, reform, and penalties. Many claims are made about the justified use of punishment in schools — but all are arguable. For example it is claimed that punishment is necessary a) when other remedies fail; b) to ensure order so that others can learn; c) because it is the only thing difficult students understand; d) because teaching conditions make the job impossible; e) as an aid to moral learning; f) not as a reformative but as a deterrent; and g) as a way of maintaining discipline. But these are only claims made as if out of desperation.

To say that punishment is necessary for these purposes is to suggest that it is a reliable method. When all else fails we use punishment as if 'that'll surely do it'. And yet we readily admit that punishment fails. It seems that the claims are excuses and not justifications at all.

Furthermore, there are very clear arguments against the use of punishment in schools. For example, how can we possibly justify a) treating violence with violence, b) attempting to decrease aggression by being agressive, and c) education based on fear? Only in desperation do educators find they must disregard these points and punish anyway. Results are poor either because it doesn't work and the situation is worse than before, or it *looks* as though it worked when in fact it merely produced superficial conformity and for all the wrong reasons.

There is a sense in which it is not logically possible to banish punishment from schools, for whether or not something counts as punishment is not entirely up to the punisher to determine. We can punish and have it 'not come off', as when the wrongdoer treats the so called punishment as a status symbol. Or we can unintentionally punish as when a child bursts into tears at the mere question, 'Why did you do that?' If anything is to really count as punishment, surely the wrongdoer must see and feel it *as* punishment and not just react to the inconvenience or the pain.

We waste time if we try to use punishment as an extrinsic disciplinary device. What we really want to do is get people to think and be reasonable about their actions and a sure way to prevent this from happening is to hit them either physically or figuratively.

Alternatively, the concept of 'penalties', as different from 'punishment', is more appropriate. When a hockey player is sent to the penalty box for two minutes he realizes the negative consequence of his having broken a rule. Whether or not he likes the rule or considers it justified is not in dispute at that time. There are rules committees to handle that aspect of the question later. He broke the rule so he must pay the price. Whether or not he feels ashamed or punished is not the point of the penalty for the penalty was given to uphold the rule — not to shame the player. Whether or not he reflects on the wisdom of his action is not the point either for the penalty was not given to teach him anything (although it may have done). If shaming, punishing, and teaching the player are necessary, it will be a job for the coach and later. It is not a job either for the referee or for the rule book.

The concepts of punishment and penalty share common ground but it is important to realize they are different. Both entail the three logical conditions of: 1) intentional infliction of unpleasantness, 2) infliction on someone for a breach of rules, and 3) infliction by someone in authority (Peters, 1966). Both are retributive by definition. But punishment also implies a further self-conscious element which is absent from the concept of penalties. It seems clear that penalties (and not punishments) are what we want for school purposes. They are objective and to the point in a way that punishments are not. Their function is merely to uphold the rules and not to pass moral judgement, deter (although they may do this), or reform.

This is not to say we should avoid the aspects that punishment tries to reach. We do want people to reflect on their actions, to think, and to be reasonable. But these are the specific tasks of 'education' and are not the territory of punishment alone. In fact the many inhibiting aspects of punishment work against the very task and are reason enough for sticking to positive educative methods. When all other methods fail we must find out what went wrong — we must not evade the real issues and merely hit back.

Much emphasis will have to be on talk, by this account; and this is full of pitfalls too. Just as pupils can walk away laughing from the cane, so can they avoid taking 'just talk' seriously. It is therefore up to educators to become expert in the techniques of discussion, argument, and reason so that it isn't 'just talk'. We teach others to reason not just by doing it ourselves but by showing them what it is to reason and by requiring them to practise.

If the logical points of penalties as different from punishment are clear, then the task of drawing up actual penalties should be fairly straightforward. The important thing is that they be unpleasant, inconvenient, and predictable. If some are found to be inneffective, the Appeal Procedure can always be used to bring in alternatives. There need not be much worry about the actual content of the penalty — what the culprit must do — as long as it is unpleasant. (For example, objections to 'writing lines' as a penalty are much stronger than they need be. Penalties are meant to be a waste of time and are not meant to be educative. Who ever learned much in a detention hall or polishing trophies either for that matter?) The educative side of things should be saved for educative times, places, and techniques. Meanwhile the minimal requirement of a penalty is simply that it should 'cost' something to have broken the rule.

As to the question of restitution, that too should not be confused with penalties or punishment. It should be dealt with as a completely separate issue which has its own justification. Having to replace a broken object is not part of what it means to be punished or penalized. It is just fair.

Finally, who should enforce the rules? By virtue of the fact that students, through the CRB, have at least agreed *to* (not necessarily agreed *with*) the rules and penalties, they should in some capacity share the responsibility for enforcement. An aspect to take seriously however is the difficulty for students to enforce rules and penalties on peers and friends. A clearly defined position of 'authority to enforce rules' will go some way in helping but it is a mistake to think it will solve the problem. Similarly, clearly publicized rules and sanctions will help. But students will need all the support they can get.

Since the purpose of school is 'to educate' and teachers are 'educators', then the participation of teachers in all phases of school discipline logically follows. If the proposed arrangement is to succeed, then in addition to normal teaching duties, teachers will be expected to a) contribute to stages of the Appeal Procedure either in staff meetings, as staff representative on the CRB, or as an 'auditor' at CRB meetings, b) know the rules and penalties, c) recognize breaches of rules and apply sanctions fairly, and d) support student 'authorities' in their attempts to enforce rules. A further task, and one that is specific to the role of educator, is to spend time and energy talking to students. One person cannot handle this aspect alone and some teachers will be better at it than others; but what is clear is that no teacher can logically claim that it is not his job.

A head may find that, justified or not, some teachers refuse to co-operate. This is serious because it can affect the morale of the entire teacher group. If it doesn't destroy others' willingness to participate, it will tend to weaken their enthusiasm. Therefore, in the interests of getting on with the job and not letting it grind to a halt, he must take specific measures. One thing he can do is to 'institutionalize' the 'rule enforcers' somehow so that it is clear which authorities are and which are not 'rule enforcers'. Thus a reluctant teacher would qualify as an authority in his field but not necessarily elsewhere. This will make life difficult for him but at least it will enable others to carry on effectively.

We have 'discipline problems' in schools because we are not all that sure a) what discipline really is, b) how to teach about it as well as whether to teach to submit to it, c) what arrangements to make in schools to promote it without stifling or alienating the students, and d) whose job is it to do all this. That discipline is an 'empty' concept, at once specific and non-specific, accounts partially for the muddle. On the other hand, that discipline is an 'empty' concept also enables educators to prescribe specifically for their own situation as reasonably as possible and maintaining a minimal standard of order and/or restriction. The measures I have outlined are positive and constructive and should be applicable in any secondary school. It is naive, however, to regard an Appeal Procedure and/or a Critical Review Board as a panacea for pressing discipline problems. These can only be effective *aids* and only if implemented successfully by the people involved. What I have tried to show is how it is possible to structure the 'outside-class' area of school life so that it can be developed into a most valuable educative arena in which to play an all important discipline-game.

References

PETERS, R.S. (1966) *Ethics and Education*. London: Allen & Unwin;
WILSON, J.B. (1972) *Practical Methods of Moral Education*. London: Heinemann Educational Books.

Discipline

Peter Newell

What, if anything, has discipline got to do with education? It has certainly got a lot to do with traditional schooling, but the relationship between education and schooling is by no means straightforward, and it could well be that the aspects of schooling which come under the general heading of discipline are the most anti-educational.

It all depends, of course, on what one sees as the aims of education. My views, and those of the people I work with in the White Lion Street Free School obviously cloud our feelings about traditional 'discipline'. In brief, we see education as aiming at the development for the individual of his capacity for real choice and control within his life. Anything which limits this development is therefore anti-educational.

To start from an average secondary school situation, and proceed to suggest institutional ways of adapting it without changing the structure, as Miss Kyle has done seems to me to be an ineffective strategy for change. I prefer to look at those things which cause discipline problems in traditional schools, to what extent they are real-life rather than institutional problems, and how they are likely to be remedied.

I can think of seven basic ones. Of course that is not a comprehensive list (there will be plenty of rich research grants around for those who wish to complicate the field still further).

1. Compulsion

'It shall be the duty of the parents of every child of compulsory school age to cause him to receive efficient full-time education suitable to his age, ability and aptitude, either by regular attendance at school or otherwise' (1944 Education Act, Section 36).

If the energies of succeeding armies of politicians, administrators and others had been directed as much at 'otherwise' as they have been at 'school', we might well not be in quite such a mess as we are. As spokesmen for the National Association of Schoolmasters and others **remind us all too frequently**, a whole lot of discipline 'problems' would disappear instantly if the attendance regulations were removed or modified. The continuing row over the raising of the leaving age to 16 would clearly be solved overnight if all those unwilling and aggressive 15 year-olds didn't have to be there. The argument for **compulsory schooling beyond, say, 13, is that the already deprived in** terms of social background would be the ones to suffer if they were deprived of schooling too, and laid open to the pressures of the unscrupulous employer or parent.

It was an argument that held a lot more weight in 1890 than it does now. That it still holds any weight is mostly due to the fact that the laws have led the school system to monopolize vast resources to become an industry with its own momentum which thwarts the development of freely available and realistic educational resources outside schools.

Plenty of others have written in great detail about the anti-educational effects of compulsion; have compared the excited, questioning approach of the pre-school child with the apathy and reluctance of the majority of secondary school pupils; have described the artificiality of the relationship between teacher and taught which forces both to obey external laws on when learning should start and stop, prolonging some experiences way beyond the point of boredom, and cutting others short just because the bell has gone or term has ended.

The attendance laws, just because they are there, can so easily overshadow the real motivation for learning. The lesson which the majority of children get from them is that learning is not their responsibility, but something other people are trying to do for them, and that it is unpleasant. The compulsion of the attendance laws is reflected in school in compulsory timetables ('options' are always limited), in the rigid divisions between learning and holidays.

Where there is compulsion, there will inevitably be discipline problems. Up to now the school system has just about been able to contain them, developing intricate theories and new professionalisms to explain truancy, and turning a blind eye to the occasional unmourned escapee. But there is every sign that containment is not a long-term policy for survival.

2. The size of teaching groups

There is so much agreement on this one that it shouldn't need saying any more. But it does. We all know that keeping between 15 and 40 lively young minds stuck in a succession of rooms for most of their school life with a single adult resource is a recipe for anything but the improvement of minds. So what do we do about it? The answer for the vast majority of schools is little or nothing, and certainly nothing which will threaten the position of the professionally trained teacher. Educational administrators have decided to use their manpower resources in a way which makes individualization of education more or less impossible. Because of rigid hierarchies and professional restrictive practices, the manpower actually used to help children's learning is very limited. The cult of professionalism inhibits people, and particularly parents, from helping themselves and their children. Communities have vast resources for learning and for self-help. But all too often the schools and the professionals within them are so inflexible and unwelcoming that they remain untapped.

To take an example, the manpower fully employed in the schools level of the education service in London gives a ratio of adults to children of well under one to ten. If you include all those employed in agencies for young people outside schools, and also those who would like to be involved in children's learning experiences if the institutions were flexible enough to have them, the whole talk of ratios becomes meaningless.

The reduction of class sizes has obsessed educationists for years now, but the only 'solution' which has been pursued with any enthusiasm is trying to professionally train enough teachers to reduce it. We all know that we will never be able to afford to beat the problem that way. So the majority of teachers continue to allow themselves to be put in an impossible situation for most of their teaching time. The discipline problems that result are ironically usually put down to inadequate training.

3. Size of schools

Experience seems to have established that any large institution which is held together as much by compulsion as by common interest generates insensitive rules and regulations, which in turn imply sanctions. Secondary education has for some years been blindly following the proposition that the only way forward from the end of **overt selection at eleven was to pursue equality of opportunity by putting** all the 'opportunities' together in bigger and bigger buildings. It does not take a genius, or even Paul Goodman to see that that is not the only way of doing things. The extreme strain put on both adults and children in trying to make these huge impersonal institutions work is obvious in any urban area. There are some hopeful signs in London and elsewhere that at long last size is being seriously questioned. But such is the investment in plant that administrators will inevitably look for any other reason for failure first.

Running a big school, like a big factory implies intricate timing and a high degree of conformity. When the workers are individual and hopefully alert children, the result can only be discipline problems.

4. Imposition of a particular value system

For some of course this is what education is all about. Rules that arise from a belief that one's own standards of dress, language, etc. are right and should be imposed on children probably cause more conflict and waste more time in schools now than anything else. Head teachers' obsession with length of hair is probably the most common example. Where they bother to defend it, probably the most thoughtful defence is that in the absence of regulations about hair length, dress codes, etc., it is not individual judgement that takes over, but the commercial dictates of fashion. It is a very short-sighted defence. Surely the reason why commercial interests can play such absurd games with young people is that conformity has become a virtue at the expense of individuality?

The education system within its basically compulsory context, has reinforced this. Young people who have been able to develop minds of their own will not wear shoes that cripple their feet, clothes that distort their bodies. It is precisely because they have not been given the responsibility of real choice, that they are unable to exercise it when confronted by commercial pressures. In encouraging conformity, the schools are working in line with the most cynical of the fashion makers and breakers.

Education defined as the imposition of a value system is propaganda, and inevitably requires authoritarian structures if it is to succeed. Few teachers would admit to this sort of aim; most pay at least lip-service to 'developing the individual'. But it is in their attitude to such apparently petty issues as the length of a child's hair that their real aims show through.

The conflicts that arise quite naturally when one person tries to impose their attitudes and standards on another become in a school situation discipline problems, because of the authority vested in the teacher and, again, because of the compulsion on the child.

The imposition of a pre-packaged curriculum based on academic theories of knowledge is all part of the same process. The aims of education have been lost sight of in the apparently justifiable struggle to get a defined body of useful information and skills across to as many people as possible in the shortest possible time. The contrast between the skills and information of use to people in their adult lives and the ones they can honestly say they learnt in school should be enough to make people rethink the process. And of course much of the theory of modern 'child-centred' education is the result of a rethink in the right direction. The trouble is that in most cases the context is such that child-centred education can only remain theoretical. Some skills (reading, writing, some aspects of numeracy, speech etc.) and some information are clearly basic to autonomous existence in the sort of society we live in. But that does not imply that coercion is going to help their learning, or that artificial packaging is going to make the learning more efficient.

The more centralized the planning of the curriculum becomes, the less sensitive it will be to the immediate learning needs of the individual child. That conflict, too, may result in more 'discipline problems'. Unfortunately all too often it only results in creeping apathy, and the loss of any desire to learn.

5. Discipline justified as protection

There are extremist libertarians around who dismiss this justification *in toto*, even when dealing with very small children. At the other end of the spectrum, there are the 'I am only doing this for your own good' school for whom adult knowledge and experience justifies a wide range of protective legislation – no smoking, no sweet eating, no fighting, etc.

This attitude in school is of course only a reflection of the dominant attitudes of **most politicians and legislators,** who for the sake of the good of 'ordinary people' (how often do you hear politicians on television contrasting their own, presumably extraordinary, personalities with us ordinaries?) propose and preserve a wide range of paternalistic laws: the censorship of books, films, plays, limitations of drinking hours, legislation covering private sexual behaviour, compulsory wearing of safety helmets, clothes, etc.

As this is in no sense a neutral academic essay, I should say now that I do believe in the need for adults to physically protect young children, and I am quite uncertain about the point at which this protective role becomes a damaging intrusion into the child's autonomy. Where there is uncertainty, there is a need for flexibility. Adults' intervention in school bullying, for instance, seems to me to be harmful when it is at the level of a form of bullying itself (the extreme absurdity being the teacher who canes for bullying – oh, yes, plenty still do). But it can be harmless when the people involved are already sufficiently close for a caring relationship to be meaningful – caring simply that someone one knows well is being hurt, and someone else one knows well is doing the hurting.

It is a dangerous theoretical type of statement, but I would maintain that in any particular school situation it is possible to define quite closely the difference between intervention aimed at preventing further violence, and intervention which is itself a form of violence.

'Protection' is in many ways the most invidious of the justifications for imposed discipline; in the short term it is often very difficult to refute. Children are thankfully naturally suspicious of it once they feel physically independent of their parents, which is why it, too, leads to 'discipline problems'.

6. 'Community necessity'

Living and working with other people implies a respect for their autonomy and happiness in return for their respect of yours.

Why should I pick up your sweet papers, do your share of the washing up? Self-discipline is the understanding and acceptance of the responsibilities of communal life. Why should this category cause discipline *problems*? Surely because society, and particularly school societies, don't pose the issues straight, but cloud them so darkly that it may actually seem extremely unnatural to a child to be asked to do his 'share' of the washing up. The hierarchical society which the school system so accurately reflects tends to minimize individual responsibility and make self-discipline an apparently irrelevant and out-dated concept.

Here again, it is the cult of professionalism that has done so much to undermine individual responsibility. The fragmentation of roles in the school — headmaster, secretary, class teacher, dinner lady, caretaker, youth worker, **counsellor, home visitor, cleaner,** — is there as a perpetual and effective teaching aid.

You cannot expect a child to play a responsible part in a community whose structure denies him and most of its other inmates any real responsibility. Judy Kyle ends: ' . . . . it is possible to structure the "outside-class" area of school life so that it can be developed into a most valuable educative arena in which to play an all-important discipline-game.' But it should not be a game, it should be a way of life which the child and adult have created together and which pervades every area of school life.

7. Conflict between home and school

In so far as this is merely schools finding that their teaching is in conflict with that of the home, it is covered by Category 4 — the imposition of a particular value system.

But not entirely. Family life frequently causes great unhappiness and strain in children as well as adults. Overcrowding, not enough money/food/sleep/warmth can provoke quite unreasonable and unexpected communal behaviour. However flexible the school situation, this can cause immediate 'discipline problems'. But they cease to be problems in the normal sense when the people — adults and children — involved know all the relevant facts. Then it is a case of judging to what extent communal life can be threatened for the good of the individual concerned, either in terms of the use of valuable time and resources on him rather than on others, or of a short-term reduction of communal responsibilities on him because of his other problems. A community's sensitivity is measured by its ability to share and work out problems together. In conventional school situations, confidentiality and the remoteness of most teachers from the reality of children's homes both work against this sort of sharing and working out. The result is often a short-cut disciplinary response to a complex situation.

II

'A load of theoretical idealism — how is all that going to help me in my classroom?'. The answer is that very often nothing is going to help the classroom situation — it is the context in which it exists that makes real change impossible.

The school has become such a highly developed institutional model, with so many highly developed supporting services, that it is often impossible to see outside it. And of course everyone now understands that the school's role as a reflection of society inhibits its role in changing society. Are there useful strategies for changing things radically, or should we all give up and get on — as most administrators are — with busily containing the situation and shoring up any cracks that appear with professional wallpaper?

Obviously those of us working at the White Lion Free School think there are strategies for changing things, and we do not think we have a monopoly of them. One strategy is to indicate that there are other ways of doing things, that the constraints that cause discipline problems and inhibit learning in conventional schools are not natural and can be removed or at least modified even within the existing educational law.

The 1944 Education Act, whatever its shortcomings, is a very flexible act, making possible a more or less limitless range of experiment, both within the maintained system and in the independent sector. There is no room here for a detailed description of our particular alternative model (that is published elsewhere).[1] But it is probably worth indicating briefly how we approach the seven basic 'causes' of discipline problems which I have listed.

Compulsion. There is no way round the basic requirement on parents to secure for their children full-time education. But there is nothing to stop schools treating attendance much more flexibly. By being open for a much higher proportion of the year, and for evenings and weekends, children can be given the possibility of attending for at least double the 400 'sessions' (mornings and afternoons) laid down as the minimum for maintained schools.

The real key to attendance of course is whether what one is offering is seen as relevant to the child — and the closer one's knowledge of the child's own experience, the more intricate a task that is.

Size of teaching groups. Removing the traditional hierarchy, and sharing the jobs that are part of communal living — cooking, cleaning, maintenance, administration, etc. — immediately provides a far better working ratio. The relationship with the family based on common interest in the child's development is a natural one, which, given time to develop, indicates the absurdity of the current fragmentation of family services. Tentative moves towards cooperation between social services and education show some official recognition of this, but progress is hampered by professional interests. We find ourselves fulfilling (in totally different ways of course) the traditional roles of social worker, education welfare officer, etc. This implies again an improved ratio if manpower were used differently. And finally, by being flexible and welcoming, we are open to a wide range of people with skills which they are anxious to use with children and other adults, given the resources and the base.

Size of schools. We at present have 50 children aged between 3 and 16, in the White Lion Free School, and developing adult activities. We don't believe this is necessarily a maximum size, but we do believe in the need for small local bases (not necessarily defined as only educational bases, but containing a wide range of community resources), 'serviced' by some centralized specialist resources (libraries, sports centres, laboratories, computers, etc).

Imposition of a particular value system. Of course there is a sense in which the absence of rules is a value system in itself. Teachers are not neutral, and it is artificial and inhibiting for them to pretend to be when playing curriculum games. But provided the setting in which they meet children is not a compulsory one, there is no imposition.

Working either individually or in very small groups, and having a close relationship with and knowledge of the family and the rest of a child's experience outside schools makes it possible to plan a 'curriculum' which really is based on their experience of the world and their learning needs. This removes the need to impose, for the sake of efficiency, a pre-packaged curriculum based on external theories. (Here of course there are no trite short-cuts: removing the constraints that so obviously inhibit effective learning in most large schools is easy compared with this task of building a curriculum based on individuals. In this everyone is a learner together.)

Discipline justified as protection. Here there can be no general rules. Justification should involve an explanation. There is obviously no simple age at which protection should always end. There are bound to be some occasions when adult experience justifies intervention before explanation. The essential, again, is to have a context in which discussion is possible, and in which adult decisions can be questioned.

'Community necessity'. A sense of responsibility and self-discipline only develops in a situation in which it can be used. A democratic structure of meetings with open agendas is a first essential, together with the removal of traditional hierarchies. The network of responsibilities which develops when any group of people try to do things together is then apparent to the child. Sharing decisions implies sharing information (on finance for instance it is important that everyone should understand the accounts, and how the money is spent). Given that large areas of society operate with a highly hierarchical system, children and adults are unlikely to adapt to full personal responsibility overnight. Conflicts will exist, and will have to be talked out. Short-cut sanctions will not help long-term development.

Conflict between home and school. Many of these conflicts occur through misunderstandings created by the distance between most teachers and most parents. The conventional structure of school-home and parent-teacher relationships often prevents the sharing of essential information. A teacher's concern for the development of a child gives him a legitimate reason for visiting families, and one which is very seldom resented. A school which is also a community resource centre, the headquarters of a local tenants association, etc., will involve parents as adults. Understanding and sharing in the education of their children can only follow this sort of involvement.

Discipline is not a side-issue in education: The current calls for more of it are the inevitable response of an out-dated school system trying desperately to contain an unworkable situation. Unless the debate is widened to question the assumptions of schooling, and how far they are in line with the real aims of education, the system will experience breakdown on an even wider scale.

Note
1 *White Lion Street Free School, Bulletin No. 2* (30p plus postage) details formation of the school. *White Lion Street Free School No. 3.* (40p plus postage, describes development up to June 1975). *How to Set Up a Free School — a Handbook of Alternative Education* (40p plus postage. All available from 57 White Lion Street, London, N.1.

Contract and Discipline in Society

Robert Lush

The concept of 'contract'

'Pacts', 'Contracts', 'Compacts', 'Solemn and Binding Undertakings': all these and many more words and phrases are used to describe varying embodiments of a single concept which, for the sake of simplicity, I will refer to as 'Contract'. It is difficult to define exactly the features common to every one of them but they have certain general characteristics. They involve an undertaking between one or more people or groups of people to carry out (or forbear to carry out) an action, in return for the other party to the contract carrying out their agreed undertaking. Reciprocity is essential, as is *some* form of sanction, for it to be a contract. The sanction can vary from mild social disapproval right up to a long term of imprisonment but without some sanction there is, in reality, no contract, but merely an agreement.

If one takes this rather wide (and not at all legalistic) view of contract and then examines the number of concealed contracts entered into daily, the results are revealing. Working and being paid, travelling by underground, using a telephone, playing a game of football, driving a car: all these, and many others, depend absolutely on quite complicated contractual conditions being observed by two parties. The contract is so basic to our society we hardly notice how much we depend on it, or rather how much we are dependent upon others to carry out their obligations under a contract. Take the examples above and imagine the results if one party fulfilled their side of the contract and the other party did not. Your employer, quite arbitrarily, refuses to pay your wages. The telephone, for which you have paid rent in advance, completely ceases to work. The opposing football team decide in the middle of the game to play according to some new rules they have just invented. As you drive, traffic approaches you at random on both sides of the road at whatever speed seems desirable to the driver.

This may seem patently obvious, but so many people act and argue as if it is *not* obvious to them that it is worth spelling out clearly. Is the idea of contract so important? Is it, perhaps, old-fashioned and out-of-date? Certainly the language of contract, particularly explicit contract, sounds archaic enough. Is there then some other system which could satisfactorily replace it?

Alternative contracts

There are really only three possible ways in which groups of people or individuals can act together to carry out a project requiring the co-operation of all of them: living in any society, from the most primitive to the most sophisticated, requires this co-operation. These are as follows:

(a) for the group to act together willingly, relying upon a continuing common motivation to carry out their part of the task;
or
(b) for the most powerful or the most charismatic individual to select the task, decide upon the course of action, and then either force, persuade or trick the other members of the group to carry it out;
or
(c) for the members of the group, having decided that the task is necessary or desirable, voluntarily to enter into contracts with each other so that each carries out his allotted part of the task.

There is a sense in which (a) and (c) are very similar and one might even argue they are identical, but I would like to make a distinction between a simple task, occupying a short period of time, in which each individual can see constantly the relationship between his task and the completion of the project, and a more complicated, long-term project, in which the individual task often appears unrelated to the aims of the project.

If one accepts this distinction between (a) and (c) then the first method (a) would undoubtedly be the best for short-term undertakings, but projects of this kind, though common in a family situation or primitive society, are less common in a more sophisticated world.

The second method is undoubtedly the worst. It is also, historically speaking, the most common. It has, I suppose, the one advantage that a task is actually performed, but as to which task, and at what cost, and for whose benefit, depends purely on the arbitrary decision of one individual or group. Clearly, this is the reverse of democracy.

It is the third method, adopted by most liberal societies, which seems to offer a combination of effectiveness and morality and seems most suited to a modern society of almost any political complexion.

Contracts in society

What then, is required for the third method? Firstly, that individuals entering into a contract are sufficiently intelligent and informed to realize the nature of the contract, 'thus exercising a real choice and control within their life'. Secondly, that they should *wish* to and physically be able to enter into a contract and, thirdly, that they are indeed 'freely' entering into the contract, without being subject to any unusual pressure such as, say, blackmail. They appreciate that they will not necessarily be expressing their personalities whilst carrying out their task; they will be accepting the discipline of the contract with open eyes. Ideally, it will be self-discipline but, failing that, discipline would be exercised from the outside by an *agreed* authority but still, and this is important, within the terms of the contract.

In the most developed type of contract sanctions are laid down in advance for infringements. For example, a contract to build a factory will include the date on which the work is to be completed. If this part of the contract is not honoured then 'damages' are deducted from the agreed price to be paid to the builder. Whether this is 'restitution' or 'punishment' I cannot say. Its object is certainly not to educate the builder, its object is to ensure that the contract is carried out. Whether the builder is governed by fear or by a feeling of self-discipline is just not relevant. It is worth noting that in this type of developed contract provision is always made for who should enforce the rules. The arbitrator is agreed by both parties before the contract is made. The arbitrator is not one of the contracting parties.

Seldom, sadly, does this ideal form of contract exist outside the world of commerce. People are not really freely 'entering into the contract'. They are under the pressure of hunger, say, to enter a contract of employment which underpays them. They are misled by ignorance or by advertising pressure to enter into hire purchase agreements whose terms they cannot possibly meet. With nowhere to live they agree to pay rents they cannot afford. But, even if the ideal contract is a rarity, I still maintain that one must choose between 'contract' and either paternalism in any one of its many guises including, of course, state paternalism, on the one hand, and the arbitrary exercise of authority by the strong on the other. Perhaps more time and effort should be devoted to creating a society in which the pressures which make the contract un-free should be ameliorated, and less time and effort to devising ways out of the contract.

Contract in education

What has this to do with education? If there were agreement on the importance of contract then one would like to see people leaving school or university having a strong feeling for its importance and, since it is not a feeling with which one is born, then it is presumably acquired both at home and at school during the period between the ages of, say, five and twenty and therefore ought to form part of the educational system, either as a subject or as a method. This could possibly form part of the curriculum as a special subject or, perhaps better, could be introduced into the study of history, especially the history of Western Europe and the Industrial Revolution, but it would be much more valuable if ways could be found to introduce the notion of contract into the day to day running of a school and into innumerable 'concealed contracts' between pupil and pupil and pupil and teacher. But this could only be achieved if teachers themselves were convinced of its importance.

Now if Peter Newell would regard this 'respect for contract' as part of a value system, then I suppose I am in favour of propaganda. Education must always be a mixture between 'developing the individual' and strongly suggesting (if not imposing) a value system, however, basic, and however undetailed. Indeed, by stating as his aim the development for the individual of his capacity for real choice and control within his life, he has already created just such a value system. One only has to imagine how that aim would be considered by, say, a nineteenth century Prussian landowner, a medieval saint, or an old-fashioned Marxist, to realize just how particular, Western and modern a value system it is. In fact, here Peter Newell has, I feel, rather evaded the issue. Length of hair, standard of dress, etc., are not really what is meant by value system though they may be rather remote expressions of its unimportant fringes. A value system is, surely, to do with some basic notions of desirable and undesirable behaviour, however unspecific, and I feel it would be difficult for anyone, especially for any teacher, not to have arrived at some position on this. The work of John Wilson and others in this area has been devoted to arriving at just such a non-partisan value system, and both the Warborough Trust and the Social Morality Council are continuing to advance this work.

Not being concerned professionally with education, any view I might have on an attempt to introduce a feeling for contract in schools is merely that of a layman. However, I do detect three problems. Firstly, the contract to be educated is not, and cannot, be voluntary on the part of the pupil. Cannot, because at the age at which the contract starts, few people would say the child was capable of making a real contract because he cannot reasonably assess its demands or understand the consequences of the alternative. Secondly, society has ordained, rightly in my view, that education should be compulsory for a certain term of years. Thirdly, that the arbitrator of this 'contract to be educated' is one of the contracting parties.

However, it seems to me that the terms of the problem change as between kindergarten and university. The contract for the latter is, firstly, voluntary in that education at university age is no longer compulsory and, because of the free nature of the decision and the age at which it is taken, it would seem fair that the discipline with this contract to be educated should be stronger and more formal. In the kindergarten, the concept of protection by authority seems more necessary. Between these two lies the area where the 'contract to be educated' starts. The question is how, and when?

An historical perspective

Morality has been described as how we behave to people we do not like and it is this same idea which gives contract its particular value. One does not have to love or even like the other party in a contract but one must respect their autonomy. In fact, the very qualities which modern educational theory seeks to develop seem to point clearly to their suitability for a contractual society. It is just the word 'discipline' which sticks in the throat. Perhaps it is the old-fashioned idea of discipline, which was, more accurately, the exercise of arbitrary power, with which people disagree, but one should beware of throwing out the baby with the bathwater.

We live, at the moment, in a 're-negotiating' society. By this I mean that, in politics and business, the inviolability of contract is constantly under pressure. Marriage without divorce is one sort of contract. Marriage with divorce by consent is another. Ministers talk quite happily about re-negotiating contracts which have already been signed. A contract to give up possession of a flat after seven years is revised by a later law. All this is done for the best possible reasons, and, in most cases, is a necessary reform, but we should beware of making the dangerous assumption that because a thing is ninety per cent good it is also one hundred per cent good.

Constantly, then, the idea of the importance of contract in society is being eroded but one should perhaps look at history to understand some of the dangers implicit in this. The evolution towards a liberal and democratic society, if one looks at this progress as it is exemplified by the changes in legal system, can be described, quite simply, as the slow increase of contract law at the expense of imperative law. A primitive society could, without too much oversimplification, be described as one in which the majority of the people were debarred from entering into contracts at all.[1] Authority, personified by the head of the tribe, the king or the priest, made contracts of a sort with other heads, kings or priests, which bound the majority, who took no part in the decision making.

But slowly, and by no means smoothly, the notion that free men could make bargains between each other, which neither advantaged nor disadvantaged the state, began to take hold, and as these other bargains became more and more important to the commercial life of society so the state became the 'discipline exercising' authority. This I see both as the beginning and as the *sine qua non* of liberal society. It is the very opposite of paternalism and treats people as free and autonomous individuals, capable of exercising choice, making decisions and abiding by them. The progress of contract has, of course, had its disadvantages. Its historical association with puritanism and, later, with *laissez faire* capitalism, has caused people to think that it is an uncaring and unfeeling system. To an extent this is true and is both its great advantage and its weakness. The feudal manor was an almost perfect model of an 'involved and caring society' but it lacked almost totally social mobility and its members, other than the lord of the manor, had very little freedom or autonomy. If we are then to have a society in which people are to create their own roles and make their own decisions then, its terms hedged about by laws, its sanctions limited by statutes, only contract offers a method of progress.

One is left with the paradox that it is not the undisciplined, free, unauthoritarian society which is really free but the one in which free people accept both discipline and authority in the common cause.

Note

1 'The point which before all others has to be apprehended in the constitution of primitive societies is that the individual creates for himself few or no rights, and few or no duties. The rules which he obeys are derived first from the station into which he is born, and next from the imperative commands addressed to him by the chief of the household of which he forms a part. Such a system leaves the very smallest room for Contract. The members of the same family (for so we may interpret the evidence) are wholly incapable of contracting with each other, and the family is entitled to disregard the engagements by which any of its subordinate members has attempted to bind it . . . The positive duty resulting from one man's reliance on the word of another is among the slowest conquests of advancing civilisation.'

MAINE , Sir Henry J. Summer, *Ancient Law*, London: Dent.

Discipline and Contract in Schools

Brenda Thompson

'Zounds. I am bethumped with words', Shakespeare has someone say, and you know the feeling! You realize that words need discipline. They need to be kept within bounds. Defer to them and they fly out of control. Restrict them and they become as droopy as battery hens. Abstract words are the most temperamental of all.

The word 'discipline' which we are studying, is an emotive one, especially in educational circles. Some people too readily allow their thoughts to be coloured by the emotional associations the word has for them. Others try too solemnly to distil the quintessential meaning of the word. Either way the word becomes mistaken for the thing. The way to avoid this mistake is to set the word against real backgrounds, to show the concept in action. I believe it will be helpful to keep a fairly broad canvas. The 'discipline problem' shows up differently in the setting of 'learning', 'teaching', 'society' and 'education'. Let us be on our guard against narrow and lazy habits of thought that ignore these levels of reality, for example offering 'social' solutions to 'educational' problems, assuming 'teaching' is the corollary of 'learning', or even that 'learning' takes place only within 'education'.

My viewpoint is that of 'a teacher', but since reading Peter Newell's paper I think of myself as 'a single adult resource' which gives me strength to handle the theory.

Society
Man is a social animal. Educational theorists tend to overlook this truism, accepting that man is social but inclined to disregard his animal nature. Isn't it curious how the study of life has such a lowly place in education? Biology is for girls and the C stream. Plenty of descriptions exist of the way our highly organized and pre-ordained society is closer to the birds and bees than we usually admit. Official education

proclaims loftily ideals of social duty and transcendental individualism, but is uncertain in respect of social relations and group behaviour. Too rarely is it acknowledged that education is a natural and integral part of society, made of the same tricky stuff. It is not some self-conscious outgrowth.

As society moves, education moves. As society is competitive, so is education competitive. As society is co-operative, so education is co-operative. As society becomes more bureaucratic, this is faithfully reflected in education. Education belongs to society the way the spots belong to the leopard. Therefore, attempting to use the education system to revolutionize society is like trying to use the spots to reform the leopard.

Do we then resign ourselves to sneezing when society sneezes? I do not wish to appear too fatalistic. I am simply against making excessive moral and physical demands on education, schools and teachers. I don't believe schools should embrace everything from pre-natal clinics to old folks' homes. It is equally absurd to ask teachers to be Dr Finlay and Father Brown rolled in one. I am totally against education being made the scapegoat for a 'discipline problem', and against its exploitation by Left or Right for political purposes. I believe schools should be places of ideas and understanding, not arsenals of dogma and ideology.

Of course schools will have to change to take care of discipline. They must become more aware of social change. But I see no need for social solutions. In my opinion the cause of· indiscipline is boredom and the answer to it will be found in the direction which Mr Newell sneers at, that of more, not less, 'professionalism'.

Learning

Man is a social animal. No harm in reminding you. If you agree with the statement you will agree that most of man's learning is social. Learning is a cradle-to-grave affair. Our formal education, even the self-teaching we do, forms only a small fraction of the ceaseless learning that comes from our contact with words and people and things, and their countless interactions. Would-be reformers sense this and say 'Wouldn't it be better if education were more to do with **'real-life'**.' I maintain that education is already a part of 'real-life'. The greater danger is to suppose that our vast social learning can be somehow annexed to the education system, even if it does mean ditching a few academic values. This leads you to make an arbitrary and picturesque selection from 'real-life' and you come up with the idea of the 'community' school. Society is simplified at a stroke into a Tin Pan Alley notion of 'friends and neighbours'. Yes by all means schools and education offices should be on good term with their neighbourhood and the parents should be closely involved. But when good communications and diplomacy are turned into a self-conscious and elaborate doctrine of 'community education' things are stood on their head. Children go on educational visits to supermarkets they've been to 'for real' with Mum. They study the local streets they already know like the back of their hands. The pure gold of everyday life is transmuted into the base metal of the school essay. This heavy footed, patronizing approach to the community has been aptly described by Rhodes Boyson. Community schools, he says, would be 'game reserves preserving a local species through centrally appointed game wardens'.[1]

Peter Newell tells us 'Communities have vast resources for learning and self-help. But all too often the schools and the professionals within them are so inflexible and unwelcoming that they remain untapped.' There's that red rag word again, professionals. Once you walk through the school gates you apparently cease to be a member of a community, living in a house, talking to people, shopping at the local grocers, drinking at the local pub and so on. The professional trap springs shut and you are transformed into a pitiless agent of alienation. Now I don't think you can use the word 'professional' as a term of rebuke if you simply mean a member of a profession or a paid performer. You must mean 'professional' in the loose sense people are using the word these days to denote a degree of competence. Now what is it about being rather good at your job of teaching that produces the Jekyll and Hyde effect? Logically we are led to believe that not being a very good teacher makes you better at running community education.

My experience in the field tells me that a parochial and sentimental view of community which ignores social trends and differences, has no validity. We are moving rapidly into a society where both parents take a job, where there are more one-parent families. Working parents are free neither in the day, nor in the **evenings** when they do the household chores or put their feet up. They are pleased to leave the children in the safe care of the school which acts as much as a child-minding service as an educational force. I am sceptical of parents coming into the school as educators. They lack the teacher's stock in trade of being able to handle groups of children and describe things coherently. And let's face it, it is parents not teachers who keep the educational rat race going. Even though it is becoming less probable that qualifications will lead to a better job with more pay, this is still a powerful motive. Even stronger is the feeling that there is something beyond money — attractive and enviable life-styles. Teachers will stress the cultural side of this, parents the material side. Either way a model life-style is unlikely to reflect traditional community values. Prolonged education produces cosmopolitan values, for good and ill. We may be clever enough one day to recreate small communities so **that people will not have** to rush about in their cars and pile into big cities. I am not impressed with the simplistic and nostalgic sketches of the new community that have come from educational reformers. In particular I dislike the idea of rechristening a school as 'a community resources centre' and giving the key to all kinds of odd people. I speak from jaundiced experience, I am afraid, since intensive use of our school by 'the community' resulted in theft, destruction and unpleasant mess.

Vandalism is the most disturbing problem of our age because we see it as 'mindless'. We see in big cities it can escalate into rioting and street warfare. But vandalism is not mindless. It has a mind of its own, a code of honour. There are two twisted virtues common to vandals, whether they are Manchester United fans on the rampage or bands of thugs in Northern Ireland. They are fiercely loyal to their group. They respond to leadership. We are dealing with a perverted tribalism that is the dark side of the community. (The Vandals after all were a tribe on the loose.) We must not lose sight of how harsh and arbitrary the tribe can be. I remember an incident in Laurie Lee's autobiography *Cider with Rosie* where the amiable village milkman is shunned, hounded from his job and the village by the community, and all because he happened to witness two fatal accidents within a few days of each other.[2]

I think there is a risk in merging schools too completely into the local community. Schools deserve their own identity and loyalty so that they can more easily offset the tribal views that prevail locally, and can assert different and wider values. It is in reconciling several loyalties that we become reasonable civilized human beings, able to balance the desire to belong and the desire for self-assertion.

Teaching

A useful witness at this point is a US educationalist, Jonathon Kozol, who from being an outright enthusiast for free schools started to have second thoughts. 'Too many of us are frightened of the accusation of being headstrong, tough, authoritarian ... In an effort to avoid the standard brand of classroom tyranny that is identified so often with the **domineering figure of the professional in the public system, innovative** free school teachers often make the grave mistake of reducing themselves to ethical and pedagogical neuters.'[3] An aimless reaction to what Peter Newell calls the 'cult of professionalism' **(Goodness,** what brutes of schoolmasters these people must have had!) can seemingly lead to a sterile cult of failure and drabness. For, says Kozol, 'an organization ... that identifies real excellence, effectiveness, or compelling life-style with the terrifying ring of despotism and authoritarian manipulation will ... drive away all interesting, brilliant and exhilarating people and will establish in their stead norms of communal mediocrity. The label reserved for those who do not learn to respect these norms is "ego-tripper".'

Do not allow these heartfelt words to scare you into the clutches of the Black Paper gang. **Stay as clear from bogus authority** as you do from bogus freedom. Remember the old Bernard Miles story where the vicar leans over the garden gate and says to the cottager, 'What a splendid job you and the Lord have made of this garden!' 'Aye', says the yokel, 'But you **shoulda seen it when** He had it to Hisself!' There are no magic formulas.

I am convinced the problem of discipline in schools can be solved by a more professionally 'green-fingered' approach. Some critics imagine 'more professionalism' as more spit and polish, a closing of the ranks against outside ideas and influences. Let us be on our guard against conservative attitudes and try to build on the strengths of professionals: their commitment, their pride, their caring and their concern for standards. The weakness of their position unfortunately is that they are at the mercy of politicians and employers who dictate what the educational product should be. As a result, teachers themselves have become a source of social disaffection or have shrunk into their academic shells. My hope lies in the great strides that have been made in progressive primary teaching. Before I describe our best efforts, that **may hold the key to more powerful and effective education,** (while *incidentally* solving the discipline problem) allow me to anticipate criticism and describe our worst mistake.

People such as myself who have campaigned and worked for freedom in primary education receive **rather grudging praise** from the avant-garde, less it seems for our achievements than for our 'child-centred' approach. Unfortunately, a lot of people interpret the propaganda as meaning an exaggerated deference to children's whims, in chaotic conditions, by a self-effacing teacher. We have more to fear from our friends than our enemies. A teacher who in the name of freedom relinquishes leadership is asking for trouble. An unrelenting law of nature makes sure that every group is dominated by someone. In the absence of leadership by the teacher a child will take over. Sometimes with most unpleasant results. A formal system of teaching makes it a lot easier to see who is boss, although it does not guarantee it by any means. An informal system can much more easily provide positive reasons for accepting the teacher's leadership.

Informal classrooms make strict but invigorating demands on the teachers and the children: Things must be made interesting. There must be variety, versatility and plenty of surprises. Therefore everything must be planned and no single activity should exceed children's attention span (adult attention can be held for at best about twenty minutes). The proceedings must seem effortless but never appear to drift; they have to be 'orchestrated' by the teacher. Everybody must be aware of the unwritten rules that govern movement and transfer of activities. Everyone has to set his own priorities but can work at his own speed. The teacher encourages talking and teamwork. Materials must be copious and arranged in an orderly way. There must be exciting output and plenty of praise.

Kid's stuff? Reflect on the absence of some of these simple criteria in the higher spheres of learning. Colossal levels of boredom and resentment may be built up when no concentrated effort is made to create interest; when learning is not a planned activity and teachers flounder; when 'lessons' are always predictable and monotonous; when sitting still in silence is a prime virtue and it is a crime to talk, to consult other children, move about or to finish something you started; when there are no interesting books, objects, pictures, or displays in the classroom; when 'work' is a never ending process with no output day-to-day or week-to-week of which you can be proud; when everybody is always doing the same thing; when the teacher always speaks to you at a distance greater than that of normal human conversation.

I should like to see a senior classroom as exhilarating as a busy and effective primary classroom on an integrated day. But what a lot of technique will have to be acquired! Is it possible that bad discipline is in fact the way that children punish teachers for their bad technique? Cast your mind back to your own schooldays. What sort of teachers had discipline problems? You remember the unpopular ones included the soft, creepy ones as well as the martinets. On balance however, tough teachers were preferred to soft teachers. Generally it was the young and inexperienced teachers who got 'the treatment'. I have laid stress on planning and preparation because this reduces the number of *situations* leading to conflict, loss of confidence, disappointment and disillusion. But style and personality must enter into it. The teacher has a role as leader as I have noted, but also as an actor playing to an audience - not just 'public speaking' but being able to amuse and shock, knowing how to overcome self-consciousness, how to use one's eyes, how to disguise or feign emotions, how to gain and hold attention. In the theatre the audience is different every night. In school the audience is the same every day so it is a difficult task and one which has been astonishingly neglected in teacher training. I believe all teachers should be given six months' drama training to give them techniques of handling people. Does that sound like too much professionalism? If we leave things to the 'born teachers' we shall be talking about six months' training in riot control!

Teachers complain that indiscipline in the classroom is imported from the 'no-man's land' of corridors and cloakrooms, stairs and playgrounds. Now if I have to give a single tip to secondary school teachers on the basis on my primary school experience, it is to make sure of being in the classroom ahead of the children to welcome them and direct them. Don't let them set the rules of occupation. What I think is essential is to have **ancillary** staff patrolling all common ground, such as stairs and corridors, where a lot of disorderly behaviour has its origin. Have you ever thought what a powerful idea is contained in the phrase 'to keep an eye on things'? Anyone interested in the effect of architecture and building design on the discipline problems of cities should read Jane Jacobs' famous book *Death and Life of Great American Cities*.[4] One of her themes is the social discipline and harmony brought about by the casual but constant supervision of all the 'eyes on the street', disastrously missing from high rise flats and perhaps from some anonymous comprehensive schools. We don't like to admit it but one of the foundations of morality is the fear of getting caught.

There comes a time when in spite of all your best efforts you must exert authority and administer punishment, knowing that failure to act decisively will store up trouble. Sometimes acting decisively in a classroom situation means handing out punishment quite arbitrarily. Consider the following real-life examples. A **five-year-old** boy went round the class cutting everyone's hair. He didn't see it was wrong. His classmates didn't particularly mind this hairdressing game. But he had to be forcibly stopped. What would you have done? You cannot always reason with five-year-olds on such matters. He was enamoured with cutting, the way a pyromaniac learns to love fire. He was ready to start on the clothes and the curtains. I mention this incident not so much to show that 'harmful' punishments may be unavoidable for 'harmless' crimes, but to draw attention to the implicit 'contracts' the teacher has to honour in his job. There is a 'contract' with the children, offering them protection against their own and other's worst instincts. There is a 'contract' with the parents to care for their children; a teacher is legally *in loco parentis*, a restraint that cannot be airily dismissed.

Perhaps one of the most important 'contracts' teachers have is with their beginning colleagues. The teaching body has a duty to embrace the enthusiasm and idealism that new teachers bring to the profession. In turn it has a responsibility to pass on to the recruits the practical techniques of classroom control. I am afraid neither side of this contract is well observed at present. The result is too many bruised and even damaged personalities among new teachers, and too many of them looking for freedom along the dangerous path of disgruntlement.

Education

If big city comprehensives did not have such a big turnover of young and **green** teachers would they have so many difficulties over discipline and morale? There might be less encouragement for the belief that educational problems demand social solutions. For if you study cases of indiscipline in schools, and you talk to children from problem comprehensives, as I have, you discover an important clue. It is that disruption rarely exceeds a certain limit. Face the fact that any group of children, even quite small ones, is more than a match for the most powerful teacher. But they do want to behave well and win respect. They would prefer not to rebel and be thrust into 'pack' behaviour. There exists what the biologist Wynne Edwards called 'the hereditary compulsion to comply',[5] the basis of 'the contract'. If we recognize this and build up our teaching techniques as I have suggested I believe we shall be well on the way to solving the discipline problem without recourse to dramatic upheaval. We should avoid another of the acrimonious debates that have distracted and disfigured education for too long. However, the inspiration must come from above and we need more than a lick and a promise. Here are my proposals.

First of all I suggest a moratorium on education-bashing and sensation-mongering about schools and teachers. Secondly, let us rebuild (by professional means) the status and self-esteem of teachers, to the level of their new salaries. Let us stop using teachers as social dogsbodies, and schools as social clinics. Then let it be officially recognized that teaching is a skill and a body of techniques that can be taught. Furthermore, let us carefully distinguish totally different problems that discipline represents when dealing with an individual, a small group, a whole class, an entire school. Discipline is not nasty green medicine, it is not the jack-booted classroom sadist, it is the respect we all owe each other.

Notes

1 BOYSON, R. (1974) *Oversubscribed*. London: Ward Lock Educational.

2 LEE, L. (1962) *Cider with Rosie*. Harmondsworth: Penguin.

3 KOZOL, J. (1973) 'Free schools - a time for candor', *Saturday Review*, 4th March.

4 JACOBS, J. (1972) *Death and Life of Great American Cities*. Harmondsworth: Penguin.

5 EDWARDS, V.C.W. Quoted by ARDREY, R., (1970) in *The Social Contract*. London: Collins.

Section Four

Religious Education in a Multi-Faith Society

'. . . Religious instruction shall be given
in every county school and every voluntary
school.'

1944 Education Act p.21,
Part II, Section 25(2).

Religious Education in a Pluralist Society

John M. Hull

What difference does it make when the society in which religious education takes place contains more than one religion?

Religious education as the nurture of faith

Religious education has usually been nurture into the religious traditions and beliefs of the educating society. This idea presents few difficulties when the society is unanimous about its religion. In Norway the religious education offered in the state schools is Lutheran. More than ninety-eight per cent of the population of Norway claims formal allegiance to the state Lutheran church. Whatever its merits, this is a perfectly straightforward situation.

But if the society is not unanimous about its religion, then there are problems. In the United States religion was denied access to the school. So diverse were the religious traditions that the school could not undertake the nurturing task on behalf of society and it was left to the individual religious communities to nurture their own young as they pleased. In Australia and New Zealand rivalry between Christian churches was intense, and since no single church was able to command a majority the schools systems became secular.[1] At a later date clergy were permitted to enter the schools and to nurture the young of their various persuasions in the classrooms. But the task to this day is not undertaken by the teachers.[2]

In England a compromise position was reached. The established church, unlike her Norwegian counterpart, did not command virtual unanimity. Even in Scotland, Presbyterianism, whether in its established or its dissenting forms, was sufficiently strong to make negotiated agreement with minorities unnecessary. So the Scottish pattern became 'according to use and wont' in each local area, thus giving Presbyterianism a strong position, since 'by use and wont' it was the prevalent form of faith.[3] But Presbyterianism did not have the formal monopoly which the State Church of Norway possessed. England was peculiar in possessing both a strong established church and vigorous bodies of dissent. Had the range of plurality been wider, we might have seen something like the American or the Australasian patterns emerge, accompanied by disestablishment. Had the range been narrower, we might have had something like the Scottish or even the Norwegian pattern.

The English compromise was reached in two stages. First, in 1870, there was agreement that if religion was taught in the maintained schools it would exclude 'formularies and catechisms distinctive of any denomination'. Second, from the mid-1920s by voluntary agreement and from 1944 by legislation, instruction would be given in the matters about which the participating denominations agreed. So a negative stage of exclusion was followed by a positive stage of inclusion, and so the Agreed Syllabus of Religious Instruction was created.

Plurality in English religious education

The English experience has thus been of plurality in religious education, and this experience is already more that a century old. But the device of the Agreed Syllabus made it possible to tolerate religious diversity without abandoning the traditional and expected role of religious education, that of nurturing the young into the religious traditions of the society. As rivalry between the religious communities declined, it was possible to move from the negative to the positive stage. But the agreement was only posible because the plurality was not very great. The English experience was confined to Christian churches.[4]

During the period of negative agreement, there was a high degree of rivalry but a low degree of plurality. During the period of positive agreement, there was a *low* degree of rivalry and a low degree of plurality. But what would happen if there was a *high* degree of plurality? If there was also a high degree of rivalry between the religious groups, religious education in the schools would not be possible. Even if there was a tolerant atmosphere, i.e. low rivalry it would not be possible to continue with religious education as normally and traditionally understood in a society with a high degree of plurality. The simple reason for this is that the more diverse a society, the more difficult it is to define the religious tradition of the society in such a way as to win enough agreement to make a syllabus. This is the situation in this country today and this is the main reason (although not the only one) for the profound changes which are taking place in religious education.

The plurality now existing is of two kinds. First, we have a larger number of people for whom life may be lived without reference to religion at all. Second, we have the appearance of a substantial number of believers in religions other than Christianity. Judaism, which never participated in the religious instruction provided in the maintained schools, has been joined by Islam, Hinduism, Sikhism, and on a smaller scale by Buddhism and the Parsis. The young person today not only encounters a wider variety of faiths, both religious and secular, but he may adopt any or none of them without losing his civic rights or his public standing.[5]

Even within the lesser plurality of the earlier period, there were limits to the agreement which could be reached in religious education. The Roman Catholics, although not prevented in law from participating along with the other non-established forms of Christian faith in the religious education offered by the state, chose not to do so. The Jewish community also took no part. The right of parents to withdraw their children from religious instruction in the schools inidicates the limits of the agreement which was possible. But now *more* people are excluded. And when the number of pupils who are specifically not Christian reaches a certain point, questions of fairness begin to be asked. So today we ask whether, when the state offers religious education to children in its care, it should offer it only to some and not to others. When the state not only offers religious education, but insists (as it does) that it be received (subject to rights of withdrawal) then we must ask this question more urgently.

Of course, it is always possible for the non-Christians, whether they be secular persons or believers in other faiths, to be present at religious classes and to consider it as information. But it is not intended as information. It is intended as nurture into Christianity.[6] This is why it appears to be more and more necessary that what should change in religious education is not only its content but its intentions. And this is what is in fact taking place today.[7]

Consequences of pluralism for religious education

The interest in establishing valid educational objectives for religious education is a direct consequence of pluralism. For now that the religions are so diverse, it is no longer possible to nurture children into the faith of their society. There are now many faiths, and this would require many nurturing agencies. A natural reaction to this situation might be to remove religion from the school curriculum. Let it be the responsibility, we might suggest, of the various religious groups. In **Britain** however it seems unlikely that this reply will win much support. Religion is too important a part of the history, culture and current experience of mankind to be left to believers alone. There is a role for the school in preparing pupils for responsible participation in a political democracy; similarly, there is a role for the school in preparing pupils to take an informed and thoughtful part in a pluralistic society. When the society contains not one but several religions, the need for a thoughtful study of religions becomes greater not less. But preparing pupils to take an informed and thoughtful interest in what goes on around them is by no means the same as nurturing them into faith in one religion or even into acceptance (as far as this might be logically possible) of religion as a whole. It is the realization of this different role precipitated by the abandoning of its nurturing function which has led religious education to take such an interest recently in educational validity. There is a sharpening distinction between nurture and education.

Of course, religious groups have the right to provide schools and to apply for aided or controlled status. Aided status leaves the school free to nurture in the faith of the religion which sponsors it. So in England and Wales we have had the dual system, whereby agreed nurture was offered in the county schools and denominational nurture in the aided schools. The dual system was thus another feature of the compromise reached in the limited Christian plurality of earlier years. The problems created by the appearance of aided schools will grow greater as plurality widens. Since Christians, mainly Roman Catholics and Anglicans, are allowed their own state aided schools, and the Jewish community is similarly supported, it is inevitable that Muslims and perhaps others will seek the same advantages. These generous and tolerant provisions by the state offer security, acceptance and financial support to religious groups concerned about the threat which pluralism presents to religious community life. To that extent these provisions are likely to make an important contribution to the domestication and integration of recently established religious communities. On the other hand, it would surely be a hindrance to community relations in the long term if by the end of the century we were to have Muslim, Sikh and perhaps Hindu systems of schools alongside the Christian and Jewish ones. Northern Ireland has illustrated too dreadfully the consequences of an education conducted along sectarian lines. And if critical, descriptive, religious education should flourish in the county schools the aided schools might find it increasingly embarrassing that they are offering something which in the vast majority of schools would not be thought educationally valid.

The study of religions should therefore continue in the county schools, possibly coming to play a more creative role than the old Christian nurture out of which it is now growing. Let us look at some of the growing pains.

School worship

In schools with considerable numbers of young people from various religious traditions and from no religious tradition at all, it is not going to be possible to continue with official school worship 'on the part of all pupils in attendance at the school'.[8] Who are they supposed to be worshipping? Worship can and should be studied in the classroom and it is very much to be hoped that schools will continue to have assemblies at which a variety of religious and non-religious attitudes and beliefs will be shared and explored. But *sharing* different beliefs is not the same as being required to *worship* the one object of belief. Assemblies for sharing will take the place of assemblies at which official Christian worship is offered, ostensibly *on the part of all* the pupils. This change will come as a great relief to everyone involved in present experiences of school assemblies in pluralist situations.

But because it will be impossible to go on conducting official school worship (i.e to go on assuming a unanimity of potential or actual faith), future Local Education Authorities drawing up Agreed Syllabuses under the terms of the 1944 Act will find their task difficult indeed. The Act can be adapted to pluralism in the sections which deal with classroom religious teaching. The expression 'other denominations', although normally taken to indicate the free churches, has been used to permit the inclusion of non-Christian faiths on Agreed Syllabus Conferences.[9] But such Conferences will have to choose between making recommendations contrary to the Act (and a Conference would not be competent to do this), making recommendations contrary to the spirit of their pluralistic syllabus, or saying nothing at all about school worship. The latter is the most preferable and we can therefore expect that the traditional content of the Agreed Syllabus Handbook, which deals both with worship and classroom instruction, will be modified so that only classroom work is dealt with. Of course, it may be that pluralism will render the religious sections of the Act so archaic that no Local Education Authority which desires to recognize pluralism will be able to accept the restrictions of the Act, and that there will not be many more significant Agreed Syllabuses. It certainly is the case that pluralism is hastening the demise of the Agreed Syllabus as it has been previously understood. We may note for example that in nurture, the parties agree to include in the Syllabus what they think is true. In pluralist education, they agree to include what they think worth teaching.

The content of religious education

One of the main problems for religious education in a pluralist society is to retain a specifically religious content. Even under the rather mild conditions which prevailed from 1870 to 1944 there was a tendency for teachers to omit religious doctrines lest they should give offence. Some Boards explicity forbade teachers when dealing with the Bible to comment on matters which were not philological, archeological, historical or moral.[10] And of course, the 1870 Act, like all its successors, forbade the teacher to include materials distinctive of any particular denomination. This meant that the religious features most characteristic of the participating denominations were excluded.

The biblical syllabuses which are still very widespread in religious education, especially in grammar schools, were the product of the impact of Christian pluralism. Alternatively, the schools treated religion as part of history, or as part of the cultural tradition. Religion itself in its living forms was rarely dealt with, because that would lead to controversy. The procedure of agreement was intended to remove the danger of controversy. Where there is low rivalry between the faiths, controversy fades away and this is why the Agreed Syllabuses of the period *c* 1938 to the early 1960s are much more explicitly religious in their content, although still cast in the biblical pattern.

But if religious education is to be effective in preparing young people for life in a pluralist society, it must present the living religions present in the society. It may deal with their history, their cultural achievements and so on, but its main concern must be with them as living religions. Controversy cannot be avoided and indeed ought to be encouraged, but the way the school ought to deal with controversy is distinctive and lies at the centre of the contribution of the school, and of education as a whole, in pluralism. No teacher will teach a syllabus made up of his own enthusiasms and no teacher will teach his own faith in a manner which gives it any privileged position. Normally the partners in a controversy argue because they believe their respective positions are true. The school however makes no assumptions about the truth (or falsehood) of any of the religions. It simply presents them, describes them, holds them up in all their beauty and their ugliness, helping the pupil to understand without prescribing what the outcome for any pupil may be should he make choices or rejections.

This does not mean that the syllabus of religion in a pluralist society will be what is sometimes called comparative religion. Comparative religion is but one way of studying the religions. There are many others. Comparative religion is one of the most sophisticated stages of the study of religion, certainly too advanced for pupils below the middle and upper levels of the secondary school. The syllabus will however consist of the study of religion in one form or another. We will no longer teach the Old Testament and the New Testament as such. We will teach Christianity, and this will include some treatment of the Christian scriptures. And the same will be true of the other participating faiths.

A cluster of subjects

Religious education is in fact not one but a cluster of subjects. In many schools, social and community service is one of the responsibilities of the religious education department and a good deal of the classroom work is preparation for this. Some religious education, particularly in the secondary school, is social and political studies, often including current affairs and world problems, and is taught with an emphasis upon values and within a framework which is generally religious or at least humanitarian. Some religious education, particularly in the infant and junior school, is sensitivity training with an intention to expand awareness and widen the emotional repertoire of the child. Much of what is called religious education is moral education. Religious education also includes a good deal of ancient history and sometimes geography, usually relating to the Jewish and Christian origins and increasingly with older students it includes study of non-religious life styles such as Humanism. Most importantly, it includes religious studies in the specific sense, i.e. the study of the religions of mankind, their customs and rituals, their doctrines and myths, their sacred writings and their ethics.

The group of subjects has been held together within religious education because of a philosophy which saw all the various aspects as being part of the Christian enterprise in education. The teacher did not simply teach the ethical problems associated with the use of money; he presented the teaching of Jesus about money. He did not only discuss the various sexual moralities which may be found in our society today; he taught the Christian sexual ethic. He did not only introduce his pupils to world problems; he studied Christian Aid. The attitudes and emotions which he sought to develop in the young child were intended as a preparation for religion and this simply meant that the emotions (wonder, love, thankfulness, penitence and so on) were central to the Christian religion.

But the effect of removing religious education from its traditional context within Christian nurture is that there is now in principle no closer relation between Christianity and religious education than there is between Islam and religious education. There is thus some danger that the subject will disintegrate. Christian faith can no longer be related to religious education in the obvious and straightforward way that once it was.

When moral education is undertaken by the religious education teacher, it will be necessary to distinguish between the study of the ethical aspects of the various religions and moral education in its own right. When the latter takes place, teachers should beware of making the moral education lessons into a form of Christian nurture. Teaching material now exists which presents moral education work units in their own right and without reference to distinctive Christian teaching. If in these lessons the teachers also use materials supplied by Christian agencies and with specific Christian applications, they should make it clear to their pupils that the material does represent a Christian or a

Humanist or whatever point of view. The proper place for the study of Christian ethics will be within a course on Christianity.

There is really no longer any reason why religious education should continue to carry so much responsibility for moral education. Every subject has its moral implications and it is encouraging to see how many books now being produced for work in English and social studies are deeply aware of this.

With the arrival of pluralism and the resulting differentiation of the cluster of subjects, many of the older concerns of religious education must now be concentrated in Christian Studies, which, along with Islamic Studies and so on, will continue to be an integral part of it. The final word 'Studies' indicates the stance which the teacher ought to adopt. The Christian churches will become more significant as the providers of materials for Christian Studies, although there are as yet few indications that the churches have realized the different approach which materials of this sort will have to adopt. Most materials from the churches still assume a nurturing aim, even when intended for use in county schools.

There is a danger that teachers will become 'specialists' in one aspect of the concerns of religious education. One teacher will teach nothing but the Bible. Another will concentrate on social and international problems; a third will deal mainly with personal relations. But it is important that teachers of religion should see, and insist to their colleagues, that although they have a variety of humane insights to offer, their main contribution is the religions of man.

Secular philosophies

The non-religious life styles have an important place too. Their inclusion is another effect of pluralism, and it is right and proper that the religious life styles should be set against the non-religious ones in order to facilitate the understanding of both.

How should non-religions be chosen? Those which may be thought of as alternatives to religion, or which are in conscious rejection of religion, or which have some of the main aspects of religions, may be included in religious education syllabuses.

So for example, Humanism should have a place, because it is in conscious dialogue with religion, rejects religion, and offers itself as a viable alternative to religion, in offering a purposeful life set within an overall understanding of man and the world. Communism and (although less relevant today) Fascism may also claim their places. Study of the 'counter-culture', the drug culture and the various 'alternative society' groups might also be appropriate for older pupils. But study of the Conservative, Liberal and Labour parties would be less suitable. These do not consciously reject religion, and any links with Christianity which they might have should be studied as part of Christian Studies. Communism has a philosophy of history, a view of man, a kind of eschatology, a detailed ethic and so on. The main British political parties do not offer this kind of comprehensiveness and do not purport to be alternatives to religion. There is of course a proper place for political studies in secondary schools, but this should take place through an expansion of social studies, community education or some such thing.

The non-religious life styles which have enough similarity with the religions to make it right for them to be included within religious education syllabuses (Humanism, Communism; possibly Fascism and the counter-culture) must be included in their own right and not simply as a foil for religion. They will be there in their own right just as sensitivity training and moral education will continue to share in this cluster of interests which we call religious education. But the central area will continue to be the religions of man. The secular areas are included both because they are important and no one else will do them if religious education fails to, and (although of value in themselves) the criterion for their selection is their similarity with the religions. All areas of the curriculum interlock, and there is a limit to what a fairly small area of the curriculum such as religious education can be expected to do. Naturally, pluralism and the consequent differentiation of religious education vastly increases the claim of religious education to be significant, and if head teachers were able to offer three or four periods a week throughout the secondary school, everything could be dealt with. In the meantime, it is important that Religious Studies in the narrow sense should not be overwhelmed. Perhaps Humanism and Communism can best be studied during a joint offering to older students from religious studies, and the history, economics, literature and philosophy teachers.

Religious studies and religious education

Let us try to express the distinction in another way. Religious studies is the study of the religions. Religious education is a wider group of 'subjects' in which things like sensitivity training, moral education, personal relations, social service, study of the non-religions and so on are set around religious studies as the periphery around a core. Religious education may thus be thought of as helping the pupil in his own quest for meaning. Religious studies is the inquiry after other people's meanings. The study of non-religious life styles is also a study of other people's meanings. So the question concerns the relation between my search for meaning and my study of other people's searches for meaning. I could not, in searching for my own meaning, do it alone. I must be with others. Those others are not only the members of the great faiths; the members of my school also have a lot to offer me. But I would surely be impoverished if I was confined to my fellows in the school community, be it never so rich. My interest is also in what men and women in all lands and at many times have thought and believed. This is perhaps the way in which the whole cluster of subjects can be held together in pluralism through the idea of informed existential dialogue.[11]

Notes

1 BREWARD, I. (1967) *Godless Schools? a Study in Protestant Reactions to the Education Act of 1877* Presbyterian Bookroom, Christchurch.

2 The situation is changing and some Australian states are considering the introduction of a critical descriptive religious education. See *Religious Education in State Schools* (The Steinle Report), South Australian Education Department, September, 1973.

3 *Moral and Religious Education in Scottish Schools* (The Millar Report), presented to the Secretary of State for Scotland, March 1972.

4 The withdrawal clauses were sufficient recognition of Judaism and other minorities. Without these clauses, if a wider pluralism had been encouraged to participate in state religious education, it would not have been possible to instruct or nurture.

5 This is what I understand a pluralist society to be. In so far as some institutions are still tied to a particular religion or denomination (the monarchy) British pluralism is incomplete. Cities are naturally more pluralistic than towns.

6 '... the Syllabus is deliberately designed as an evangelistic instrument, and the Christian teacher should have no reservations in using it as such. Before 1944 many teachers rightly felt that they had to be discrete in teaching religion because of denominational suscep-tibilities, but happily the situation has now been transformed. The subject to be taught is not Biblical knowledge nor morality but the Christian faith, and the aim is to lead the pupils to a personal knowledge of Jesus Christ and to active life within a worshipping community. To achieve that purpose the Christian teacher may zealously use all his influence.' County of Lincoln — Parts of Lindsey Education Committee. *Agreed Syllabus of Religious Instruction* 1964 p.10 ff. Needless to say, this is a statement of nature and aim which almost nobody in Lincolnshire or anywhere else in England would espouse today.

7 The change antedates the impact of wide pluralism. Edwin Cox's *Changing Aims in Religious Education* was published in 1966.

8 Education Act 1944, Section 25, para. 1.

9 The fifth schedule of the Education Act (1944).

10 *Return: School Board Schools (Religious Teaching)*, House of Commons, 4th March 1879, *passim*.

11 Many of the questions raised in this chapter are discussed in greater detail in my *School Worship, an Obituary* (SCM Press, 1975). See also my chapter 'Agreed Syllabuses, Past, Present and Future' in *New Movements in Religious Education* ed. D. Horder and N. Smart (Maurice Temple Smith, 1975) pp. 97–119.

Pluralist Education

Harold Loukes

We may, if we are that way inclined, be bewildered and distressed by the necessity of bringing up our children in a society marked by a multiplicity of faiths. It would be so much easier, would it not, if everybody *adhered*, stuck together, in one world view, and agreed to support the institutions that expressed it. All we should have to do then would be to get our children to join in, to like joining in, and to enjoy practising the accepted forms. They would not need to understand very much: they would not need to worry their heads or their hearts about the truth: they would just tag along. And this, if we liked this kind of thing, would not be very difficult. Children are easily persuaded to join in; and need no persuasion at all to avoid worrying their heads or their hearts. We could have the whole thing fixed up by the age of seven.

Education in choice

But this is no longer possible. We must now *make* them worry, and think, and make choices. Thinking and making choices, we should want to say, is what *education* is about. In the old, single-faith days the only people to be educated were those who would later have to make choices, the rulers of state and church, who would face unpredictable situations, engage in conflict, and offer leadership. The rest were simply 'brought up', persuaded to fall in with the institutions – social, economic, religious – and not to worry their heads about what they did not understand.

But now we *want* people to understand. We live not only in a multi-religious, but a multi-skill and multi-problem society; and we want the multitude, and not merely the élite, to face their own problems and devise their own solutions with responsibility and understanding. There is still the production line, that men must tend and be enslaved by; but even here we want men to understand the whole task and be generously responsible about it. So we want to educate them too, and not merely 'bring them up'.

So if everybody is to be educated about their work, and social life and economic condition, they must be educated too about their religious condition; and religious education must be of the same order, and follow the same methods, and have the same objectives, as any other sort of education. If it does not, we cannot call it education at all, but should have to call it training, or conditioning, or indoctrination.

What I want to welcome, and not be sorry about, in the present situation, is that we can no longer get away with training or indoctrination, while imagining that we are educating. Exclusive sects still survive, but only by shutting themselves up in other ways besides the religious, cutting themselves off from the theatre, the concert, and the pub. They are not educated at all.

Education in religion

The painful process we are now engaged in of re-examining religious education is thus not a *re*-examination at all: it is a *first* examination. We are for the first time asking the questions: how can we bring up children so that they will question and discover in the religious area as they must question and discover in other areas? We are asking how to treat them so that they can have religious knowledge instead of adherence to somebody else's knowledge. 'Knowledge' is a difficult word to use in an area where different opinions exist vociferously together; but in any area we should want to mark out knowledge from belief as some sort of seeing for oneself – some sense-experience on one's own senses, some act of interpretation or judgement by one's own mind. Such experience and act of judgement are forced upon our children in a multi-faith society, in a way they are not even suggested by a single-faith society; our children are compelled to be ready for education, instead of being able to accept – which would be so much easier for them, as it would be easier for us – **training** and indoctrination.

I have set out the opposition in over-simple terms. Single faith societies throw up individuals who see for themselves (Jesus, for one); and multi-faith societies contain many who would prefer not to see anything beyond the parish pump. Indeed the contemporary problem is bedevilled by the millions who want nothing better than to hang on to any plausible leader, be he *guru*, radical socialist, or just whimsical about diet, or breathing upside down. Our educational problem thus becomes more urgent: to persuade the young to accept education in an area where they would prefer just to be indoctrinated; and to do it quickly, before everybody goes mad.

Now there are two immediate, large, tasks to be performed before we can educate in religion. The first is to be clear about what 'religion' is: to examine the items in the package that was passed on for acceptance and adherence and which we must now use as the material for our education. The other is to apply the principles of education to this material, and to see how we can teach it in such a way that it will be understood, instead of being merely accepted.

The examination of religion

The first task is now well under way. We are busy unpacking the concept of religion so that we can set the items side by side, and see which of them involve disagreement and disputation, and which don't. 'Christians worship in church' and 'Hindus worship in temples' provoke no conflict: there is nothing to argue about here; but when we begin to examine the *object* of worship in these two places, argument begins, and we can start to establish a language and criteria of judgement, for conducting the argument. Similarly, 'Christians worship God', 'Atheists don't worship God' is not an argument until we ask 'What do Christians mean by worship?' and 'What do atheists do instead, to meet the human need that Christians meet by worship?' This is an illustration of my claim that the present situation is more educative than the old one, because Christians are now compelled to examine their own package, as part of the process of examining the other packages. They can no longer dismiss Hindus on the grounds that they bow down to wood and stone, because they patently do nothing of the sort. Much remains to be done here, and if religions remain alive there will always be plenty to be done, but it *is* being done. It is the task called for by John Hull under the title of religious studies.

One important distinction, as he also observes, has been already made clear: The distinction between the moral insights of a particular religion and the morality that all men must have if they are to relate to each other at all. Some of the preliminary work on this developed from a kind of anthropological stew, demonstrating that all religions taught a similar set of moral principles — the Golden Rule, for example, appears in all of the world religions. But now we can go further than this, and claim that the Golden Rule is in the world itself: it is part of the situation with which we deal, and life for anybody is wrong without it. We view it not as a commandment backed by all the religions, but a law of human encounter as binding as the law of gravity. We can no more establish human relationships without it than we can walk on cliff edges without knowing the law of gravity.

Moral reasoning has established its autonomy against religious reasoning as surely as scientific reasoning has done. 'Why be good?' becomes a question to be examined in just the same way as 'Why not jump off a cliff?' Neither question is properly answered (at any rate to a child we are trying to educate) with the words 'Because God says so'. They may both be answered by the same kind of demonstration of consequence: certain fundamental moral laws are broken at the same inevitable risk as certain physical laws. The consequences are not so easy to demonstrate, but then living-in-relationship is more complicated than walking on cliffs, and a false step in one is not so dramatic in one as on the other. This only means that there is more to moral learning than there is to walking on cliffs, but it is, at root the same *kind* of learning, by observation, by the development of skill, and by the achievement of insight and responsibility.

And so with all the rest of the 'cluster of subjects' with which religious education has been traditionally concerned, we are now free to ask of all of them, what are their own concepts, and structures of thought and criteria of validity? And this sets the study of religion free as surely as it sets free the study of morality, or society, or politics. There will still be some to blench at this. 'Setting free' sounds like a 'free for all'; and if I say 'morality is morality' am I not also saying 'business is business' in the fearsome sense we usually attach to that phrase? This is not what I mean at all. Business *is* business, in the sense that anyone who is in business has to obey certain laws. Even the church must pay its way, make ends meet, and the like; and there are certain conditions attached to making ends meet which apply as rigorously to the church as to a supermarket. Being well-disposed, and saying one's prayers, is not enough for a managing director, any more than going to church is enough for a scientist. What matters to them all is the understanding of the task in hand *now*, and the rules that are built in to this particular situation. I can drive a car morally or immorally; but I cannot drive *morally* unless I understand about driving. I cannot drive *morally* unless I know that in England one drives on the left, which is not a God-given rule, but a part of the local situation that I must grasp.

The examination of education

I am not here saying that morality has nothing to do with religion. Morality is a dimension of everything, including religion, but it is always a *moral* dimension and not a religious dimension. So when we educate in morality (or society or politics) we educate in their own terms, and not in religious terms. So this brings me to the second of my large tasks: the scrutiny of what it means to educate in religion, or morality, or indeed anything else. It would arouse no great opposition nowadays if I were to say that the educative process involves an individual in experience, meaning, and commitment − all three, and none without the others. Merely experiencing without meaning (whatever that could be) is not educative; repeating meanings *without* experiencing the data for meaning is not educative; perceiving meaning but not standing by it is uneducated. There are many things to be said about all these 'levels' of activity if that is what they are; but they are easily recognizable for what they are. Children who while learning number play with tiddleywinks or cuisenaire rods or jugs of water are just 'experiencing' number; they begin to perceive — and are trapped by their teachers in strenuous perception — of the meanings numbers can carry; and, in the end, they want to get their calculations right.

In the light of this analysis we can see why the single-faith religious education was not education at all: It reversed the true order of progress. Commitment first, it said; then understanding; then experience. But what would be meant by applying the analysis in the *right* order? What 'experiences' do we want to start with? What meanings do we want our learners to perceive? And what kind of commitment would we hope for? What are our tiddleywinks? What our numeracy? What is 'getting our sums right'?

The answers we shall give to these questions will turn on the answers we shall give to the other set of questions, about what religion is. In the present imperfect state of consensus, the answer may go something like this. A religion, of any sort, carries some kind of bidding from the universe to the individual soul, some lifting out of apathy or mere impulse, some word, if you like, that is to be listened to. This is where the 'non-religious secular philosophies' to which John Hull refers carry the appearance of a religion: they carry a message that transcends the individual and pulls him out of his selfish corner. Apart from nihilism or 'hippy-dom', they all make an approach, and call for an answer, and indeed in the context we are contemplating, of a study of religions, even nihilism and hippy-dom pose a question about all the others.

Now for the child, this bidding or nudging begins in the first hours of life, when the mother, supported by her medical advisers, urges the infant to say 'Yes' to the universe. 'Do you respond.' she says, 'to the warmth I give you, the cuddling, the breast, the milk? Do you approve when I come to answer your cries? Do you discover, when you do not get everything you want precisely when you want it, that I am, myself, real, and have my own needs and purposes? And so do you come to trust my authenticity, my difference? And so do you hear the bidding, to transcend your own preoccupation with your stomach and your bowels, and become a person?'

These are the first religious experiences; and many psychologists tell us that if what the baby goes through at this time makes him say 'No', then he will find it hard to say 'Yes' later on (though he may well put on a religious disguise, and say his 'No' with absurd Puritanism or sectarian hate or neurotic guilt). If he emerges from this stage saying 'Yes' (for most of us, of course, it is 'Yes — but . . . ') then he is ready to continue the process at a less radical but more expansive level. He can now be shown things and people, and be helped to savour them. A good infant school curriculum is, no more, no less, than a curriculum of religious experience. 'Look,' the mother-substitute now says, 'here are bits of the universe − a bird, a hamster, a rock, the rolling tide, the swinging stars − they bid for your attention: *savour* them.'

Now there is nothing sectarian, or racial, in all this. A child viewing the universe from the Sahara desert may well see the world differently from a child born on a French vineyard; but two children in an English housing estate, even if one is called Abdul and the other Arthur, share the same bidding, and may share the same response. When we come to grasp the meaning of it all, we may find differences that call for imaginative tact and an eternity of patience. To a Parsee child, even in England, the sun has significances we should not share. But granted the tact and the eternal patience (and these are the ordinary workshop tools of the teacher anyway), the adding of meanings is an enrichment of the experience itself. Children are the better for their myths.

But what about getting their meanings *right*? In the past it has been assumed (by Christians) that Christians were right, and the rest lamentably (though not culpably, because they couldn't help it) wrong. We are not quite so sure of this nowadays, but we are still capable of advancing Western criteria of rightness and wrongness − scientific positivism, causability and the like − in full confidence that if only everybody would do their sums in our way they would in the end come to our answers. Well, perhaps they would; but they might be the wrong answers after all. There are those, even in our culture (Michael Polanyi for one) who suspect that Descartes, Laplace and the rest have been leading us up a garden path; and we may, for all our certainties, be in the compost heap. In any case, I should want to suggest that educational criteria of rightness are not so much concerned with having solved all problems correctly so much as being ready for, equipped for, and interested in, the problems that lie ahead. An educated mathematician is not one who has worked out all the sums, but one who can correctly identify the terms of the *next* sum. On this analogy, I would want to say that the man educated in religion is the man open to further religious experience: a man listening and compassionate, outreaching and outgoing.

I do not want to imply, by this, that all religions, and all sects in all religions, are equally valuable. I would not want to suggest that a belief-system has only to call itself a religion to place itself beyond the reach of critical judgement. But I *do* want to claim that the mark of being religiously educated is more this kind of openness and sensitivity than any kind of correctness or orthodoxy. A man can be a well-educated literary critic and yet be misguided about a particular writer; but if he were, I should want to attack his views, but not try to make out that he was a 'bad' critic. And in the same way I should hope to be able to accept as religiously mature a man whose thought-forms I found uncongenial.

If this be accepted, there is open to the teacher of religious studies a positive neutrality. He can take into the situation his own commitment without challenging another person's commitment. He can bid his students to commitment without trying to force upon them the way of thought within which his own commitment operates, for it is not a commitment to a particular form of truth, but to a serious search for truth.

Education in morality

Something of the same sort can be said about the study of morality. Here, too, we have the same rhythm of experience, meaning and commitment. As moral experience I should count any human relationships in which respect for each other, and the compassionate understanding of each other, was expressed. Again, like religious experience, it starts early in life, as the mother's feelings flow out and she welcomes feeling back; and as the mother's service of the baby demonstrates her respect for him, setting up a pledge of the recognition of his rights. For his part the baby soon learns to know what she is feeling like, and to allow for her ups and downs, and to accept her rights as of importance beside his own. 'Now Mummy have some,' he will say, as he nibbles at his cake.

If it be agreed that the nuclear moral experience consists of this mutuality of respect and feeling, then it is clear that all good teaching-and-learning is moral experience. We cannot teach anything to anybody without a degree of respect for them, at least to the degree that we regard them as worth teaching, and capable of learning. And we cannot teach without at least some understanding of what it feels like to be ignorant; we must learn to view our knowledge, that we are so confidently on top of, from underneath: we must have a child's-eye-view of it. And, *per contra*, the child cannot learn from us unless he respects us, trusts that we are qualified to teach him, that we understand what we are doing, that we are telling him the truth. And he cannot learn unless he senses something of our value for what we teach, unless he catches a little of our enthusiasm. This respect and this feeling are not, most of the time, overt: it would be boring if they were. But they are implicit and inescapable. At this point, then, of the provision of moral experience, all education is moral education.

The exploration of moral meaning is, much of it, conducted by the children themselves, as they reflect on their own experience. 'It isn't fair', 'It doesn't pay': these are the first advances of the young mind towards moral principles. It becomes more explicit, and we play a larger part in it, as we *impose* consequences, with reward and punishment; or we discuss an offence, and try to get the offender to see what went wrong; or as we move into deliberate moral discourse, examining the moral conventions of our society, comparing them, as our pupils grow older, with the conventions of other societies; and, in the end, trying to establish criteria by which we may perceive moral principles, such as truth-telling, that are built in to any relationships; and further, establishing such methods of casuistry as will permit the analysis of special cases, where one in-built principle, such as truth-telling, may rightly yield to another, like respect for persons.

The outcome of all this, we should hope, would be some degree of moral commitment, but as with religious commitment, it is not to a particular position but to the search for a position: not to specific conclusions, but to passionate moral thinking and concern. The mathematically educated man is deeply committed to solving mathematical problems mathematically; and it does not occur to him to try another method, such as reading up his horoscope, or feeling some seaweed, or just thinking of a number, still less ask the Gallop Poll or the Party Executive for an 'acceptable' answer. If we set out to educate mathematicians, and failed to produce this commitment, we should know we had failed; as we should know we had failed if our Muslim pupils were regularly coming up with answers different from our Christian pupils.

There is, of course, a difference between mathematics and morals. The folkways of different folk have their own content, which sets up moral expectations which affect the case. Differences in sexual convention, for example, may, *sub specie aeternatis*, be merely conventional; but what a girl expects of a young man is a moral fact, not to be ignored in the way he approaches her. What in one society would be no more than a flattering attention becomes in another an assault on the personality. It is to be expected, therefore, that a multi-faith group can go through the same form or moral reasoning and, perfectly properly, arrive at different decisions on what is right for them, now, in the present case.

My argument would be, however, that the moral reasoning would be the *better*, and not the worse, for being conducted in a multi-faith group. We are already familiar with the way our own received moral conventions have been changed by the findings of cultural anthropology. Some of us may be alarmed by this, and judge the process to be corrosive of morals. Be that as it may, the process cannot be reversed, and it offers the possibility of a morality based, not on local habits, but on a fuller understanding of the nature of man.

A multi-faith society is uncomfortable to live in. Any rapid change is uncomfortable to live in. But we have them both; and my case has been that if we adopt an open, questing attitude to questions of faith and morals we may devise the education appropriate to discomfort. Education is, after all, a kind of 'making uncomfortable'. It would be so much easier to say to our children, 'Copy the cow: feed on your grass, be milked and produce your calves; and you will be happy.' It would be easy; but they would not listen to us. And we should have failed in our educational task.

The Politics of Religious Education

Brian E. Gates

'Why do you think there are all these different Religions?'

'In the beginning God drove Adam and Eve from Paradise and told them to go and live with the other peoples of the world . . . in different places. These simple people like the Red Indians saw the sun and the earth and the stars around them, they saw thunder and lightning, and they made up gods. They said it is the sun who does everything for us, it is the earth who grows our crops. But if someone came along and said there is a person called God up in the sky who does everything for us, they'd not be inclined to believe them. Because if someone came along and told us that it was the Sun and the Earth that do everything for us, we wouldn't believe them because we've believed in God all our lives. So it's no use going to a Communist and telling him your belief. They'll just say: 'And how do you know it's been changed into the body and blood?' We'll say: 'We believe it'. They'll say: 'Well you don't know do you? It's only because it's your silly religion. You believe too much! Are you sure it happened 2000 years ago?' They would be very questionable. Like if I went up to a Muslim and asked why he believed this and that, because their ideas are a bit hard for us to grasp. . . .'

'How does anyone decide what Religion to be?'

'If you're brought up in the Catholic community, people go to Catholic Church. You learn to believe and you've got faith in it . . . But when you grow older, you might find that you don't like the idea of your religion, you might not think it's any good and you look around. You might find another religion, it's usually pretty similar . . . I could become a Protestant if I wanted to. A Protestant could become a Catholic . . .'

10-year-old Catholic girl

How resilient are children? They must be tremendously so for their individuality to survive institutionalization. For from conception forwards a child is prey to institutional expectations. The family near or far, the local community, the school, the banks and businessmen, the advertisers and entertainers, the police, politicians, preachers, all exude the nation's norms. And as well as saving, these can crush or kill.

No more blatantly is this true than in the sphere of moral and religious sensitivity. The local church or synagogue, the neighbourhood school, teachers, parents and society at large may all intend to open doors of delight to every boy and girl. But these doors may hinge open in opposed directions. Another's gentle push may unwittingly trap the child groping on the other side.

In the midst of so many institutional pressures, there are good reasons to be sceptical about the value of religious education (RE). So easily it can be just another dungeon door, or be treated as the way to an empty attic. Yet it might be otherwise. Institutions are generally the vehicle of life as well as death, and children may have the power to be discerning given proper opportunity. The arguments of the previous papers have demonstrated the potential relevance of RE to such discernment. What evidence is there that RE is already helping children make sense of the plurality of religions? Can schools and religious communities agree to collaborate in overcoming present limitations?

I Unfamiliar faiths

Both Hull and Loukes agree that the process of becoming religiously educated (religiate) should include for every child study of the religious experience of mankind and opportunity to ponder and probe their personal situations of being in the world at all. The corresponding brief for teachers (and parents) is considerable. It requires of them both a grasp of the range and richness of religious traditions, and an ability to be at once caring and impartial about the outcome of the child's exploration of them.

A recent Schools Council survey of multi-racial education in primary and secondary schools[1] revealed incidentally that of all subjects in the curriculum, RE is the one where teacher aspirations and syllabus content match most closely in seeking to prepare children for life in a multi-cultural society. However, the reasons quoted by teachers and heads for this overlap of interest varied greatly. On the one hand, there were those who spoke of 'study of religions of the world and relationships of cultural and social attitudes of each faith', involving contact with different religions in the community. On the other hand, some spoke confidently of 'the Christian way of life' providing the basis for their approach to multi-racial living:

'From the religious aspect — as members of God's family the Church — we have a duty to help each other, no matter what our colour or creed.

The New Testament is the only ancient religious book which teaches the absolute equality before God of all races and levels of society. The answer to racialism is not to teach more Comparative Religion but to teach more Christianity — with the love and understanding which St. Paul showed to people of varied religious background.'

Unfortunately, it is not clear what proportion of respondents was working with the first presupposition or the second. However well meaning, the latter's naiveté can be singularly insensitive to the faith and doubts of other folk, and in effect discouraging of genuine inquiry on the part of the pupils.

Research evidence

A more selective indication that RE may yet be failing in this way to respond to its proper horizons has emerged from research being completed on children's religious development.

Representatives of different religious backgrounds or none were involved in the research. Initially, a thousand pupils were interviewed in eight schools, four in the north-west of England, and four in the south-east, two primary and two secondary schools in each region. According to information given during these written sessions, 80 Anglicans, 38 Non-Conformists, and 80 claiming no religious association were selected for oral interview. Subsequently seven other schools were involved, all in the south-east, for 40 Catholics, 40 Jews, 40 Sikhs (20 primary and 20 secondary in each case), plus 17 Muslims (all secondary). In this small way the varied religious complexion of the nation was acknowledged at the outset of the research. With the exception of the Muslim pupils, each group had equal numbers of boys and girls, and of each age from 6 years to 15.

The topics dealt with in the interviews included both ones which were explicitly religious (e.g. prayer, beyond death, God, religious institutions) and others involving an interplay between moral, natural scientific, political, and religious thinking (e.g. space exploration, atomic war, important(?) people). But of particular relevance to the theme of pluralism was a sequence on different religious identities.

Each subject was asked the following questions and encouraged to elaborate wherever possible on immediate responses:

'What do they call people who go to church? . . . What is a Christian? . . . Could you recognize one in the street? . . . What is

a Jew? ... What do they believe? ... A Muslim? ... A Sikh?
... A Hindu? ... A Buddhist? ... A Catholic? ... A Communist? ... An Atheist? ... Could you be a Christian and a Jew
at the same time? How/Why not? ... Could you be a Christian
and a Muslim at the same time? How/Why not? ... Could you be
a Christian and a Catholic at the same time? How/Why
not? ... Could you be a Christian and superstitious? How/Why
not? ... Why do you think there are all these religions in the
world? ... Are they all true? ... Or, are they all false? ... Or, is
one better than another? ... How does anyone decide which to
be? ... Can you change your religion?'

In the case of Catholic, Jewish, Muslim and Sikh boys and girls, the
questions were begun with their own communal identities and the
sequence as a whole adapted accordingly.

There was humour in some of the responses to the religious identity
sequence of questions: people who go to church are called 'Prime
Ministers' (6-year-old-boy). 'If they speak funny, they are Catholics'
(13-year-old girl). 'A Jew is a person that doesn't believe in God, like a
Viking ... A Communist is a person that wants to go to church but
can't because he's got things to do' (8-year-old boy). 'You don't have to
be a Christian to go to church' (12-year-old girl). Nevertheless,
amusement is little compensation, especially at the secondary school
level, for the general level of ignorance revealed by an analysis of all the
responses.

Variations by age

Starting with the most familiar, the identification *Christian* was
unknown to 32, not surprisingly, half of them six-year-olds, the others
seven to nine years. Eight of these were Sikhs, three were Catholics, but
the remainder were Anglicans or Unattached from the four original
primary schools. The identification *Catholic* was unrecognized by 86,
again most especially by junior children (60 were nine years or under);
26 not knowing were Sikhs and 9 Jews, the rest were evenly drawn
from the other groups. Since even the slightest recognition was scored
positively; it is interesting to note that 26 of these, all nine to
15-year-olds, followed popular caricature in identifying a Catholic as
one who believes in Mary more than Jesus.

Recognition of *Jewish* identity was slightly poorer than for Catholic,
this time going unrecognized by 129, of whom 34 were 11- to
15-year-olds (almost exactly six a year); only just over half of the 160
primary children had heard of a Jew. The extent of the knowledge
varied, unhappily for 13 (at every age except six and ten) being limited
to the non-religious attribution of 'meanness'. For another 34 (even age

spread) the recognition was historical only, relating to the distant biblical time and place. Almost 100 considered Jesus central, but only 22 in the positive form that the Messiah was believed to be awaited by the Jewish community; of the other 75, 26 put this same belief in negative form — Jews do not believe in Jesus — the rest had it confused that Jews believed in Jesus, but not in God. Except for the Jewish pupils themselves, only 34 had any more elaborate references to make (18: Jewish scriptures and sabbath; 11: the chosen race; 5: these references and others besides). Considering the long-established Jewish settlement in this country and their fate in Christian Europe generally, this ignorance is devastating.

None of the other religious identifications were even half so well known as the Jewish community however. In addition to any treatment they may have received in RE this may simply reflect their relatively recent settlement in this country. The *Muslims* were unknown by 227; only 20 under 11 years recognized the name, and of the rest only five non-Muslims showed more than minimal knowledge (i.e. a reference to either Mohammed, or the Koran). The *Buddhists* were unknown by 252, only 18 under 12 and but six in all with more than minimal knowledge (most of it, apparently picked up from Blue Peter!). Similarly, the *Hindus* were unknown by 270 (17 under 11 had any recognition, only two in all with more than minimal knowledge). *Atheists* went unrecognized by 254 (only seven under eleven years knew the term) and *Communists* by 253 (known by nine under eleven-year-olds). Sadly the *Sikhs* were recognized by only 15 non-Sikhs.

Although, as might be expected, recognition was consistently greater according to the age of the pupils (see Table I for summary), being in a secondary school, or indeed reaching school-leaving age, was no guarantee of even superficial recognition of major religious communities.

Table I: Distribution of recognition of different religious identities — by age 6–15 years.   *N = 335*

Identity	6	7	8	9	10	11	12	13	14	15
Christian	13	22	31	32	30	35	30	35	34	41
Catholic	8	18	21	23	24	27	27	33	32	36
Jewish	5	10	14	18	18	27	24	29	26	35
Muslim	0	0	2	11	7	16	15	19	14	24
Buddhist	0	1	1	5	6	5	10	14	14	27
Hindu	1	2	3	4	7	9	6	11	9	13
Sikh	4	4	5	4	4	6	4	5	9	10
Communist	2	0	2	2	3	10	8	13	19	23
Atheist	1	0	1	2	3	8	8	12	20	26
Number of pupils	31	30	35	34	30	35	30	35	34	41

Variations by religious belonging

Significant variations were evident according to the religious belonging of the pupils themselves. The following facts stood out: the Unattached group included 16 per cent who did not recognize Christian, 22 per cent not recognizing Catholic (plus 12 per cent quoting the Mary preference over Jesus) and 35 per cent not recognizing a Jew. Otherwise this group was as near each mean as the Anglican and Non-Conformist groups usually were. The Roman Catholic contingent (well-defined for being from two church schools) was strong on Jewish and Buddhist identifications, much weaker on Muslims and Hindus, but had only nine per cent failing to recognize Christian, whereas Anglicans had 21 per cent. The Jewish group was more knowledgeable of Muslims, partly no doubt for historical and cultural **reasons** (Jews and Muslims alike respect Abraham and Moses, they also share the dietary restriction against pork) than any other group, and also of Buddhists. The Sikhs were generally least knowledge-able, except, again perhaps for historical reasons, they were second only to the Jewish group in their recognition of Muslims, and ahead of all in recognizing Hindus. (Although now a separate religion the Sikhs emerged from the parent Hindu and Muslim traditions in the 16th century.) With the exception of the Catholic and Jewish pupils, these variations are independent of the schools; in a small way this is a reminder of the extent to which religious education (positive and negative) occurs beyond the school.

One may doubt the extent to which these findings are genuinely representative of the school situation nationally in 1975. In particular, the limited sample size and relatively few schools from which pupils were interviewed invalidate atempts at easy generalization. But the very least that can be concluded is that in the eight original schools, including two selective grammar schools, as well as in the seven approached for strength in 'minority faiths', the increasing plurality of religious life in England, not to mention the world at large, meant very little to most of those interviewed. Could it be that the traditional pattern of Agreed Syllabus RE (such as predominated in all but the Catholic schools and the Jewish secondary school in the sample) has too well succeeded in presenting a consensus version of Christianity, and now conceals the diversities of man's religious life generally? Weaknesses in this regard may not be confined to RE, but possibly extend to social and political education as well. Evidence that this is so, plus consideration of possible psychological limitations on a child's understanding of different religious points of view, is treated more extensively in the main study.

True or false?

All that has been mentioned so far by way of evidence about the current effectiveness of RE in preparing children for life in a plural world has been concerned solely with factual understanding. An equally important aspect of becoming religiate is attitude. Here Loukes stressed openness and sensitivity as especially vital. It is relevant therefore to conclude the research reference with a summary of children's responses to the question of truth and falsity of religions.

Table II: Distribution of attitudes to questions of the truth of religions — in five age groups

Response	6 — 7		8 — 9		10 — 11		12 — 13		14 — 15	
don't know	7	35.8%	5	18.2%	5	15.5%	8	1.6%	1	1.4%
all equally true	5	24.8%	9	31.8%	9	38.1%	19	38.1%	24	44.6%
all true some more so	2	10.1%	4	9.1%	4	15.5%	8	7.9%	5	5.4%
one true rest false	6	29.3%	9	22.7%	9	17.2%	9	28.7%	18	14.9%
may be true/false		0%	4	13.7%	4	12.2%	6	18.8%	12	27%
all untrue		0%	2	4.5%	2	1.5%	1	4.9%	3	6.7%
	(20)		(33)		(51)		(63)		(74)	

The breakdown by age (Table II) reveals marked variations in response to this sequence of questions, but little systematic pattern. Only 241 of the 335 interviewed are included in the chart; responses to the questions on particular religions at the beginning of the sequence showed that for the rest the terms of the question were not understood. The number responding in each age group increases accordingly, therefore percentages have been used to facilitate comparison. The percentage affirming that *all* religions are true rises to 44 at 14 to 15 years of age, of those with an open mind about the truth or falsity of all religions the percentage rises to 27.

It is when these responses are broken down by religious belonging that the degree of discrimination, even exclusiveness, takes rather a different perspective. Anglican, Non-Conformist and Sikh groups each have more than half claiming that all religions are true; less than a quarter of all the others think this. Of the Unattached, 40 per cent think religions may be true, maybe not; the average of all the other groups is ten per cent. But proclaiming the truth of one religion, and the falsity of the others are 51 per cent of the Jewish group, 54 per cent Catholics, and 64 per cent of the Muslims. The average for all the other groups is 9 per cent.

These figures highlight the major problem of pluralism — theological diversity. Very clearly there are religious traditions characterized in part at least by a spirit of breadth and inclusiveness. This might be in the form of a church that has been nationalized, or a faith like Sikhism that historically sought to remove barriers between religions (notably between Hindus and Muslims). How fortunate for them to hear talk of open RE! To those with liberal views and to an unattached humanist one acceptable outcome of being religiate might well be indecisiveness about the truth of religion. Yet that very indecisiveness or openness is under judgement from the other kind of view held by 53 of the boys and girls: that one particular religion is the true faith and that all others are false.

This confrontation is basic to the denominational schools issue mentioned by John Hull, or the matter of folkways admitted by Harold Loukes. Whatever shall the poor liberal educator do with those who shun his liberality as though it were a trojan horse for deicide? How is it possible for RE in English schools to justly resolve so fundamental a tension?

II Religions galore

To be confronted with the plurality of religious communities and their alternative, even rival, claims to truth can actually create a sense of buzzing confusion and chaos in the human condition. Traditionally religion has been a central institutional means of domesticating the chaos of existence. Whether in the Ancient Near East, Medieval Christendom, or the Australian outback, religious symbols have articulated a framework within which man could live. But faced with the range of Christian denominations, Hindus, Jews, Muslims, Sikhs and other traditions of long standing, plus a proliferating variety of small sects, an adult as well as a child may see only confusion. Instead of religion as a source of harmony, it becomes as Babel. Even the professional theologians may be discomforted by the extent of the diversity in religion. But there are repercussions also for avowedly secularist credos, in Marxist, psychoanalytic, or any other guise. The repercussions will be all the greater, the more genuine is the openness to the variety of religious experience. For no one world view is immediately and self-evidently proven against all alternative claims to truth. Oppositions exist between every kind of doctrine.

Two very different reactions to the flux of uncertainty are common. One withdraws to a singular citadel of truth; within its own peculiar territory at least there is semblance of order. The other accepts the plural facts of life, but seeks a ready synthesis. However inadequate one or both may be, they represent real concerns that no third alternative could reasonably overlook. Examples of both can be found in the classroom practice of moral and religious education.

Sanctuary on insured premises

An important institutional example of education drawn up in exclusive terms as over against the widespread worldly confusion is to be found in the official Roman Catholic position prevalent for much of this century. According to Pius XI,[2] Catholic children must be taught in Catholic schools, by Catholic teachers that the whole curriculum may be an expression of Catholic conformity:

> 'For such conformity it is necessary that all the teaching, all the ordering of the school staff curriculum and text books, in every kind of discipline shall be regulated . . . under the direction and maternal vigilance of the Church . . . without this knowledge of whatever kind will be of very little profit, often indeed will only result in serious harm.'

By implication, RE by any other means is of little worth.

A more specific example of retreat from public education can be instanced from à South London comprehensive school. As part of integrated humanities teaching (involving English, History, RE and Geography) a fourth form was launched into a six week project on Christmas; the timetable was blocked so that four half days could be devoted to this in each week. On learning that this was to happen, the Jehovah's Witness parents of one of the pupils exercised their rights to conscientiously object and he was withdrawn from all this work. Again, where education is seen not to confirm a confessionalist viewpoint, it is rejected as contaminating. Neither of these examples favours an education that is public and plural.

Salvation by synthesis

A second reaction to pluralism is to seek to synthesize. An example of this emphasis coming through in moral education is in part reflected in the position of Peter McPhail and the Schools Council Moral

Education Projects.[3] Taking as the starting point the claim that to adopt a considerate life style is a self-rewarding activity, the recommended technique for motivating moral action is an exploration of the situation of being faced with moral dilemmas. But the outcome of such exercises in group sensitivity is more likely to be a morality of adjustment than one which is alive to all the value issues pertinent to the situation.

Too earnest a desire for synthesis may even tempt a teacher to play down the differences between religions. Indeed the temptation may be all the greater in view of the timetable constraints under which many an RE specialist operated, or the limited opportunities afforded for primary teachers to resource themselves in this field. Anyway, a 'founders and festivals' view of religions can be very impoverished. With an instant juxtaposition of Gautama, Jesus, Abraham, Mohammed, Confucius it is hard not to misrepresent the religious tradition in question; Gandhi is frequently invoked as saviour to fill an otherwise embarrassing gap in Hinduism. Similarly, that Pesach, Diwali, Id and May Day are variously celebrated, can no doubt be colourfully conveyed. But to get inside the significance of any festival will demand the extensive work in myth and theology at children's level that is so often missing from equivalent treatments of Easter. Neither of these two examples from moral or religious education do full justice to the distinctively plural perspectives which inform peoples' lives and cultures.

Tensions of dialogue

For all the weaknesses of these two approaches however, any attempt to realize some more effective alternative must needs heed them. The emphasis on *synthesis* is in part a concern for common sense. If the religious experience of mankind is to be appreciated at all an element of translation will be necessary wheresoever another country, culture, or century is approached. Otherwise, that which is distinct will remain alien or unintelligible. And in translating and selecting from these traditions past and present, the teacher will need an artist's imagination for human resonance. Or again, if the varying moral consequences of alternative belief systems are to be understood it would be helpful if certain elements in man's experience were discovered to be trans-cultural (e.g. anthropologists speak of the exogamy taboo against incest, Loukes specified the Golden Rule). McPhail's social-interactionist approach has just this strength, besides any weakness, of one who would reconcile the one and the many through appeal to intrinsic norms, to a 'natural law' of social psychology.

Such concern for common sense and public meaning may seem far from the other *exclusivist* emphasis. Yet that too, reflecting as it frequently does a proper concern of religion with claims of revelation, is necessary for any common programme of RE. For though RE without reference to revelation might flourish in schools, it would scarcely convey the sense of claim from without known to, for instance, a Chasidic Jew, a Sunni Muslim, or an evangelical Christian. In turn, the Second Vatican Council, while maintaining the Catholic claim to objective truth, so commended the importance of the individual's free response in faith, of mutual understanding between men of different faiths, that the impressions of rigid superiority conveyed by an earlier decree are considerably qualified.[4] In the interests of RE there is every reason to explore the conviction and care that looks for total commitment.

III The future of RE: secular and plural

It is likely that England has always been a pluralist society in terms of ethnic composition and of individuals who have held 'heretical' beliefs or behaved in 'eccentric' ways. But the pluralism of contemporary society is far more overt and televised. Even so, in institutional terms these differences are only partially acknowledged. The Christian monarchy, the Parliamentary prayers and bishops, Civic Sundays and laws relating to Sabbath observance are all signal vestiges of the aspiration that England be a Christian nation. It is within this context that John Hull placed the traditional provision for RE in schools.

The time has clearly come to advertise the distinction between the confessional RE properly practised in the parent religious community and that which ought to be part of any county school curriculum. This latter will be *secular* RE rather than nurture into any particular parent faith. Secular, not in any sense antipathetic to religion, but in the same way that India describes herself as a secular country: though religions and ideologies abound no assumptions are made constitutionally about the truth claims of any, nor is one allowed protected status. Within these terms secular RE is a necessary element in understanding man and his situation in the world. Professional RE associations (ARE, ATCDE, CEM) take this as axiomatic and the work of the Schools Council RE Projects has done much to gain more general recognition for the change.[5] In this light the extensive ignorance revealed by the research interviews could be overcome.

No doubt RE can stand its own in secular terms; it now needs no 1944 Education Act to justify itself. But will enabling legislation be needed to acknowledge just this academic status quo, and confirm its plurality?

To be sure it did appear at the beginning of 1974 that the law on RE could be adapted to include representatives of other than just the Christian faith in drawing up Agreed Syllabuses. The ILEA had done this in the late 1960's,[6] Birmingham and Bradford[7] were developing the logic of this position in their own arrangements for syllabus revision. There were signs that the DES might not object at a school exploiting the parliamentary defeat of William Temple's 1944 proposal that worship in school be specified as Christian; after all that word was expressly ruled out of the Act. But such flexibility as this has recently been engulfed by the legal wrangle that has given Birmingham its first **Disagreed Syllabus.** Thus the national picture too is in different perspective.

An official Anglican report on education has favoured an RE that includes faiths other than Christianity in county schools, and ruled out domestic denominational teaching even from church schools.[8] The consistent application of such a policy would require acceptance that the privileged position of the Christian churches in syllabus making is a thing of the past. Neverthless, it would not be inconceivable in these latter days of the *established* Church of England that such generous-minded changes in RE could come to be seen by some as threats.

If this were to happen, the feuding atmosphere that infected the earlier history of board school RE could in a trice be re-created only this time the battle lines would be inter-religious, and not just denominational or secularist. Another major difference would be that the academic groundwork underpinning secular RE is there as a sufficient guarantee of the subject in a way that was not true in 1970, 1902 or 1944.

The danger then might be that RE could become devitalized in the self-denying interests of academic respectability. The faiths that were met in the classroom would be frozen fruits, not fresh. For subject disciplines in education can be as escalators moving ever more quickly away from ground level. Ironically, over-sensitivity on the part of some members of the largest religious community could do more to eliminate from RE the proper tension of openness and commitment than any amount of anti-religious propaganda.

Slowly there has been forged in England, as nowhere else in the world a public provision for RE which has at heart the sympathies of both educationists and believers. A National RE Council was set up in 1973 conjoining exactly these interests: the entire range of religious and humanist communities found in England, plus school, college and university professional RE organizations, all are represented on it. This Council holds the promise of a secular-unaligned-RE and an RE that is plural in a living sense. For Christians and Muslims and Jews, as those of other faiths, realise that their individual understandings of revelation daily interact with the faith and doubt of others.[9] Here is the quick of today's religious communities, on their own premises, but also in the secular school. In these developments it is not difficult to detect an educational model that is worthy of international imitation.

An end to it

To return to the image we began with: a child is fragile, yet resilient. There is little reason to suppose that spiritual over-protectiveness is any more productive of personal well-being than its physical equivalent; on the contrary. Far better that he meets with different persons, different religious identities. With a teacher's careful help he can meet them directly, or vicariously through stories and plays. At least he can find out their names and begin to understand who they actually are. Through them he may even begin to weigh and wonder at all the promises held out for him, and be changed accordingly. So very much depends upon the politics of RE.

Notes

1 TOWNSEND, H.E.R. and BRITTAN, E.M. (1973) *Multiracial Education: Need and Innovation.* London: Evans/Methuen. pp. 26, 41.

2 VOELTZEL, R. (1966). 'Religion and the question of rights: philosophical and legal problems in the European tradition' In: BEREDAY, G.Z.F. and LAUWERYS, J.A. *World Year Book of Education: Church and State in Education.* London: Evans pp. 222–3.

3 McPHAIL, P. *et al.* (1972) *Moral Education In The Secondary School.* London: Longmans.

4 ABBOTT, W.M. (1966) *The Documents of Vatican II.* London: G. Chapman.

5 SCHOOLS COUNCIL (1971) *Religious Education in the Secondary School.* London: Evans/Methuen.

6 INNER LONDON EDUCATION AUTHORITY (1968) *Learning for Life.* London.

7 BRADFORD METROPOLITAN DISTRICT (1974) *Guide to Religious Education in a Multi-Faith Community.* Bradford.

8 RAMSEY, I.T. (Ed.) (1970) *The Fourth R.* ('The Durham Report'). London: SPCK.

9 HICK, J. (Ed.) (1974) *Truth and Dialogue.* London: Sheldon Press.

Dreams and Realities in Religious Education

Cynthia D. Evans

'I still have a dream today that one day the lamb and the lion will lie down together and every man will sit under his own vine and fig tree, and none shall be afraid.'[1]

Martin Luther King's dream of a world at peace appears at times somewhat removed from reality. Yet in these words,he has drawn attention to one of the greatest destructive forces of human life. Fear of other people is largely the result of ignorance and misunderstanding, and an instinctive desire for self-preservation. Fear divides men, and hinders natural growth; it may cause suspicion and hatred, and it will undoubtedly impede the development of personal integrity, the perfection of inward integration.

A society consisting of individuals fearing and feared, can know no peace. It is the concern and desire of all communities that their children should not be enslaved by fear and the educational provisions are designed to give them the confidence and competence which will set them free.

To educate today the people of tomorrow is perhaps the most awesome task any society can undertake. The highest aim in such an educating process must be the introduction of men and women of integrity, in the true sense of the word, into the life of the ongoing community. To educate is to provide for the fullest possible development of the human individual, physically, mentally and spiritually, and a willingness to be truly educated is a commitment for life. Hence to speak of education in relation to merely formal schooling is at once to recognize the restrictions of application such a definition imposes.

While all academic disciplines need to be fully aware of their merely partial control of the educating process, nowhere is this more essential than in the field of religious education. A child's education, the bringing out of the character and personality of the individual and the acceptance of that single unit as an integral part of the society which has nurtured him, is one of the most intricate and fascinating mysteries of human life. That formal education may play an important role in this mystery is not disputed, and it is for those engaged in religious education to decide what role their subject will play in society's commitment to individual freedom and integrity.

Need for a new approach

It has become increasingly clear that if religious education is to make a valuable contribution to the educating process, it must, as Harold Loukes has said, be approached and ordered by the same criteria applied to any other subject. It is essential that pupils feel able to question and search for themselves, even if they are coming to the subject with a variety of preconceived ideas, and different cultural backgrounds.

There will of course be pupils whose parents have brought them up to believe in one particular faith, and who already appear to be convinced personally about the part they will play in that faith. For them, examination of their own position is important and will lead to a deeper understanding of the issues involved. Moreover, they should be given the opportunity to view beliefs and gain insight into traditions which differ considerably from their own, that they may be educated to a greater understanding of beliefs they do not share, and to a firmer, clearer appreciation of the faith they themselves possess.

It is of course vitally important that all pupils should have the opportunity to learn about the culture and traditions of the country in which they live. If justice is to be done by them to the musical, artistic, and literary heritage, to the history, customs, principles and structures of the society in which they live, then religious education in British schools must include teaching about Christianity. Moreover at present, most of the people pupils will meet, who will talk of their religion and its meaning, will inevitably be Christians. For the many who do not adhere to another tradition any religious experience of their own is likely to occur within a Christian context and will probably be discussed within the language framework of traditional Christianity.

The importance of pupils receiving a thorough grounding in Christianity and biblical background, with sufficient opportunity for questions and discussion cannot be underestimated. Yet the presence, in many schools, of pupils from other faiths, and the certainty that all pupils will meet those from other religious traditions at some point in their lives, necessitates the equally vital programme of religious education in a wider context — an opportunity for all pupils to study religious ways of life other than their own, and to be confronted with solutions to common problems which differ markedly from those with which they have previously come into contact.

Religious education and morality

In former decades, the concept of 'nurturing' in the Christian faith associated with religious education, naturally gave rise to a certain amount of moral teaching based on Christian doctrine. This can be seen from the Agreed Syllabuses. One such syllabus states, 'the aim of the syllabus is to see that children . . . may seek for themselves in Christianity the beliefs and principles which give true purpose to life, true standards of values, and light on the problems and difficulties of life . . .'.[2] It was only reasonable that pupils should be shown how the faith in which they had been nurtured could affect the daily lives of those who were committed to it.

Recently however, with the increased plurality to which John Hull has referred, and the introduction of a broader-based **approach**, it is **necessary that the traditional attitude** to moral education undertaken by the religious education teacher, is closely examined. For although much has been achieved in introducing a study of the different religions into the classroom, the moral education being undertaken has generally fallen well behind this development. This is perhaps especially true of the religious education being taught to fourth- and fifth-formers, which sometimes tends to verge on moral education exclusively, and which in other cases takes the form of a course in Christian ethics. This is not entirely the fault of the syllabus or of the religious education teacher himself; for much of the material available, specifically designed for these age groups, is either prejudiced towards a Christian solution, or does not concern itself at all with religious implications. In the case of the latter, often designed for use in moral education rather than religious education lessons, the teacher, aware of the lack of moral education facilities within the school, while at the same time concerned to show the relation between religious belief and an ethical code, has tended to introduce Christian material in an attempt to increase the religious content of these lessons.

Moral education cannot be divorced entirely from religious education — for the relevance of the study of the worship and beliefs of the religious faiths to our contemporary world, may to some extent be seen to lie in the effects which such faiths have on the lives of people and the events of history, in the search for truth and the meaning of reality. Yet now the right place for the teaching of Christian morality, as John Hull has made clear, is in the study of Christianity and it is right that it should be so included. In the same way, each ethical system founded on a religious faith should be introduced at a point appropriate for the pupil's understanding of its implications.

However, it has for many years been widely accepted that many subjects are responsible for moral education in one form or another, and the religious education teacher should not feel that he is waging a lone crusade here in allowing pupils to discuss and examine their actions and those of others. Social studies, history, English and other subjects are naturally concerned with education in morality, and in some schools, moral education has become part of the curriculum in its own right. The teacher of religious education has not been and should not be content to substitute morals for religion, for his task is already extraordinarily complicated and varied and it is for him to contribute to the wider issue of educating in religion.

It is therefore no longer sufficient for the religious education teacher to be a practising, committed Christian, with high moral standards which may be 'caught' by his or her pupils. If education involves integration into a full and active life in the community, then the moral standards of any educator, whether teacher or parent are likely to be influential. Moreover, whenever an individual professes commitment to one faith, his behaviour is always open to close examination, especially by highly critical, often idealistic pupils. Thus responsibility for integrity in religious commitment and the upholding of an ethical code is not the prerogative of the religious education teacher, but falls on any 'believing' member of staff or public. For the specific and peculiar responsibilities of the religious education teacher, we must look elsewhere.

The role of the teacher

For some years now, the role of the religious education teacher has not been seen to be that of 'nurturing' in the Christian faith. As John Hull has pointed out, modern educational research has been moving steadily away from ideas of 'instruction' or 'implanting' towards a more child-centred approach, where information and ideas are presented to the child, in order that he may possess the ingredients for educational growth, and that in the case of religious education, he may be in a position to decide for himself what conclusions he is to draw about the religious quest of man.

Such an approach requires teachers who are qualified and trained specifically in religious education. Some schools experience great difficulty in recruiting suitably qualified staff, while in others there are specialists now teaching according to Agreed Syllabuses, who are perhaps naturally reluctant to undertake the change of approach research would seem to suggest is desirable. Many feel unqualified for a new approach, or are unwilling to teach about religions they have little sympathy for and less experience of. It is important to recognize the fact that, as in any other teaching subject, a degree in Theology or

Biblical Studies, or any specialist training in religious education will provide the teacher with only the basic tools of his trade, and not a complete syllabus ready to be regurgitated. Such reticence to teach of other religions, while revealing a sensitive awareness of possible difficulties, is an underestimation of basic training, which has outlined the questions about man, the world and the nature of divine experience which religion claims to answer, and has given an awareness and understanding of difficulties. Of course, more study and wider reading will be involved but previous training will equip the teacher to discern more easily the distinctive features of other religions. Moreover, it is often possible to enlist the aid of local religious leaders, who may provide an introduction to their faith from first-hand experience which the teacher himself may lack.

Naturally no teacher would claim to bring pupils to the brink of deciding for or against each religion discovered in the classroom, and few would consider this desirable or within the capabilities of one teacher. Yet it is to be hoped that sufficient insight will have been encouraged and developed for the pupils to gain a basic idea of the structure of the religion studied and the wider implications such a study has raised concerning man and his world. The individual will then be able to follow up any line of investigation he may himself undertake, and may emerge with some fundamental understanding and respect for the beliefs which members of his community hold, even if, and perhaps especially if, he shares none of them.

There is of course room for religious instruction in denominational schools, and it is not here to be condemned, since such instruction takes place by common consent. Yet in the state schools, where plurality is a growing phenomenon, it is important that children are educated in religion, and not instructed.

Such an approach will enable pupils from non-believing backgrounds and those who are themselves sceptical about faith or religious belief, to enter into lessons with a clear conscience, prepared to make a positive contribution, and to take a full part in a study of religion. To nurture in one particular faith is not to educate in religion and in a pluralistic society the former task must rest with the parents, should they so desire, and must also be seen as the responsibility of the various religious denominations and communities themselves.

Hence many teachers prefer to talk of religious education, rather than religious instruction or religious knowledge or scripture, and a number seeing the gross inadequacies of the Agreed Syllabus in many parts of the country, have constructed their own syllabus to suit the aims of their department and the needs of the particular pupils and communities concerned.

Religious education teachers may be personally committed to one particular religion or denomination, they may be agnostic or atheist. While personal experience of how religion can affect the life of man may be advantageous, personal beliefs need have no direct relation to the teacher's ability to present his subject accurately and enthusiastically. Yet one thing all teachers will have in common, as will any subject group of teachers, is commitment to the belief that their subject is a serious matter, that it is worth studying, worth exploring and that a search for meaning in this field is significant in the development of the individual.

The 1944 Education Act

A recognition however restricted of the worth of such study was perhaps involved in the drawing up of the 1944 Act. There is now however an urgent need to review the Act in relation both to school worship and the teaching of religious education. A united experience of worship is increasingly difficult in a pluralistic society where pupils are constantly requested to make their own search for answers, and where individuality is encouraged and hypocrisy deplored.

In the last ten or fifteen years, teachers and pupils have begun to feel the effects of research on the work undertaken in school, but further progress in this direction may be said to be impeded by the provisions of the 1944 Act. New situations and contingencies have arisen which were difficult to foresee, and the attitude towards religious education adopted in many schools is now the very reverse of the Act's intentions. Then religious education was regarded as so desirable that it was singled out for special reference. Yet now in many schools, religious education has been assigned the minimum time to fulfil a legal requirement, instead of being regarded as a subject of educational value and validity, with as much to contribute to education as history or geography.

Children have always objected on principle to doing things because they had to, because there was no alternative, or because it was the law — such is human nature. Hence pupils naturally resent a subject which they believe has been alloted timetabling space only because of a law. Parents, it seems, still wish their children to take religious education, even more so, it would appear, when they are shown the vast range the subject can offer and the exciting possibilities for exploration in this field. The future of religious education in a pluralistic society lies in its ability to stand on its own merit, to provide for all an acceptable introduction to the religious sphere of man's existence and experience, an investigation in which pupils are encouraged to understand the insights of others and to explore for themselves man's search for ultimate truth. This is clearly part of an educating process. It does not need the law to support it, nor should such an approach warrant the withdrawal of pupils (except perhaps from the most exclusive sects) anymore than it is the present practice to withdraw children from science or history lessons. As two teachers have written, 'We feel that the conscience clauses are anomalous and imply doctrinal bias in the presentation of the subject'.[3]

Those elements of the curriculum regarded as educationally valuable do not require legal support. The task of many who regard religious education as an essential feature in the development of the individual is to present, and be seen to present their subject as a valuable entity. It may be said that the existing legal provisions do not now support such an approach and were not designed for the sort of society John Hull describes or the type of education envisaged by Harold Loukes. Perhaps the most difficult issue at the present time here is that of worship in the school.

School worship

At present school assemblies are designated by the 1944 Education Act as occasions for worship, 'the school day . . . shall begin with collective worship on the part of all pupils in attendance at the school',[4] and it has been taken as axiomatic that such worship was intended to be Christian. Many schools have found this a nearly impossible task, with the growing opposition expressed by pupils, parents and some members of staff to any form of religious worship, as well as the increasing problems entailed in educating a multi-racial society. Once again past dreams have not reached their fulfilment in present realities.

Assembly was envisaged by many to be the first uniting act of the day, bringing the school together for the worship of God and thus putting education in a 'fitting' context. In many schools, this would not be an accurate description of the proceedings. Some schools are too large for all the pupils to meet together regularly for worship and such assemblies are often found organized on year or house systems, which while valuable, do not have quite the same impact. Many children are withdrawn from assemblies, some such as the Jehovah Witnesses, because all religious instruction is to be given at home or by the denomination itself, some because their parents are atheists, others because they belong to a different faith. Some of these, if they form a sufficiently large group, may find another separate assembly organized for them, as in schools where there is a high proportion of Jewish pupils, and others may experience instruction in the school from their own religious leader — the Imam, for example, may pay the school regular visits. Thus the original uniting of the school for worship has become the moment when the differences between children and their backgrounds have become the most obvious, and school assembly has no longer the same role for the school community. Moreover what is not witnessed by all, is too easily misunderstood and distrusted.

Perhaps an even greater problem in this respect is the vast number of children who do attend the Christian Assembly regularly, but who have no intention of worshipping God or of contributing at all to a shared experience of worship. For some, of course, the assembly is treated in the same rather grudging manner with which lessons are approached, but for others, the assembly poses a real problem, a true crisis of conscience; for pupils do not wish to be hypocritical or to be seen to be taking an active part in things they do not yet understand or have already begun to reject. Staff also, while technically able to withdraw, often feel it their duty to attend assemblies and pupils are quick to charge them too with hypocrisy. As H.J. Blackham has said, 'The school is thus brought together either as an incomplete community or as an insincere one'.[5]

Many schools have of course long recognized these difficulties and have attempted to solve them by introducing 'assemblies for sharing', as John Hull has termed them, in which different aspects of life are introduced and explored. This may have provided a form of assembly acceptable to a wider section of the school community and yet cannot be said to have resolved the dilemma posed by the 1944 Act. Pupils with a Christian background, and particularly those from evangelical churches regard such sharing assemblies as a poor substitute for worship, and the usual addition of a hymn and a prayer still makes the assembly unacceptable to many of different faiths.

The Durham report states, 'The exploration of religious beliefs through classroom study and discussion requires to be complemented by that exploration of religious practice which the experience of worship provides'.[6] While this may still be a distinct possibility in a denomination school, it is neither possible nor desirable to undertake this in a state school, where a common experience of worship is generally unacceptable. Moreover, the normal conditions in which assemblies have to be held are hardly conducive to a worshipful atmosphere, and such worship as is provided is seldom a typical example of Christian worship in any denomination. Voluntary assemblies for worship, would seem a more attractive and educationally valuable possibility but would undoubtedly cause administrative problems. Furthermore, this could not in the same way be seen as part of life in a multi-racial school.

Having spoken of the role the school should adopt in presenting religious instruction, John Hull comments that 'The school, however, makes no assumptions about the truth (or falsehood) of any of the religions'[7] and this, of course, is a necessary position to adopt in a multi-racial pluralistic society. However, at present, each morning school assembly gives the lie to that statement, for here assumptions are being made about truth. Pupils and parents in many cases do perhaps

not unnaturally, connect the work of the religious education department with the school assembly. In practice there may be a wide
variation in the extent to which the religious education department is
involved in school worship. It may well be that religious education staff
are better qualified to prepare assemblies, having received some training
for this, and often committed Christians, prepared to involve themselves as individuals in the preparation of school worship, are to be
found in the religious education department, among others. However,
this connection between the traditional type of school assembly and
religious education is to a large extent a disadvantage. For while one is
calling for a definite commitment, the other is undertaking an
exploration into religion, and the approach of the Christian religious
education teacher to school worship will in all probability differ
enormously from the approach in the classroom.

Success or failure?

The assessment of success or failure in any educational field is
always a hazardous undertaking. There are norms by which society
judges success, but if we are to adhere to the belief that to strive for a
complete education, as stated earlier, is a life-long commitment, then
we must move from a position where success in education is measured
in terms of examination results, or indeed in numbers of facts learned.

Since it is apparent that many children have an incomplete,
inaccurate idea of the religion to which they have been introduced by
their parents from a very early age, it is hardly surprising that, as Brian
Gates reports, primary school children have little understanding of their
own faith, and still less of others. This situation is not the fault of
parents or school, of a narrow-minded home background or a
reactionary Agreed Syllabus. Children of primary school age are
generally unaware of difference or accept it as natural, unless informed
to the contrary, and because religion is essentially intangible, will have
little conception of difference in this respect. Of course children may
be told stories about other peoples, may examine customs or festivals,
but such outward indications of a difference in outlook or behaviour,
will not at primary level be automatically associated with religion.
Indeed teachers have been wary of introducing their pupils to any
stories or systems of belief they might confuse or misconstrue. One
cannot expect many children, even those from families committed to
one particular faith, to be able to express coherently and accurately the
distinctive features of their own faith, much less be able to comprehend
differences between their beliefs and those of others.

One cannot conclude automatically from weaknesses in factual
knowledge or understanding that the religious education syllabus or the
teaching offered is to blame. Certainly by the age of fifteen one might

hope that a pupil had been given and had grasped a reasonable understanding of the faith which he might hold and of the distinctive customs, worship and beliefs of others. But if the school is the only educating factor in these matters, then it is clear that, as in any other subject, understanding before the completion of a five year secondary course will be limited, and if never reinforced by other influences will remain only partial and superficial, easily forgotten.

However if religious education in schools is merely an explicit introduction into the area of religious awareness, it is impossible to assess further developments which may take place as a result of such initiation. Moreover, in this field of study perhaps more than most, it is clearly difficult to define the areas of influence exercised by the various educating parties. Some assessment of understanding can be made, but such results cannot clearly be demonstrated to have issued from the good or bad, adequate or inadequate teaching the school provides. Perhaps a developing sensitivity to religion may be observed and pupils unsolicited comments may be as good a criterion for the teacher as any systematic testing.

Practicalities

The dreams of the teacher, and the idealistic enthusiasm of the pupil are only too often thwarted by grim reality. In a society where increasingly more emphasis is placed on examinations and qualifications, there is a widening gulf between work possible in the junior school and the study necessary in senior work. Too frequently pupils who have enjoyed and benefitted from courses in a broader-based religious education are suddenly confronted with the prospect of an unjustifiably narrow path of study, often offering little opportunity for individuality and investigative skill. Many 'O' and 'A' level syllabuses are almost exclusively Christian based, and little account has so far been taken of the Hindu or Sikh pupil, or for that matter the agnostic, who might wish to take religious education as an examination subject. Jewish pupils have in the past been allowed to offer two Old Testament papers, which in some cases have been entitled 'Old Testament'. There are new syllabuses now being produced with these problems in mind and this is encouraging. On the whole CSE syllabuses are at present more enlightened, especially in Mode III, but a thorough reconsideration of aims and methods would be beneficial.

The question of textbooks is yet another area where progress appears to be very slow, and the demanding courses now strongly advocated, require good, weighty textbooks, able to be used for children of varying background and ability. For a number of the examination syllabuses there are no adequate textbooks, far less a choice, as one would find with the other humanities. Even the study of

Christianity becomes problematic, when textbooks assume a confessional approach. Some recommended for examination purposes, particularly those concerned with a Christian approach to morality, still use the unhelpful phrase 'We Christians' or while correctly posing problems for discussion, then proceed to outline not merely the Christian answers, but the 'right' ones. Similar comments could be made of many films and filmstrips available. Pupils are quick to see behind such an approach and would-be agnostics and atheists soon feel 'caught' out of their depth. They can no longer engage in research, and must content themselves with rebellion and rejection. Lack of adequate facilities and practical aids becomes increasingly embarrassing in a multi-racial society.

An important factor, greatly influencing the effectiveness of the transformation of relgous education now underway, and one frequently neglected, is that of public opinion. Religious education must not merely be done; it must be seen to be done. This will necessarily involve individual departments in publicizing their work, to the staff, the parents and the local borough authorities. The debate concerning religious education in schools continues, and feelings run high, but it is staggering to be constantly reminded of how little most parents know about the particular form of religious education their child is receiving. Surprisingly few parents look at textbooks or exercise books, and many wrongly assume that their children receive religious instruction identical to that they themselves once received. Parents, while sometimes making difficult opponents, become enthusiastic and firm allies, once they are informed of the aims and content of the work being undertaken. Many taken aback by their child's enthusiasm for a subject they always disliked, will understand and gain pleasure from their child's sense of excitement once they have been accurately informed of the facts about religious education, and nowhere is this more essential than in a multi-racial community with inbuilt fears and prejudices. Parents are the most important group to whom publicity must be directed, for they will have greater influence on their children than any other single agent, but the importance of a general public, well-informed of the nature and significance of religious education and its vital contribution to the education of its young people cannot be overestimated.

It is always a grim task to match the realities of a situation with the dreams which gave it birth. Moreover one is frequently tempted to concentrate on the reforms of present, obviously unsatisfactory conditions while at the same time losing sight of the ultimate goal. Research in religious education during the last ten years has certainly shown that there is much misunderstanding about the nature of religion, and even more ignorance of factual information. Children appear more ready to offer the value judgments of their parents on matters of religion, than to undertake an independent investigation. Hence fear of the unknown and misunderstanding of the known goes unchecked, for it is naturally more likely that children will be influenced by their parents, than by the hour or so in the week, when religious education may be offered to them in school.

We are however still in the infancy stages of religious education, for most of the parents of present pupils experienced the confessional approach of religious instruction, and may well have learnt very little about the beliefs, customs and forms of worship of faiths other than their own. We may need patience to wait for the next generation of parents who accepted themselves a more open and broader-based religious education, and who may be anxious to ensure their children receive the same. This of course is not to ignore the inevitable prejudices of any individual or the sincere and whole-hearted commitment of many to one particular faith. Yet it may be hoped that this present generation will have less fear and suspicion of other faiths and more understanding of their contribution to the search for meaning and the achievement of purpose.

This is the dream, and it's fulfilment is the mystery. The ability of religious education to realize the dream must not be overestimated. Education within the schools will include an introduction to possibilities, an investigation of probabilities and an invitation to commitment. It must ensure no less but can do no more. What may be initiated within the schools may find its fruition through the many and varied influencs affecting the human environment. A world at peace is a world perfectly integrated. Educator and educated dream, and the dream challenges the reality.

Notes

1 Martin Luther King, Speech at Lincoln Memorial, Washington Monument, Aug. 27th, 1963.

2 Surrey County Council, *Agreed Syllabus*, 1963, p. 8.

3 P. MILLER and K. POUND, 1969, *Creeds and Controversies*, Preface to the Second Edition. London: English University Press.

4 1944 Education Act. Section 25.

5 H.J. BLACKHAM 'A Humanist Approach to the Teaching of Religion in Schools', p. 53. In: J.H.R. HINNELS, (Ed.) *Comparative Religion in Education*, 1970, Newcastle upon Tyne: Oriel Press.

6 Durham Report *The Fourth R*, 1970, p. 135, Section 297, London: SPCK

7 See John Hull's preceeding article (p. 200).